No foreign conflict has had a greater impact on modern British politics than the Spanish Civil War (1936–9). More than other conflicts of the 1930s in Abyssinia and China, or more recent wars in Vietnam and Bosnia, the Spanish Civil War served to galvanise political activity in Britain, in support both of the Republican government and of Franco's Nationalist rebels. In this book, Tom Buchanan offers the broadest account yet published of Britain's response to the Civil War. Familiar aspects, such as the role of the British government, the intellectuals, and the International Brigades, are reinterpreted alongside the first detailed accounts of previously neglected subjects such as right-wing and religious opinion. In addition, Buchanan shows how the Civil War acted not only as a symbol of anti-fascism for the Left, but also as a positive example of a 'New Spain' arising from the ashes of the old. For the British Left (and also, it is argued, for the Right) Spain's experience during the Civil War appeared to offer both hope and inspiration. Tom Buchanan draws on many new archival sources to offer a concise, stimulating, and readable new interpretation of a subject of great significance to twentieth-century Britain.

BRITAIN AND THE
SPANISH CIVIL WAR

BRITAIN AND THE SPANISH CIVIL WAR

Tom Buchanan

Lecturer in Modern History and Politics
University of Oxford

CAMBRIDGE
UNIVERSITY PRESS

PUBLISHED BY THE PRESS SYNDICATE OF THE UNIVERSITY OF CAMBRIDGE
The Pitt Building, Trumpington Street, Cambridge CB2 1RP, United Kingdom

CAMBRIDGE UNIVERSITY PRESS
The Edinburgh Building, Cambridge CB2 2RU, United Kingdom
40 West 20th Street, New York, NY 10011-4211, USA
10 Stamford Road, Oakleigh, Melbourne 3166, Australia

First published 1997

Printed in the United Kingdom at the University Press, Cambridge

Typeset by Computape (Pickering) Ltd, Pickering, North Yorkshire

A catalogue record for this book is available from the British Library

Library of Congress cataloguing in publication data
Buchanan, Tom, 1960–
Britain and the Spanish Civil War / Tom Buchanan.
p.   cm.
Includes bibliographical references and index.
ISBN 0 521 45500 6 (hardback). – ISBN 0 521 45569 3 (pbk.)
1. Spain – History – Civil War, 1936–1939 – Participation, British.
2. Spain – History – Civil War, 1936–1939 – Foreign public opinion, British.
3. Public opinion – Great Britain – History – 20th century.
4. British – Spain – History – 20th century.   I. Title.
DP269.47.B7B8   1997   946.081'341–dc21   96–45538   CIP

ISBN 0 521 45500 6 hardback
ISBN 0 521 45569 3 paperback

CE

For A. N. B.

In one word it is the lure of a civilisation near to ourselves, closely connected with the historical past of Europe, but which has not participated in our later developments towards mechanism, the adoration of quantity, and of the utilitarian aspect of things. In this lure exerted by Spain upon so many foreigners . . . is implied the concession, unconscious very often, it is true, that something seems to be wrong with our own European civilisation.

Franz Borkenau, The Spanish Cockpit (1937), p. 300

CONTENTS

PLATES

All plates reproduced courtesy of
the Hulton Getty Picture Collection Limited.

ACKNOWLEDGEMENTS

I would like to record my gratitude for all of the help that I received in many libraries and archives in the course of researching this book. I would like to thank the following for permission to quote from archive material: the Public Record Office, Kew; the Trades Union Congress; the Trustees of the National Library of Scotland; the House of Lords Record Office; the Trustees of the Liddell Hart Centre for Military Archives, King's College, London; the Master, Fellows, and Scholars of Churchill College, Cambridge; Alexander Murray; Save the Children; the Library Committee of the Religious Society of Friends; the University of Liverpool; J. D. Stapledon. Parts of my article in *Twentieth-Century British History* are reproduced with the permission of the editors and of Oxford University Press.

I am especially grateful to Martin Conway for reading the manuscript in draft. I am also grateful for the helpful suggestions of the anonymous readers of both the draft and the original proposal. The encouragement of Richard Fisher at Cambridge University Press was invaluable in bringing the project to fruition. I would like to thank Joanne Dacre for her help in preparing the manuscript. I would also like to thank Jim Fyrth for his helpful advice on archival sources, and David Bradshaw and John Walton for allowing me to see copies of their articles prior to publication. Needless to say, the responsibility for views expressed in the book is entirely my own. Above all, I am grateful to Julia for her support and encouragement during the writing of the book.

ABBREVIATIONS

BUF	British Union of Fascists
CEDA	Confederación Española de Derechas Autónomas, or Spanish Confederation of Autonomous Right-wing Groups
CNT	Confederación Nacional del Trabajo, or National Confederation of Labour
DOBFP	*Documents on British Foreign Policy*
ILP	Independent Labour Party
LNU	League of Nations Union
LSI	Labour and Socialist International
MML	Marx Memorial Library, Clerkenwell, London
MRC	Modern Records Centre, Warwick University
NMLH	National Museum of Labour History, Manchester
Parl. Debs.	*Hansard Parliamentary Debates*
POUM	Partido Obrero de Unificación Marxista, or United Marxist Workers' Party
PPU	Peace Pledge Union
PRO	Public Record Office, Kew, London
PSOE	Partido Socialista Obrero Español, or Spanish Socialist Workers' Party
SCIU	Save the Children International Union
UGT	Unión General de Trabajadores, or General Workers' Union

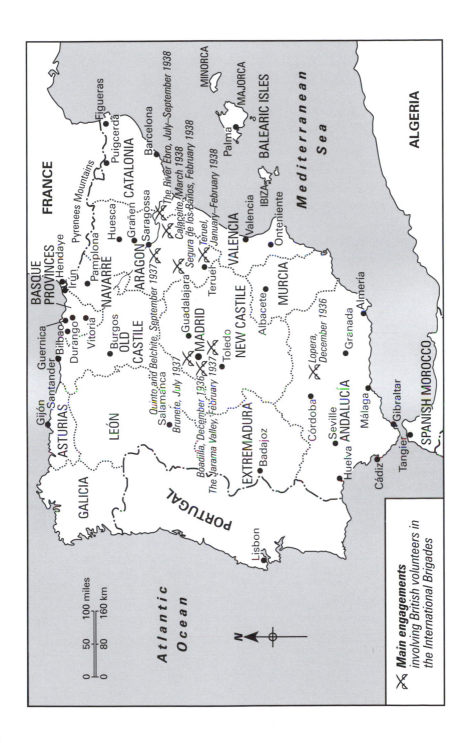

FRANCE

BASQUE PROVINCES

Pyrenees Mountains

Figueras

Puigcerdá

CATALONIA

Barcelona

The River Ebro, July–September 1938

Hendaye

Irún

Pamplona

NAVARRE

Huesca

Grañen

Saragossa

ARAGON

Calaceite, March 1938

Segura de los-Baños, February 1938

Teruel

Teruel, January–February 1938

MINORCA

MAJORCA

Palma

BALEARIC ISLES

IBIZA

VALENCIA

Valencia

Onteniente

Mediterranean Sea

Guernica

Durango

Bilbao

Santander

Gijón

ASTURIAS

Vitoria

Burgos

OLD CASTILE

LEÓN

GALICIA

Quinto and Belchite, September 1937

Guadalajara

MADRID

Brunete, July 1937

Salamanca

Boadilla, December 1936

The Jarama Valley, February 1937

Toledo

NEW CASTILE

Albacete

MURCIA

Almería

PORTUGAL

EXTREMADURA

Badajoz

Lopera, December 1936

Córdoba

Granada

ANDALUCÍA

Seville

Málaga

Huelva

Cádiz

Tangier

Gibraltar

SPANISH MOROCCO

ALGERIA

Lisbon

Atlantic Ocean

0   50   100 miles

0   80   160 km

N

Main engagements
involving British volunteers in
the International Brigades

INTRODUCTION

The British have not always been as greatly moved by other people's wars as they were by the Spanish Civil War. Indeed, of all the foreign conflicts of the twentieth century in which Britain was not directly involved, the war in Spain made by far the greatest impact on British political, social, and cultural life. In contrast, the Italian invasion of Abyssinia in 1935 and the Japanese aggression against China in 1937 were too remote; the Hungarian revolt in 1956 was too swiftly crushed. Stronger comparisons can be drawn between the Spanish Civil War and the campaigns for solidarity with Vietnam in the 1960s and Nicaragua in the 1980s. But Vietnam, while having an impact on national politics, appealed primarily to the young; the Nicaraguan revolution had a wider range of supporters, but they had no effect on Margaret Thatcher's government. Most perplexing of all has been the war in Bosnia (1992–5), in the shadow of which this book was written. Repeated attempts were made by some journalists and politicians to present Sarajevo as a second Madrid. Yet, despite humanitarian assistance from Britain, Bosnia remained tragically marginal to British politics; for the British public the conflict was too 'Balkan', too 'incomprehensible'.

And yet, the Spanish Civil War was also initially seen to be incomprehensible: a savage and inconsequential struggle that was of no concern to Britain. Indeed, many British citizens remained unmoved by the conflict and were convinced that Britain's best course was to avoid any entanglement in it. Far more than in the case of Bosnia, however, perceptions changed during the course of the war. Increasingly, the British public began to believe that this was a war of universal significance, and that it both could and should take sides (overwhelmingly with the elected Spanish Republican government against Franco's Nationalist rebels). Why, then, was Spain so different?

1

Two complementary explanations will be proposed. The first is that the war appeared to embody the great ideological conflicts of the day. For many the war was a struggle between democracy and fascism; for others between Christianity and communism. In both cases, however, the common theme was the defence of civilised values against a barbaric enemy. Secondly, it will be argued that many British people came to identify closely with their chosen side in the Civil War, and that they did so not only with a defensive mentality, but also because they were inspired by the values that their side claimed to represent. Both the Republican cause and the Nationalist cause offered a vision of social and political progress that was particularly attractive at a time when British politics appeared exclusive and deadlocked.

In seeking to explain why the Spanish Civil War acquired such importance in Britain, one inevitably, therefore, turns first to the fact that it occurred during a period of mounting international crisis and seemed to possess a significance that went far beyond the borders of Spain. In short, the Civil War could not have made such a profound impact in Britain and elsewhere had it not coincided with the rise of fascist regimes challenging both the peace of Europe and the future of democracy.

For many British observers Franco's rebellion appeared to be but one facet of the menace posed to the international order by the rise of fascism: the latest, indeed, in a series of fascist aggressions. Ever since the coming to power of the Nazis in 1933, the European settlement that had followed the First World War had been repeatedly challenged. German rearmament and the remilitarisation of the Rhineland in March 1936, as well as German demands for territory from its neighbours, all demonstrated that the Nazi regime was bent on reasserting Germany's position as a great power. This process gathered pace in 1938 with the *Anschluss* (union) with Austria in February and the German acquisition of the Sudetenland from Czechoslovakia at the Munich conference in September 1938. The mid-1930s also witnessed renewed international aggression by the Italian Fascist regime. In October 1935 Italy embarked on the conquest of Abyssinia, and the prestige of the League of Nations never recovered from the abortive attempt to discipline Italy through the imposition of sanctions. Mussolini's ambition to create a new Roman Empire alienated him from the western democracies and pushed him closer to Germany, despite the two countries' competing interests in Austria and central Europe. Mussolini's intention of turning the Mediterranean into an 'Italian lake' created a situation of considerable danger for the British Empire, with its communications resting on Gibraltar and Suez.

The rise of fascism did not only cause alarm in the sphere of international relations. Quite apart from Nazi Germany and Fascist Italy, by the mid-1930s undemocratic regimes were the dominant form of government throughout central, eastern, and southern Europe. With the exceptions of Czechoslovakia and Spain, democracy was increasingly confined to the northern and western margins of Europe. In Austria the Catholic authoritarian government of Engelbert Dollfuss had violently suppressed the Viennese Socialists in February 1934. Dollfuss was himself soon afterwards to be assassinated by Austrian Nazis in an unsuccessful *coup d'état*. Even in the surviving democracies, forces hostile to parliamentary rule were on the march. In France anti-government demonstrations by the right-wing Leagues resulted in riots on the night of 6 February 1934 that left fifteen dead and over a thousand wounded. In Belgium the Catholic Rexist movement of Léon Degrelle won over 11 per cent of the vote in the elections of May 1936, and a tenth of the seats in parliament. In Britain, the former darling of the Labour Party Sir Oswald Mosley had created the British Union of Fascists in 1932, and his 'Blackshirts' were organising violent anti-semitism in the East End of London. Fascism, in its many forms, appeared to offer a terrifying threat to democracy and to civilisation itself. Thus, the outbreak of the Spanish Civil War in July 1936 was seized upon by many as the first occasion where fascism had been resisted by a people in arms, and provided a lesson in how this thuggish, nationalistic, and dictatorial force could be stopped. Moreover, they believed that, if Franco and his Fascist backers could be defeated in Spain, then countries such as Britain could be spared a similar ordeal. When demonstrators blocked Mosley's East End march at Cable Street on 4 October 1936, the slogan of 'They shall not pass' was taken straight from the defenders of Madrid.[1]

The rise of fascism and, correspondingly, of 'anti-fascism', was clearly central to the impact that the Civil War made in Britain. George Orwell spoke for many who volunteered to fight when, *en route* to Spain, he told a friend that: 'This fascism, somebody's got to stop it.'[2]

The Civil War brought the threat of fascism to life in all too human terms, as well as presenting the first real opportunity for it to be defeated.

However, the concept of anti-fascism tells us what was being fought *against*, but not what was being fought for. It does not explain the full range of emotions that the Civil War engendered in Britain. Moreover, it reinforces the view that Spain was merely the battlefield for the contending European ideologies – a 'world war in miniature' – within which Spain itself counted for little. This book seeks to redress that balance. It argues that, if anti-fascism provided the immediate political context and sense of danger within which the Civil War could be understood, it was Spain, its people, and their struggle for freedom that provided the emotive power. The campaigns in solidarity with the Spanish Republic were not only defensive, but were inspired by the passionately held belief that a new and better society was being created in Spain. The romance of the Civil War lay above all in the emergence of the Spanish people from out of the geographical and historical margins of Europe: from feudalism to democracy, from backwardness to social progress, and from oppression and disunity to national pride and liberation.

Thus, the Republic was worth fighting for not because it was the equivalent of British democracy, but because in many respects it seemed to be superior to it. The emphasis that has traditionally been placed on the 'anti-fascist' motivations that drew British people to the Republican cause has hampered a full appreciation of the enthusiasm that existed in Britain during the Civil War for Republican Spain's experiment in democracy. This experiment had started with the creation of the Second Spanish Republic in 1931. In Britain, conversely, since 1931 democracy had brought the political supremacy of the Conservative-dominated 'National Government', a government that those on the Left saw as dangerously sympathetic to fascism, as well as one that had presided over unpalatably high levels of unemployment. Nor was criticism of the government confined to the Left: British right-wingers drew inspiration from Franco's Nationalists at a time when they felt their own government to be weak on imperial issues, especially India, and misguided in refusing to align with authoritarian anti-communist states. Thus, Spain during the Civil War became the repository of the hopes and aspirations of all those critical of the National Government, as well as appearing to provide the key to political change in Britain itself.

The emphasis that will be placed on this strong identification with the Spanish Republic in understanding the impact of the Civil War has two further implications. One is that it draws attention to the similarities between those who sided with the Republic and those (admittedly fewer) who sided with the Nationalist rebels: both saw a new and attractive society being created in their favoured part of Spain, and they personally gave the Civil War a much higher priority than the British government was willing to accord it.

The second point concerns the historical context within which the British response to the Civil War should be viewed. As we look back from a distance of sixty years it is important to emphasise the gulf that separates us from the events of the late 1930s. The paramount feature of British involvement in the Civil War was the degree to which individuals, not government, intervened in an attempt to affect the outcome. When the British government refused to side with the Spanish Republic, British citizens not only tried to force it to change its policy, but also themselves intervened directly in the Civil War. The most obvious example was that of the volunteers who went to fight, but the supply of medical units to support the armies on both sides, the dispatch of foodships to avert starvation, and the evacuation of refugee children from Bilbao were also all intended to influence the course of the war. All, moreover, emphasised the fundamental inability of the British state to control its own citizens, even in such a vital area of foreign policy. While subsequent solidarity campaigns have sought to influence events in other countries (for instance, the economic and cultural boycotting of South Africa in the apartheid era), none has offered such a comprehensive range of responses as emerged during the Civil War.

The comparison was often drawn at the time between the enthusiasm created in Britain during the early months of the Civil War and the patriotic fervour of the summer of 1914. Perhaps equally appropriate, however, is to compare the campaigns in support of the Spanish Republic to the great liberal causes of the nineteenth century: Greek independence, the First Carlist War in Spain, Italian unification, the 'Bulgarian atrocities', and (to a lesser degree) the American Civil War. Even though in the 1930s the rhetoric was as likely to be spoken by a Communist as a Liberal, the content was remarkably similar in presenting the Republic as the representative of liberty, progress, and freedom from foreign and religious oppression.

This was but one of many ways in which, for Britain, the Spanish Civil War evoked the politics of the nineteenth century. 'Non-intervention', the guiding light of British government policy throughout the war, had been the great liberal precept for foreign relations in the 1860s and 1870s. The ineffective banning of volunteers was attempted through reference to the 1870 Foreign Enlistment Act, itself an amended piece of legislation from the 1820s primarily designed to prevent the sale of arms during the Franco-Prussian War. For many, the diplomatic humiliations and political frustrations of the Spanish Civil War served to recall a golden age of undisputed British power and strong moral leadership. A seamen's leader hankered after the days of gunboat diplomacy in response to rebel attacks on British vessels.[3] Others looked back with affection to the days when British governments had sided with liberal and humanitarian causes. The liberal academic Gilbert Murray believed that the British government was turning a blind eye to Italian atrocities in Abyssinia and Spain, whereas 'in previous times, when crimes or atrocities were committed in Armenia, or on the Congo, or the Putamayo, the British government published the facts fearlessly and allowed no mistake to be made about its attitude'.[4] A Liberal student leader consoled himself with the thought that: 'If Mr Gladstone had been alive today, he would have stumped the country denouncing the barbarities committed by General Franco against the civil population of Madrid.'[5]

It is not surprising, therefore, that the agitation surrounding the Spanish Civil War looked self-consciously backwards to a mythologised nineteenth century as much as it looked forwards to the anti-fascism of the Second World War. It clothed itself in the language of the nineteenth century, from the description of the International Brigades as 'volunteers for liberty' to Harry Pollitt's instruction to the poet Stephen Spender to 'go and get killed, comrade, we need a Byron in the movement'.[6] Those who campaigned for the Spanish Republic drew inspiration and legitimation from the Romantic nationalist movements of the past. This retrospection was positively encouraged by the Communist Party which was trying to establish itself in the mid-1930s as a wholly British radical party, appropriating the liberal internationalist tradition. As the Communist *Daily Worker* proudly proclaimed: 'If history is to put the fate of freedom and liberty, the fate of democracy and culture, into the leadership of the Communists, rest assured that they are strong hands.'[7]

Thus, there was more to the impact of the Spanish Civil War in Britain than anti-fascism alone. For a British audience this was a war understood partly in terms of the ideologies of the 1930s, but also one that was seen in the context of Britain's peculiar relationship with Spain stretching back over many centuries. It was not only the prelude to World War II, but the last great European war of national liberation. In 1862 during the American Civil War Gladstone had said of the Confederate leaders that they had 'made an Army. They are making, it appears, a Navy. And they have made – what is more than either – they have made a nation.' This was a sentiment with which both pro-Republicans and pro-Nationalists would have concurred during the Spanish Civil War. Both would claim of their chosen sides that they had 'made a nation'. Tragically for Spain, two such discordant visions of the nation could not co-exist in one country.

Chapter 1

OLD SPAIN, NEW SPAIN

When a military rebellion broke out in Spain on 17 July 1936 few in Britain could have predicted that it would develop into a prolonged civil war that would threaten the peace of Europe. More acute observers recognised that this rising was different from previous *pronunciamientos* by disaffected Spanish officers – more brutal and desperate – and that it might represent a climax to the social and political tensions that had troubled Spain for decades. Even so, the common verdict was that the rebellion would succeed or collapse within a short time, and that, whichever side won, Spain's fundamental problems would not be solved. The editorial in *The Times* on 29 July encapsulated some characteristic features of the – initially condescending – British response. 'The Spanish Tragedy' was an anachronistic struggle irrelevant to modern Europe. The labels 'fascist' and 'communist' were inappropriate: this was a conflict framed not by the ideologies of twentieth-century Europe, but rather by Spanish history. Thus, the 'characteristic pitilessness of Spanish civil strife' was blamed on the Goths and the Vandals, and the political intolerance of July 1936 on the religious intolerance of the Inquisition. Neither side offered any solution to Spain's 'lawlessness, ignorance, and black poverty', and the country appeared doomed to dictatorship. The message was that Britain had no interest in the dispute and should on no account take sides.

Such Olympian detachment was soon to be challenged. The surprising strength of resistance to the rebellion, the rapid military intervention by Germany and Italy and the escalation into full-scale war all ensured that the impact of the Spanish Civil War on Britain could not be ignored. More than any other event, it gave flesh to the great political issues of the late 1930s. More even than appeasement or mass unemployment, Spain galvanised political action. The Cabinet may have seen the war as a distraction from more important business, but it was still forced to give it a high priority for almost three years. In both Houses of Parliament the Civil War was debated ceaselessly, if to little effect. It created divisions between the parties, but also within them. Most memorably, some 2,500 Britons volunteered to fight on the Republican side – at least 500 died – and thousands more participated in the political and humanitarian campaigns that the Civil War spawned. For many individuals support for one side or the other became the focal point in their lives during these three years – and often for decades afterwards.

The impact of the Civil War was particularly surprising because Spain in many ways still seemed remote from Britain in the 1930s. According to the writer Rebecca West, Spain in 1936 was 'in normal times a country not at all interesting to the man in the street; it is a long way off, it is not easy to visit, its economic ties with England are neither many nor obvious'.[1] And yet, for all its remoteness, Spain's history and culture were familiar to Britain in a way that much of modern Europe was not. The Civil War was emphatically not, in Neville Chamberlain's infamous description of Czechoslovakia's problems in 1938, a 'quarrel in a far away country between people of whom we know nothing'.[2] In practice, however, British knowledge of Spain often amounted to little more than a fog of assumptions and stereotypes that was just as dangerous as Britain's alleged ignorance of the affairs of Czechoslovakia. Thus, an understanding of Britain's involvement in the Civil War must begin with the eventful development of the relationship between these two countries.

In November 1936 the Catholic peer Lord Rankeillour spoke of the problems that bedevilled any discussion of the Spanish Civil War in Britain: 'It is the tradition of Philip the Second, the Armada, Westward Ho, and all that which comes to people's minds.'[3] He was addressing a point specifically of interest to Catholics – that the British still viewed contemporary Spain in the light of the Golden Age of Spanish power and did not realise, for instance, that the Catholic Church had since lost much of its wealth. However, his comments also highlight the degree to which British understanding of Spain's history was significant in forming perceptions of the Civil War itself.

By 1936 Spain had existed in relative isolation from Europe for many decades. Accordingly, politicians and opinion-formers found it difficult to interpret Spanish politics within a contemporary European context and sought analogy in other continents or centuries. W. H. Auden's description of Spain as 'that arid square, that fragment nipped off from hot / Africa, soldered so crudely to inventive Europe'[4] has often been quoted. But likewise it was noted in Cabinet that conditions in Spain during the Civil War were 'more analogous to South or Central America than to Europe';[5] for the Catholic journalist Raymond Lacoste, Spain's diversity was 'like the fifteenth-century in the middle of the twentieth, and like Africa in Europe';[6] and for the Anglican writer Henry Brinton, Spain at the inception of the Second Republic in 1931 was 'as backward as other countries in the Middle Ages'.[7] This gulf of understanding meant that the Spanish Civil War was often branded as 'incomprehensible' to a British audience, but more frequently the search for explanation resulted in the enthusiastic pillaging of images of Spanish history stretching back to the 'Golden Age' and even to the medieval Reconquest of Spain from the Moors.

Lord Rankeillour was certainly correct in believing that the age of Spanish supremacy had left an enduring legacy in Britain, although one that mingled fear with respect. While the 'Black Legend' of the brutality of the Spanish Inquisition had depicted an intolerant and backward-looking society, Spain under Philip II (1556–98) was also an empire at the height of its powers, squandering the wealth of the New World in pursuit of hegemony in the Old. As Robert Southey observed following a tour of Spain in 1797, after Philip 'the name of Spanish glory survived, but the glory of Spain was extinguished'.[8] The replacement of the Habsburg dynasty by the Bourbons in 1700 added a new dimension. British travellers to Spain in the eighteenth century were fascinated with Spain's decline, especially at a time when Britain was forging its own empire. The changing balance of power between the two countries was symbolised by the British seizure of Gibraltar in 1704, the dogged defence of the Rock in the siege of 1782, and its development as a strategic imperial base. Spain's decline was routinely blamed by Britons on the Bourbon centralising 'despotism', to be remedied with a large dose of liberty. The Black Legend had been brought up to date, with the Bourbons taking the place of the Inquisition as the main obstacle to Spain's integration into modern Europe.

The real crucible for Britain's modern relations with Spain lay, however, in the first four decades of the nineteenth century. Between 1809 and 1814 British troops under Wellington fought the French in Spain, sharing a common enemy with the Spanish if rarely co-operating harmoniously as allies. As Raymond Carr has observed, perceptions of this conflict were strikingly different – for the British this was the Peninsular War, fought to weaken Napoleon and defend Portugal as a strategic base; for the Spanish it was the War of Independence in the course of which Spanish liberals hoped to create a constitutional monarchy.[9] However, although the first Spanish Constitution was promulgated in 1812 by the deputies besieged by the French in Cadiz, the great political issues raised by the war were not easily resolved. The Constitution was abolished by Ferdinand VII on his return to Spain in 1814. Apart from a brief revolutionary interlude in 1820–3, a watered-down version was only reintroduced in the year after his death in 1833.

Between 1834 and 1840 Spain was again disturbed by civil strife. The First Carlist War broke out on the death of Ferdinand between the supporters of his infant heir Isabella (and her mother Cristina) and those of her uncle Don Carlos. This was no mere dynastic struggle: Carlos represented the forces of traditional conservatism, integralist Catholicism, and Basque provincialism in defence of that region's medieval privileges; the *Cristinos* stood for constitutional monarchism and mild liberalism. The Spanish struggle soon involved the European powers, just as it would a century later. Palmerston, foreign secretary in the Whig administration, strongly supported the government of Queen Cristina and initiated the Quadruple Alliance with France, Portugal, and Spain to preserve stability in the Iberian peninsula. The official British policy of 'non-intervention' was defined loosely enough to permit the Royal Navy to assist the defenders of Bilbao against the Carlist siege, and for the Royal Marines to venture inland with government forces. In addition to permitting the supply of arms, the British government also sanctioned the formation of a 10,000-strong British Legion which fought for two years alongside the *Cristino* forces. The Legion was led by George de Lacey Evans, the Radical MP for Westminster who had fought with Wellington in Spain and who would live to command a division in the Crimea in the 1850s. Despite a respectable record of service in Spain, the Legion's performance was denigrated by the Tories in Britain who tended to sympathise with the Carlists. However, comparisons with the British volunteers of the 1930s should not be too strongly drawn. The Legion of 1835–7 was not only primarily a mercenary force with an officer corps of serving (if second-rate) officers, but also acted as an unofficial arm of government policy.

After 1840 British interest in Spanish politics waned until the 1930s. Indeed, in many respects British perceptions of Spain were frozen at the end of the Carlist War. In 1843 George Borrow published *The Bible in Spain*, an account of his three visits for the Bible Society to 'the land of old renown, the land of wonder and mystery'.[10] Much that Borrow had to say about the Spaniards was still thought to be valid in the 1930s – their nobility and generosity, the incompetence of their governments, and the spiritual oppressiveness of their Church. Although Borrow brought Spain alive for a British public as had no other contemporary author apart from Richard Ford, one consequence of his success was to reaffirm a British perception of Spain as an exotic backwater, geographically and culturally remote from the mainstream of European life. The Carlist wars and their aftermath reinforced the conviction that Spain was inherently politically unstable, and that Spanish nature tended towards a quite unnatural ferocity in the settling of political scores – in 1936 *The Times* would even complain that the contemporary Spanish atrocities lacked the 'grandeur' of those of the 1830s!

Spain experienced further political turmoil in 1868–74, when Isabella was forced from the throne, the feckless new King Amadeus of Savoy gave way to a short-lived First Republic, and the Carlists again rose in unsuccessful revolt. Spain's pretensions as a great power following the restoration of the Bourbons in 1874 were brutally exposed by the loss of the most valuable remnants of empire (Cuba and the Philippines) in a war with the United States in 1898–9. The response from the most brilliant of the young Spanish intellectuals was to call for the 'regeneration' of a country that one of their number, José Ortega y Gasset, lambasted as 'invertebrate Spain'. Yet, despite the carving out of a new pocket-empire in Morocco, Spain remained a symbol for international failure and decline – and a warning for imperial Britain. In 1930 when Sir Oswald Mosley resigned from government he alluded to Spain in these terms:

What I fear much more than a sudden crisis is a long, slow crumbling through the years until we sink to the level of a Spain, a gradual paralysis, beneath which all the vigour and energy of this country will succumb.[11]

Under the restricted democracy of the restored Bourbons, the latter years of the nineteenth century saw dramatic economic and social change in Spain. Two peripheral regions flourished – the Basque country, the centre for iron and steel production, and Catalonia with its rapidly developing textile industry. Economic success revived regional identities and movements for self-government that would contribute markedly to the Spanish crisis of the early twentieth century. The period also saw the growth of British economic interests in Spain. Two British companies, Tharsis (in 1867) and the even more successful Rio Tinto (in 1873), bought a dominant share in the previously state-owned pyrites and copper mines of southern Spain. British investment allowed for a fuller and highly profitable exploitation of these reserves. Rio Tinto in particular remained a leading exporter of pyrites, used in the production of sulphuric acid and crucial to the armaments industry, into the 1930s.

Industrialisation sharpened social divisions within Spain. Two movements of social protest arose in competition for the loyalty of the workers and peasants. In 1879 Pablo Iglesias founded the Socialist Party (PSOE) in Madrid, and subsequently the General Workers' Union (UGT). The Socialists, a moderate parliamentary party despite their Marxist rhetoric, were strongest in central Spain and the Basque country, and in the twentieth century shared a common international affiliation with the British Labour Party and Trades Union Congress. One of Europe's most significant anarchist movements also developed in Spain at this time. Anarchist theory had arrived in 1868 through Fanelli, a follower of the Russian exile Bakunin. He found a ready audience as communal organisation and hostility to the state were Spanish political traditions, and the concept of federalism was a powerful factor in the politics of the ill-fated First Republic. Anarchism, with its unambivalent rejection of corrupt party politics, its utopianism, and its violent antipathy to the Church, army, and ruling elites, was particularly attractive to the alienated landless peasant communities of the south. It also flourished amongst the workers of Catalonia, in the revolutionary trade unionism known as anarchosyndicalism. From its foundation in 1910 until the Civil War the anarcho-syndicalist National Confederation of Labour (CNT) was a major force in Catalan politics. The constant struggle between Socialists and Anarchists for hegemony over the working class was a serious source of weakness for the Left, and a factor in Spanish political instability until the anarchist movement's destruction during the Civil War.

Spain's neutrality in the First World War (due to irreconcilable differences over which side to join) re-emphasised its lack of international significance. However, the role of the Basque seamen, continuing to carry iron ore despite the submarine menace, was remembered with gratitude in Britain in 1937 when Bilbao was under attack. Others recalled that Britain's friends in Spain during the war had become the Republicans of the 1930s, and that the military had generally sided with Germany. The war increased social as well as political divisions in Spain, resulting in the near-revolutionary chaos of 1917–19. Order of a sort was restored under the dictatorship of General Miguel Primo de Rivera (1923–30) who, it was hoped by one official at the British Foreign Office, would purify 'the highly diseased Spanish body politic'.[12]

In the 1920s the dominant British image of Spain remained one of a country that had ceased to be a major power, that was stifled by tradition and by 'feudal' institutions, and that was adrift from the main paths of European development. Even the modernising dictatorship of Primo de Rivera could do little to change this, although his construction of a new road network was warmly welcomed by British travellers.[13] Spain was an anachronism. In December 1930 the British ambassador was able to comment smugly that a recently failed Republican rising was like the revolutions of nineteenth-century Europe, in countries where 'the kind of liberties for which progressive Spaniards are still struggling have long ago ceased to be political issues'.[14]

This vision of Spain was challenged in May 1931 when municipal elections precipitated the bloodless overthrow of the monarchy and the creation of the Second Republic. Created in a mood of euphoria, the new Republic appeared to offer an era of democratisation, modernisation, and equality between the classes and sexes. It was greeted with sympathy by liberals and socialists in Britain, who saw the Republic as the 'New Spain', striving peacefully to break the shackles of the past. Writing in 1933, Sir George Young posed the question of why Spain, which in 'ethnic and economic' terms might have moved towards communism or fascism, 'so far chooses an evolution by way of parliamentary radicalism such as we might follow?'[15] Non-violent change, however, proved an illusion. The radicalism of the new Constitution alienated the Church and other powerful forces in Spanish society such as landowners and the army. The supporters of the Republic were soon at odds with each other, while the Right evolved new forms of political mobilisation to oppose it (most notably the Catholic CEDA party led by the young lawyer José Maria Gil Robles). The break-up of the liberal–socialist coalition of 1931 resulted in defeat for the divided Left in the election of 1933. Between 1933 and February 1936 Spain was ruled by the parties of the centre-Right under the increasingly conservative prime minister Alejandro Lerroux, leader of the Radical Party.

The Left watched with dismay the growing power of the CEDA and its bullish leader Gil Robles, especially in the light of the suppression of socialist movements in Germany and Austria. In October 1934 the Socialists, aided locally by Catalan nationalists and Anarchists, launched an abortive rebellion to prevent the entry of members of the CEDA into the government. The only serious fighting occurred in the Asturias where coal miners from all of the left-wing organisations held out for three weeks under the slogan of 'UHP' ('United Proletarian Brothers') before being brutally suppressed by the army. Ominously, Moroccan soldiers were employed for the first time on Spanish soil to suppress the revolt. Despite the defeat, however, the revolt acted as a catalyst for political change. Through fatal indecision the Right failed to exploit its advantage, and allowed the imprisoned Socialist leaders to appear as martyrs. Moreover, the gaoling of many of their militants encouraged even the Anarchists to contemplate voting, if only to secure their comrades' release. In 1935 Socialists, Communists, and liberal Republicans united in a Popular Front, and defeated the divided Right in the elections of February 1936.

The Popular Front election victory solved little. The Socialists refused to join the government, which was drawn entirely from the Republican centre. The government was further weakened when the strongman of the regime, Manuel Azaña, was elevated to the presidency in May. The remaining months of peace saw increasing political and social tensions. Peasants and workers took the chance to make gains after the 'two black years' of right-wing rule, and there was a spate of strikes and seizures of land. The Socialist leader Francisco Largo Caballero made clear that, while in the short term he was willing to support the parliamentary system, he might well sanction a workers' revolution in the near future. Within the army, networks of officers plotted rebellion despite the efforts of the government to dispatch suspect generals, such as Francisco Franco, to distant commands. Right-wingers, disillusioned with the CEDA's incapacity to win power through electoral means, moved into the more overtly fascist Falange Party of José Antonio Primo de Rivera, son of the former dictator. Falangist gunmen provoked their enemies with a series of assassinations which culminated in the murder of Lieutenant Castillo of the pro-Republican Assault Guards. In response, his outraged colleagues abducted and murdered the Monarchist leader Calvo Sotelo on the night of 13 July. For the plotters this was the excuse that they had sought: the army rebellion began on 17 July 1936, supported by paramilitary groups on the Catholic, Monarchist, and Fascist right wing, especially the well-trained Carlist Requetés of Navarre.

British reactions to the Republic had been predictably mixed. For those on the Left it had represented, at least under the governments of 1931–3 and again after February 1936, a noble attempt to transform a benighted country by democratic means. Such sympathy was reserved for the Liberal and Socialist Parties – the Anarchists were little understood and, apart from some minuscule groups, had no one to put their case in Britain. Few politicians gave much priority to Spanish politics, although the suppression of the 1934 rebellion attracted the attention of two leading women in the Labour Party, Leah Manning and Ellen Wilkinson, who would each play a prominent role during the Civil War. On the Right, the Republic aroused the hostile interest of a small clique, including Douglas Jerrold, Sir Charles Petrie, and the Australian-born Marquis del Moral, who favoured a monarchist restoration, and who became the core of Francoist support in London after July 1936.

For the British government the Republic brought instability after the relative calm of the dictatorship, although even Primo de Rivera had latterly courted popular support by raising the level of taxes on foreign companies. Despite sympathy for King Alfonso and his British wife, however, the Republic was eventually offered diplomatic recognition, and the Foreign Office was initially confident that the Republican government of Manuel Azaña could hold off any threat from the Left. Relations were soon dented by Azaña's government's economic nationalism and pro-labour policies. Moreover, in 1932 Spanish trade with Britain was seriously hit by the British government's introduction of tariffs and imperial preference: Spanish orange exporters, for instance, now found it hard to compete with their rivals in British-ruled Palestine. Spain responded with exchange controls to reduce the repatriation of profits from British companies. The replacement of Azaña with Lerroux's more conservative regime in 1933 was broadly welcomed, especially as his government strengthened the hand of British companies in dealing with their workers and adopted a more conciliatory stance on trade. Less helpfully, however, the new government was also sympathetic to Italy over its invasion of Abyssinia.

The Popular Front's victory in the February 1936 election alarmed the British government. British officials in Spain, led by the ambassador Sir Henry Chilton, warned in increasingly hysterical terms that the new government was too weak to resist pressures from the Left. The government was portrayed as a 'Kerensky' regime, with reference to the short-lived liberal-democratic interlude in Russia before the Bolshevik revolution of October 1917. Although it was not yet clear which side would first turn to violence, by the summer of 1936 the Foreign Office viewed Spain as a country sliding into turmoil.[16]

The military rising was initially successful in Spanish Morocco, and in some mainland cities. General Franco arrived in Morocco from the Canary Islands on a privately chartered British plane to lead the Army of Africa, although formal rebel authority initially resided with a *junta* headed by General Cabanellas. The rebels' inability to capture the largest cities, and assistance from Italy and Germany, turned a failed rebellion into a Civil War. The Republican politicians of the Spanish government were unable to defend themselves and were forced to rely on the militias of the Socialists, Anarchists, Communists, and smaller left-wing parties such as the anti-Stalinist POUM (Partido Obrero de Unificación Marxista, or United Marxist Workers' Party). In much of the Republican zone (especially in the Anarchist stronghold of Catalonia) civil war gave way to social revolution as soon as the rising had been crushed. Industry was collectivised, churches were burnt, and all those seen as enemies were massacred. Order was only slowly brought to the Republican side following the appointment of the Socialist leader Largo Caballero as prime minister in September 1936, leading a broadly based coalition government. In the course of the summer the chaos of the first phase of the Civil War was slowly resolved into coherent blocks of territory. The Republican zone, with its capital initially in Madrid, comprised Catalonia and much of Aragon, central Spain (Valencia and Murcia), and part of Andalucía. Most of the northern Spanish coast was also held by the Republic: the Asturias, Santander, and the Basque country. The Catholic Basques, who had little in common with the parties of the Popular Front, chose to throw in their lot with the Republic in return for self-government, which was granted in October 1936. Meanwhile, the Nationalists held a swathe of territory across northern Castile, Galicia, and Navarre which was soon united with their southern conquests in Extremadura and Andalucía.

The attitude of the foreign powers soon began to influence the course of the war. The Italian and German dictators both decided to help the rebels, Hitler for primarily ideological reasons, Mussolini in pursuit of strategic advantage against Britain and France. The German airlift of Franco's Army of Africa from Morocco beginning in late July constituted the first decisive moment in the war. The Spanish government appealed for help to the fellow Popular Front government of France, led by the Socialist Léon Blum, elected only a month before. While elements of Blum's divided administration wished to help, however, he was concerned that French aid might trigger a conflict with Italy and Germany, one in which Britain might not automatically support France. Blum's solution was to announce French 'non-intervention', and to call for an international agreement to prevent the flow of arms into Spain. After prolonged diplomatic wrangling twenty-seven countries eventually adhered to the non-intervention agreement, and from September 1936 a Non-Intervention Committee sat in London to deal with the many complaints that it was being disregarded.

Already desperately short of weapons and trained men, and denied supplies by non-intervention, the Republicans faced disaster in the autumn of 1936 when Franco's army marched on Madrid. Franco paused only to relieve the rebels besieged in the Alcazar at Toledo, and used the resulting political kudos to be named as 'Head of Government of the Spanish State' on 28 September. His position was greatly strengthened when, two months later, Germany and Italy gave his regime full diplomatic recognition, thus committing themselves to a Nationalist victory. The second great turning point in the war came in late September 1936 when the Soviet Union decided to help the Republic militarily, and Soviet tanks and planes, alongside the International Brigades organised by the Communist International, arrived in time to prevent the fall of Madrid.

The cost for the Republic was both financial and political. Spain's gold reserves were shipped to the USSR to pay for the arms, and the Soviet influence over the Republic grew through the rapidly expanding Spanish Communist Party as well as through the presence of Soviet intelligence networks in Spain. Stalin was anxious that the Spanish Republic should be politically acceptable to the western democracies and it was promoted as a 'parliamentary democracy of a new type', utilising democratic forms to sweep away the vestiges of feudalism. However, the Communist strategy of emphasising continuity with the pre-Civil War Republic and seeking to reverse the revolutionary changes of the war's early months inevitably resulted in political tensions between the Communists and the Anarchists and POUM (the main advocates of the idea of a 'revolutionary war'). A major battlefield was the Socialist Party itself, already bitterly divided between Right and Left factions before the Civil War. Largo Caballero, prime minister and leader of the Socialist Left, was increasingly wary of Communist pressure and struggled to maintain his freedom of movement. Tensions on the Republican side peaked in May 1937 when there was a week of street fighting in Barcelona between the Anarchists and the forces of the central government. The fighting broke the Anarchists as an oppositional force, and also the resistance of Largo Caballero, who was replaced as prime minister by another Socialist, Juan Negrín. In the aftermath the POUM was suppressed, and its leader Andrés Nin was seized and assassinated by the Soviet NKVD.

Increasingly the conflict evolved into a struggle between two centralising regimes. Franco, too, crushed potential opponents within the Falange in April 1937, and forcibly united all political groupings under his command in the portmanteau Falange Español

Tradicionalista y de las JONS – better known simply as 'the movement'. His authority was reinforced by the deaths of all of his potential rivals: Calvo Sotelo's assassination had triggered the rebellion, and José Antonio Primo de Rivera had been executed by the Republicans in September 1936, while Generals Sanjurjo and Mola both died in plane crashes. Gil Robles was politically marginalised, and spent the war years in Lisbon.

Madrid was secured for the government by a series of battles in the first months of 1937, culminating in the Republican victory at Guadalajara in March when Mussolini's Italian 'volunteers' were routed. In July the Republic launched its first major offensive at Brunete which, while good for morale, proved to be the first of many such campaigns which the Republic would be unable to sustain, and resulted in heavy losses of men and materiel. The Nationalists, meanwhile, conquered the enclave on the northern coast (the Basque country, Santander, and the Asturias) as well as taking Málaga in the south. Republican hopes soared in December 1937 when a surprise attack captured the Aragonese city of Teruel – the first substantial victory for the new People's Army, without help from the International Brigades. But Franco, ever loath to concede any territory, ground them down in bitter winter fighting, and in March 1938 launched a massive offensive that took his armies to the Mediterranean sea at Vinaroz and divided the Republic.

With the Republic again facing imminent defeat, more time was purchased by the brief opening of the French border to supplies of Soviet arms. Although this lifeline was finally severed in mid-June, under intense British pressure, the Republicans had recovered sufficiently to launch one last offensive on 25 July. A surprise attack across the river Ebro disconcerted the Nationalists, but again resulted in an unwinnable bloodbath. When the Republic pulled back in September the way was open for the fall of Catalonia in January 1939. Although there were still many men under arms in Madrid and central Spain, Republican resolve now collapsed. Negrín was overthrown by a Military Defence Council lead by Colonel Casado, seeking a compromise peace. But compromise was not possible, and Casado's coup merely precipitated Franco's bloodless occupation of Madrid on 1 April 1939. Even before the Republican collapse was complete, Britain had recognised the Franco regime on 27 February.

Franco had won due to a favourable combination of international and domestic factors. Firstly, he had received more and higher quality military assistance from Germany and Italy than his opponents had from the USSR, and this assistance was sustained until victory. Meanwhile, non-intervention, championed by the British and (less and less enthusiastically) the French governments, prevented the Republic from purchasing military assistance on the open market, pushing it deeper into the Soviet embrace while doing nothing to deter large-scale intervention on the Nationalist side. Secondly, Franco was able to resist pressure from his foreign supporters much more successfully than the Republic. Mussolini and Hitler were often dismayed at what they regarded as Franco's sloth in pursuit of victory in a war that was costing them dearly. Franco, however, was following his own time-table, preferring a slow victory, which would encompass the complete defeat and demoralisation of his enemies, to a speedy end to the war.[17] On the Republican side, military decisions (from the location of offensives to individual promotions) were too frequently taken for political reasons. Finally, Franco's side was more politically united than his opponents. The Nationalists broadly accepted the one-party state, backed by the Catholic Church, that Franco had created in return for victory – although many questions remained about the nature of the regime that would emerge after the war was over. The Republic achieved an uneasy uniformity after May 1937, but the events of March 1939 showed the degree to which latent antagonisms survived.

What did the British public make of the Spanish Civil War, and did its opinion matter? The evolution of British opinion towards the war has to be understood within the context of changing public attitudes towards foreign policy more broadly. The First World War had shattered the idea that foreign policy was an elite preserve, beyond the scrutiny of the public. In 1919 Lord Cecil heralded the new era of universal suffrage and open diplomacy in the journal of the League of Nations Union: 'In a democratic age everything depends on public opinion. This means that the public must have an opinion on international politics, and that its opinion must be right.'[18] Cecil's enthusiasm was countered by an enduring suspicion that the public lacked the knowledge to hold useful opinions on the whole gamut of political issues. As Lord Grey remarked in 1923, it was a fallacy to suppose that 'the supreme statesman in democratic government is public opinion'.[19] Even so, public opinion on foreign policy undoubtedly concerned politicians in the 1930s. In 1935 hostile letters from constituents to MPs contributed to the fall of the foreign secretary Sir Samuel Hoare following the controversial Hoare–Laval Pact.[20] Stanley Baldwin, prime minister for a final term between 1935–7, was acutely aware of the need not to offend pacific public sentiments through any premature rearmament. His conviction was reinforced by the surprise Labour Party victory in the 1933 East Fulham by-election, where the successful candidate was believed to have won on a 'pacifist' ticket. Even so, the Spanish Civil War exposed very starkly the difficulty of defining exactly what the public really thought about foreign policy. The pro-Republican Duchess of Atholl, in a letter to Anthony Eden, was reduced to citing a conversation with a taxi driver as evidence that the public would not stomach a Franco victory.[21]

In the 1930s 'public opinion' was conventionally regarded as being the public views of opinion-formers, who interpreted the sentiments of their voiceless fellow-citizens. Considerable power was seen to reside in the editorial columns of leading newspapers, especially The Times – hence the attempts by government to manage their views on sensitive issues such as appeasement. Public opinion was not an entity to be scientifically tested, but rather an amorphous public morality, to be interpreted and moulded by politicians and journalists.

However, the 1930s did witness the beginnings of a new conception of how public opinion could be both measured and mobilised. The 1935 Peace Ballot offered the first unofficial referendum on foreign and defence policy, even though the results were vague enough to be open to political manipulation. This voluntary ballot of eleven million people, organised by the League of Nations Union, revealed overwhelming support for the League, for measures to reduce armaments by international agreement, and for economic and non-military measures to stop aggression. On a more sensitive question, the ballot divided by 6,784,368 to 2,351,981 in favour of military measures 'if necessary' to restrain an aggressor.[22]

By-elections were increasingly fought over pressing defence and foreign policy issues, from East Fulham in 1933 to the post-Munich contests at Oxford and Bridgwater, and the Duchess of Atholl's decision to force a by-election on the issue of appeasement in

December 1938. However, by-elections were held much more frequently than in the later twentieth century, and had still to be seen as referenda on government policy. Bridgwater and Oxford were part of a series of contests in October and November 1938, many of which were safely held by the Conservatives and where domestic rather than international issues dominated.[23]

The most intriguing development in the understanding of public opinion was the Mass Observation movement, created in 1937 as an enthusiastic mixture of sociology, anthropology, and surrealism. It intended to gather information on popular culture and attitudes through a group of some 1,500 volunteer 'Mass Observers'. The initial levity of some of the activities had by 1939 matured into a critique of Britain's democracy – the 'hiatus between the millions and their leaders'.[24] In *Britain by Mass Observation* (1939), a study of popular attitudes to the Munich crisis, Charles Madge and Tom Harrisson noted the growing sense of alienation of ordinary people from world affairs, and the tendency of the newspapers to speak on behalf of the public without seeking to establish their views by scientific means. They argued the need for more active and better-informed citizens, who would be able to contribute genuinely to national decision-making: 'We must have knowledge, at least sufficient for us to come to personal decisions.'[25]

While movements such as the Left Book Club sought to fill the gaps in the public's knowledge, the criticism made by Mass Observation was also being met by the development of opinion polling. As this was still in its infancy, however, its value must be seen as limited, and there is no evidence that the few polls that were taken influenced the contemporary debate on the Spanish Civil War. The British Institute of Public Opinion first polled on Spain in January 1937, and the response to the question of whether Franco's *junta* should be regarded as the legal government of Spain revealed only 14 per cent in favour and 86 per cent opposed. Further polls continued to show a preponderance of sympathy for the government side. In March 1938 57 per cent supported the Republic and 7 per cent Franco, with 36 per cent offering no opinion. These results were repeated in October 1938, but in January 1939 a final poll showed 71 per cent supporting the Republic, now in its death throes, compared with 10 per cent backing Franco, and a mere 19 per cent backing neither. The breakdown of the last two polls is also interesting, even though it largely confirmed the assumptions made at the time. Support for the Republic was stronger amongst supporters of the opposition parties than Conservatives, and amongst men, younger people, and those of below average incomes. Support for Franco was, in composition if not in size, broadly a mirror image of the other results. Significantly, however, even 48 per cent of supporters of the Conservative-dominated government backed the Republic in October 1938, and this rose to a striking 64 per cent in January 1939.[26]

The value of the polls needs to be qualified. The questions posed dealt in generalities of sympathy rather than practical policy, apart from one occasion in February 1938 when 78 per cent supported 'direct retaliatory measures against Franco's piracy'. It is also unfortunate that no polls were taken in the early months of the war – it is probable that the confusion and atrocities of that period would have resulted in less support for either side. Crucially, there were no polls on the thorny question of non-intervention, and it is important to bear in mind that in the latter stages of the Civil War, when undecided opinion was swinging towards the Republic, opinion poll support for Neville Chamberlain and his policy of appeasement was remarkably buoyant. Thus, passive support for the Republic did not necessarily imply backing for a course of action that might result in war.

Given the limited value of the polls, the evidence that they provide on British attitudes towards the Civil War needs to be located within a wider assessment of the evolution of British opinion and of the ways in which opinion was produced and influenced. Other kinds of opinion-forming, such as politics and the views of intellectuals, will be discussed in later chapters. However, it is worth at this point analysing the attitudes of the press, especially as a Mass Observation survey in 1938 showed that those polled still saw newspapers as the main source on which they based their opinions.[27]

There was a clear division within the British press over the Spanish Civil War. Of the national dailies, The Times (which had a small circulation and considerable influence) supported British government policy, especially over non-intervention. However, its special correspondents (who included Kim Philby in Nationalist Spain) enjoyed considerable freedom of expression. George Steer's reports on the bombing of Guernica had a powerful impact in Britain and temporarily undermined The Times's carefully built reputation in Germany, to the distress of the editor Geoffrey Dawson. Of the other major conservative papers, the Daily Mail, the Morning Post, and the Sunday Observer were strongly pro-Franco, and the isolationist Daily Express less so. The Daily Telegraph was supportive of government policy in general, though critical of the appeasement of Germany. On the Left, the Daily Herald had a large readership and little influence, and, as the mouthpiece of the Labour leadership, faithfully reflected Labour policy on the Civil War. Thus, while pro-Republican, it initially supported non-intervention. The liberal papers (the Manchester Guardian, the News Chronicle, and the Sunday Reynolds News) were freer in their support for the Republic and in their condemnation of non-intervention once its shortcomings had been revealed.

Loyalties within the national press were, therefore, fairly evenly divided, and, in terms of circulation, the Republic may even have had the edge. This does not allow, however, for the relative degrees of influence of the leading titles, and ignores both the important regional and religious newspapers and also the weeklies. Catholic papers were overwhelmingly pro-Franco, while the Anglican and Free Church papers adopted a neutral stance which, indirectly, counted against the Republic by bolstering non-intervention. With the exception of the left-wing New Statesman and Time and Tide, the great majority of weekly reviews were also neutral or pro-Franco.

Of the other news and discussion media, the BBC pursued balanced reporting, and in the corporation's journal (the Listener) reports from Republican Spain tended to be juxtaposed with those from the other side. Despite this care, however, the BBC's continued use of the term 'insurgents' was irksome to the Nationalists. The newsreels spent little time on explaining the political complexities of the conflict, but rather used film of the war to illustrate the evils of civil strife and to reinforce a conservative view of British life. A Pathé report of 3 August 1936 concluded that:

> while we watch this grim struggle let us be thankful that we live in a country where men are free to express their political opinions without being shot, where internal strife is a thing unknown. While we here live under the protection of the Law, young Spain learns to shoot.[28]

In the opening months of the Civil War, British opinion was over-whelmingly non-interventionist. Although both Republicans and Nationalists had their firm supporters in Britain from the outset, the image of each side had been severely tarnished in the eyes of uncommitted opinion. The Second Republic's dream of peaceful reform had given way to the collapse of government authority and the tyranny of 'uncontrollable' elements. In particular, a succession of images were presented which were unlikely to have much appeal in Britain – rampant anarchists, militia women on the barricades, forcible collectivisation of land, and murders of priests and nuns. However, the rebels were equally hampered – military rebellion against a recently elected government, the massacres of Republicans, and the use of Moorish soldiers were no more palatable to British taste.

The atrocities, especially those committed by the Left, were par-ticularly influential in forming public opinion. The new Spanish ambassador, Pablo de Azcárate, taking up his post in September 1936, was fully aware of the damage that had been done to the Republican cause in Britain across the political spectrum, from 'the City to Transport House'.[29] The right-wing and Catholic press (in particular Lord Rothermere's Daily Mail) published atrocity stories with great zeal. Ironically, they overplayed their hand by exaggerating the extent of what had, in fact, been a shocking slaughter: thirteen bishops and over 4,000 priests had been killed.[30] By making the stories appear too grotesque to be credible they offended a readership still sensitive to the way in which these same papers had stampeded men into joining the army in 1914 with invented stories of German barbarity. Moreover, while rebel atrocities were less widely reported, the massacre of the Republican defenders of Badajoz in August 1936 made it hard to differentiate between the two sides on this score.

These events merely reinforced the belief that Britain should not become involved in the conflict. The Marquis of Zetland, a Cabinet minister, wrote in support of non-intervention that a new world war must not start 'because one set of desperadoes insists on cutting the throats of the other set of ditto'.[31] This sense that there was little good in either side was widespread in the early months of the Civil War. However, 'non-interventionism' on these grounds was not always the reason for the cross-party support that was offered to the policy of non-intervention. Non-intervention was undoubtedly seen by many as genuinely desirable, but was also supported (for instance by the labour movement) because it would reduce the risk of war and because they believed that it would favour the Republicans. Even newspapers which would become very hostile to non-intervention, such as the *News Chronicle* or *Reynolds News*, offered it their initial support on these grounds. Broad public support for non-intervention lasted well into the autumn of 1936. Philip Noel-Baker, a Labour politician who criticised his party's support for the policy, accepted in mid-September that 'there is probably a good deal of public opinion in favour of "non-intervention", and that for the Labour movement to take the lead in this matter means going against a pretty strong tide'.[32]

The seal was set on the public perception of the opening phase of the Civil War as essentially a Spanish problem in October 1936 with the publication of an influential book by E. Allison Peers, professor of Spanish at Liverpool University and the leading Hispanist of his day. The book was well reviewed and went through six editions in a matter of months, not because it was a model of scholarship (it was concocted primarily from press cuttings) but because of Peers' standing as a 'neutral' academic. Moreover, the book's message, encapsulated in its full title *The Spanish Tragedy, 1930–1937: Dictatorship, Republic, Chaos, Rebellion, War*, chimed with majority sentiment at that time. While not endorsing the anti-communist conspiracy theories of the Right, Peers wrote from a deeply religious and conservative viewpoint. He presented the Republic as a disaster that had failed to take account of Spanish sensibilities and had unleashed a violent reaction. His analysis was convincing, amongst those who wanted to be convinced, in subtly delegitimising the Republican side, and in arguing that this was a fundamentally Spanish conflict which Britain should stand above.

While non-intervention remained popular, however, sympathy was swinging towards the Republic as its supporters articulated the case in its favour. In October a 'Committee of Enquiry into Breaches of International Law Relating to the Intervention in Spain' made effective use of captured documents supplied by the Spanish government to show how non-intervention was being flouted by Germany and Italy. While organised by Communists, the committee contained weighty independent pro-Republicans such as Professor J. B. Trend and Eleanor Rathbone. Even more influential was the report of a cross-party group of MPs, marshalled by the Liberal Wilfred Roberts, that visited Madrid in November. The report, signed by two of the three Conservatives in the group, was authoritative in its account of the aerial bombing of

Madrid by the rebels and drew attention to the humanitarian crisis in the city. While broadly sympathetic to the Republic, it was an even-handed document that also expressed concern at the fate of the estimated 14,000 political prisoners held by the government.

In addition to highlighting foreign intervention and the bombing of civilians, Republican sympathisers also exploited Franco's use of Muslim Moroccan soldiers from the Army of Africa. In terms of public relations (if hardly of military effectiveness) this was Franco's most serious mistake. The Left seized on the incongruity of a Catholic 'Crusade' making use of Muslim forces. The presence of the 'Moors' encouraged the view that the Nationalist rebellion was essentially alien to Spain, hiring savage mercenaries to subdue the Spanish people. The Moors realised 'that it was now their turn . . . they came nursing age-old wrongs, neither giving nor seeking quarter'.[33] The Left's propaganda pandered to racist sentiments in Britain, so that the horror of an invasion by 'black' soldiers allowed the war to be brought home in a particularly dramatic way. This issue helped to dispel the negative images associated with the Republic in the early months of the war, and placed Spain firmly within the community of civilised nations threatened by the most ancient of foes. With the Moors at the gate there could be little doubt that the boundary of 'civilisation' rested on the Spanish rather than the French side of the Pyrenees.[34]

In addition to exposing the dangers facing the Republic, sympathisers also had to defend its record on the issue of atrocities. These were generally located within the context of a timeless Spanish struggle. Rebel atrocities represented the bloody reckoning of a feudal order with those who had dared to challenge it; Republican atrocities were explained either on the grounds that the rebels had used the churches as military outposts, or because the church-burnings and priest-killings represented a culmination of ancient animosities. This view was expressed strikingly by Ralph Bates in his essay 'Compañero Sagasta Burns a Church'. Bates, who had lived in Spain since 1923, was a Communist who claimed an understanding of what he saw as the fundamentally 'religious' anarchist mentality: their violent anti-clericalism was a response to political and sexual oppression by the Church. Witnessing a church-burning in a Catalan village, Bates helped to choose which statues to save and which to burn. Despite his claim neither to 'condone nor to condemn' these actions, he still concluded that: 'The street is brighter, purer, it seems to Compañero Sagasta, *and to me*, when the church is burnt down.'[35]

After the autumn of 1936 British perceptions of the Civil War shifted steadily. It was far less frequently seen as a conflict that was incomprehensible and anachronistic. Instead, it began to be interpreted, even by previously uncommitted observers, as a war that was central to the modern world, both in terms of the issues at stake and the methods of warfare used. This corresponded to changes in the conduct of the war itself, as foreign intervention gave both sides (to differing degrees) the capacity for modern warfare. Moreover, the consolidation of centralised governments on both sides allowed for greater discipline in the armed forces and on the home front. Nothing symbolised this change of perception more clearly than the bombing of Guernica on 26 April 1937, which profoundly shocked opinion in the western democracies. Although it followed other raids by the German Condor Legion on Basque villages such as Durango, the attack on Guernica was particularly disturbing because in the words of the famous *Times* report on 27 April:

> In the form of its execution and the scale of the destruction, no less than in the selection of its objective, the raid on Guernica is unparalleled in military history . . . The object of the bombardment was seemingly the demoralisation of the civil population and the destruction of the cradle of the Basque race.

British opinion, already in a subdued panic due to the fear of mass destruction from the air, now for the first time witnessed the reality in terms easily transferable to British towns.

Guernica accelerated and made irreversible the shift in British sympathies during the Civil War. It was particularly shocking in that its victims, the Basques, were seen in British eyes as uniquely blameless. This was expressed nowhere more clearly than in the writing of George Lowther Steer, *The Times* correspondent whose report did much to form British opinions about Guernica and to undermine the rebel claim that the town's destruction had been caused by retreating Anarchists. Steer passionately identified with the Basques as a classless and democratic people, at odds with the ideologies of the modern world. In his gripping account of the Basque campaign, he argued that they had paid for upholding such unfashionable doctrines as freedom, decency, and truthfulness by succumbing to a two-pronged Spanish attack of 'military Fascism from without [i.e. the rebels] and proletarian pressure from within [i.e. their Socialist and Anarchist allies]'.[36]

The bombing of Guernica was merely a foretaste of how the war would develop. The shocks to public opinion were now overwhelmingly delivered by the Nationalists and their allies as they used their aerial and naval superiority to cripple the Republic. Henceforth all of the miseries of modern warfare – the bombing of defenceless cities, the killing and injuring of civilians, the mass movements of refugee women and children – were suffered by the Republicans. The submarine attacks on British shipping in the summer of 1937 and the bombing of British merchant vessels a year later offended British sentiment and pride. The bombing of Barcelona in March 1938 killed 3,000 citizens and, even more than Guernica, indicated what an aerial attack on London might actually be like.[37] It is, therefore, hardly surprising that opinion polls showed rising sympathy for the Republic in the final two years of the war. The task for the politicians, however, was to turn that sympathy into an instrument that would overturn the government's support for non-intervention.

Although the British, as an island people, have always had the option not to become involved politically in foreign conflicts in which they are not participants, British politics has, in fact, regularly divided over foreign wars and crises. Indeed, this was the case far more before the Spanish Civil War than since. Thus, K. W. Watkins' observation apropos the Spanish Civil War that 'probably not since the French Revolution had a "foreign event" so bitterly divided the British people'[38] deserves qualification: from the First Carlist War (1834–40) and the American Civil War (1861–5), to the agitation surrounding the 'Bulgarian atrocities' (1875–80), 'foreign events' had a striking capacity to arouse and divide British opinion.

Where foreign causes have become major political issues in modern Britain it has usually been for at least one (and generally more) of the following reasons. Firstly, there has been a pressing sense of national peril making the conflict appear directly relevant to British interests; secondly, one side in the conflict has been seen as representative of political or religious values with which a section of the population is in profound sympathy, and opposing an equally well-defined ideological or religious enemy; thirdly, there has been a strong sense of humanitarian identification with one side, generally those regarded as the victims. These categories can, for convenience, be reduced to two: the factors concerned with the implications of a foreign conflict for British interests; and the factors that relate to a direct concern for and identification with one group of participants in a conflict. The case of the Spanish Civil War is particularly notable not only because all of these factors applied, but because they also applied to two distinct constituencies – pro-Republicans and pro-Nationalists – within Britain.

A major determinant for British attitudes was the mounting concern for international peace and stability. Four main groups, which were by no means mutually exclusive, were apparent on the pro-Republican side. These were liberals, left-wing anti-fascists, intellectuals, and those for whom the Civil War raised fears for the security of Britain and its empire.

'Liberal opinion' represented not only the Liberal Party itself, but also internationalist Conservatives and the mainstream of the Labour Party. Such people still believed in the new world order, based on the League of Nations and collective security, envisaged at the end of the First World War. They had watched with dismay the progressive abandonment of international law in favour of power politics ever since the Japanese invasion of Manchuria in 1931. The Spanish Civil War appeared to represent this betrayal in its starkest form. Here was a democratically elected government attacked by its own army, and then denied the means for its defence by an international agreement that was deliberately flouted by the rebels' supporters. Thus, it was believed that the victory of the Republic would have a stabilising effect on European politics by reasserting the primacy of international law and forcing the fascist powers to act within it.

Left-wing anti-fascist opinion, which was far less concerned with international law and regarded the Peace of Versailles itself as largely misguided, was primarily concerned with the rising tide of fascism throughout Europe. This view was particularly to be found amongst Communists and left-wing members of the Labour Party. Although international communism had been slow to respond to the threat from Nazism in the early 1930s, when it had been following a deeply sectarian course, the Nazi take-over in Germany had alerted the Communist leadership to the need for a change in policy. In 1935 at the Seventh Congress of the Communist International the new line of the 'Popular Front' was adopted. Communists would now work in defence of peace and democracy and against fascism, building partnerships with whoever would co-operate with them. The Spanish Civil War, as the quintessential anti-fascist struggle, became the focus for Popular Front activity world-wide in both politics and culture.

For intellectuals, the Civil War was seen as having a cultural, even spiritual, significance. Fascism was equated with a new barbarism in which freedom of thought and expression would be eliminated. Not surprisingly writers and intellectuals felt with a particular intensity the threat to their own future – and the debt that they owed to the Spanish defenders of freedom. Belief in the essential anti-cultural barbarity of fascism was reinforced by the news of the murder in Granada of Federico García Lorca, the pre-eminent Spanish poet and playwright of his generation. This concern for the future of culture ran most visibly through the statements of 127 writers published in support of the Republic in June 1937 as *Authors Take Sides on the Spanish War*: in the words of one contributor, the journalist John Langdon-Davies, 'Art and Anti-Fascism are synonymous.'

For a fourth group, the Civil War was significant primarily in strategic terms. Many who would not have been naturally sympathetic to the Republic came to hope for its success because they dreaded the consequences of a Franco victory: a client state of Germany and Italy threatening the French border, French communications with North Africa, and, above all, Gibraltar and British imperial interests in the Mediterranean. Perhaps the best example of this position was the Duchess of Atholl, a Conservative MP and resolute imperialist and anti-communist, whose pro-Republican sympathies ultimately destroyed her parliamentary career. Basil Liddell Hart, the well-known military writer and a supporter of the Duchess, was another who believed that a Franco victory would be a national disaster. At one point he noted that those who wanted such a victory in Britain (including many of his own circle of contacts) were 'traitors to England'.[39]

Similar arguments, though with the positions reversed, were advanced by the Nationalists' supporters in Britain. For them, the Civil War was not a symptom of a rising tide of fascism, but rather of the continuing threat of communist world revolution. They saw the rebellion as a justifiable riposte to plans for a communist revolution in Spain, and the conflict came to loom just as large in their view of the world in the later 1930s as it did in that of the Left. A Nationalist victory, Franco's supporters believed, would check Soviet expansionism, defeat the forces of atheist communism, and save western civilisation. While active supporters of the Nationalists were far less visible, and less numerous, than those of the Republicans, they were to be found throughout British society. Supporters were most likely to be found amongst two groups. One was the right wing of the Conservative Party and the fascist Right, for whom the Nationalists were seen as leaders in the world-wide anti-communist struggle. Secondly, Catholics were a prominent and disproportionate element in pro-Nationalist circles. For them, admiration for Franco's anti-communism was combined with admiration for the Catholic principles on which he was intending to rebuild Spain.

The international context of the Spanish Civil War explains the urgency that lay behind the British response, but it does not, alone, explain the strength of its appeal in Britain. For the most remarkable aspect of the British response to the Civil War lies in the degree of positive identification with both sides – the sense that this was not simply a front in the increasingly polarised international crisis, but a significant event in its own right. The explanation for this lies in the fact that Spain not only represented a world war in miniature, but that it also represented a New World in miniature.

On the Left, the relatively small group that had taken an interest in Spain before 1936 was already accustomed to seeing the Republic as attempting to establish a 'New Spain', breaking peacefully with the 'Old Spain' of feudal landlords, dictatorial generals, and oppressive clerics. This image was accepted even more widely after the outbreak of the Civil War, although only once the confusion and mayhem of the early months had died down. Indeed, left-wingers who went to Spain were initially more likely to see the New Spain as a revolution that had swept the proletariat into power. The young Communist volunteer John Cornford wrote in the autumn of 1936 that:

> In Barcelona one can understand physically what the dictatorship of the proletariat means . . . the real rule is in the hands of the militia committees . . . It is genuinely a dictatorship of the majority, supported by the overwhelming majority.[40]

This view was shared by George Orwell, who remembered his first view of Barcelona in December 1936 (however misleading with hindsight) as 'startling and overwhelming. It was the first time that I had ever been in a town where the working class was in the saddle.'[41] Hewlett Johnson, the left-wing Dean of Canterbury, recorded in his diary during a visit to the city in April 1937:

> The hotel was a 'has-been', very well fitted but now deserted of those for whom it was fitted. I walked in the streets before breakfast. The shops had lost their splendour, posters were placarded everywhere; one felt that the new civilisation, at any rate at its start[,] did not need such buildings or streets as these, the well-to-do, well-dressed people of yesterday were gone.[42]

This revolutionary vision of the changes taking place in Spain did not last long, and was mainly found amongst those who had visited Spain. As political and social order were restored to the Republic, images of proletarian dictatorship soon gave way to those of the Spanish people united in defence of their Republic and in pursuit of democracy and reform. The wheel had turned full circle, back to the early days of the Republic, as if the turbulence of the summer and autumn of 1936 had never happened. According to the Duchess of Atholl, in her best-selling book *Searchlight on Spain*, there was complete continuity between the pre-war Republic and the wartime regime: 'changes at the centre of government brought no political revolution in their train'.[43] The Republic was humane, progressive, and uplifting. Eleanor Rathbone, writing to the grieving mother of a volunteer ambulance driver, conjured up this remarkable vision:

> Though it is a dreadful war in a way, one did not hear of the kind of horrors (apart from the excesses and cruelties of the early stages) that made the Great War so terrible. It is on such a much smaller scale that the atmosphere is much more normal and I have hardly seen anyone in Spain who looked shell-shocked or dispirited or in painfully bad health. Everybody seemed extraordinarily cheerful, even jolly, and the bright sunshine and beautiful scenery and extraordinarily invigorating air no doubt help to produce this mental and moral atmosphere.[44]

Republican sympathisers emphasised in their reports not only the military front-line, but also the work that was going on to complete the work of the Republic on the home front: education, the elimination of illiteracy, the promotion of mass culture, and the transfer of real responsibility to peasants and workers. Thus, the extent of support for the Republic has to be seen in the context of how low Spain seemed to have fallen in 1931. A country that had been a symbol of undemocratic, reactionary backwardness had now risen up. The ability of its new People's Army to initiate increasingly sophisticated military operations was an index of the social transformation within the Republic as a whole. Ralph Bates, speaking in July 1937 at the Madrid Congress of the International Writers' Association, boasted with reference to Ortega y Gasset that: 'invertebrate Spain has now produced a magnificent and vertebrate army'.[45] As a result of the Civil War, therefore, Spain had been regenerated within the Republican zone.

With hindsight it can be seen that this interpretation was seriously flawed. If there was a New Spain during the latter parts of the Civil War this reflected the defeat of other alternative visions – the New Spain of the Anarchists or of the Socialist Left. The Republican governments of Juan Negrín were geared towards war rather than social reform, and failed in both. The Soviet Union was more concerned to eliminate its political enemies in Spain than to promote social change, however mild. Yet this is to miss the point that these criticisms received little hearing in Britain at the time. The image of a New Spain emerging from the bombed ruins of the Republic and defying fascism was the strongest and the most enduring perception of the importance of the Civil War.

Nor was it only the Left who were mesmerised by the vision of a New Spain. Not all on the amorphous British Right identified with Franco's regime – some, for instance, were monarchists and wished to see the restoration of the old order rather than the birth of the new. But many, especially Catholics, came with time to see more in Franco's movement than mere anti-communism. The rebellion marked a break with the corrupt monarchy and compromised politicians of the past. Franco's New Spain would mark the rebirth of the Spanish nation in arms. All divisive class-based institutions such as trade unions had been suppressed, and the regime would develop elaborate projects of poor relief, urban reconstruction, and land reform.

Franco's New Spain was even emptier than that of the Republicans. Yet it is apparent that, from the British perspective, two competing visions of Spain's future were in conflict. Indeed, within British political debate the division between those who adhered to the idea of a New Spain and those who continued to see the Civil War as a side-show in international politics was perhaps more significant than the more immediately obvious division between Right and Left. Thus, political attitudes were moulded by contrasting perceptions of the nature of the Civil War, and the different priorities that were accordingly given to it. Distinctions can be drawn between, for instance, trade union bureaucrats and passionate pro-Republicans on the Left, as well as between mainstream Conservatives and passionate pro-Nationalists on the Right: it also emphasises the congruities between otherwise ideologically opposed views. In this sense the dividing line ran through, rather than between, Left and Right. But none, it will be argued in the next chapter, were more immune to the idea of a New Spain than the British government.

Chapter 2

GOVERNMENT

On 10 August 1936 the *Daily Herald* published an article by Lord Strabolgi, a Labour peer and former minister, which denounced British policy in the Spanish Civil War as one of 'malevolent neutrality' towards a democratically elected government. Motivated by its fear of Bolshevism, the British government, he claimed, was facilitating the creation of a fascist state in Spain that would threaten the security of the British Empire. Such was Strabolgi's standing that he received a personal reply from Lord Halifax, who asserted that Britain's only aims were to 'localise the disturbance' and to prevent outside assistance from prolonging the war.[1] Strabolgi, now on holiday shooting grouse, remained unconvinced and, indeed, this exchange encapsulated the two poles of argument in subsequent debate over the British government's response to the Civil War. Ever since, argument has oscillated between praising the government's 'statesmanlike' containment of a dangerous conflict, and damning it for abetting a Nationalist victory that was at odds with Britain's own interests. The reality was more prosaic. The British government undoubtedly contributed, intentionally or not, to the defeat of the Republic through its vigorous advocacy of non-intervention. Apart from during the first weeks of the war, however, its policy owed far more to events outside Spain (especially the dictates of relations with Germany and Italy) than to those within it. The complex international problems caused by the Civil War resulted in a policy that gave offence to both sides, cushioned only by the belief that whichever side won would look to Britain for financial assistance. This cynical calculation received its unjustified rewards during the Second World War when, more by luck than by judgement on Britain's part, Spain remained neutral.

Britain's self-styled National Government was created during the economic and political crisis of 1931 when the Labour prime minister James Ramsay MacDonald, with a handful of supporters, abandoned his own party to form an administration with the Conservatives and Liberals. The new government was confirmed in office with a crushing majority in the general election of October 1931, and re-elected with a still considerable mandate in 1935. Ostensibly a broadly based coalition, by 1936 the government was effectively dominated by the Conservatives. Stanley Baldwin had replaced MacDonald as prime minister in 1935, and he made way for his fellow Conservative Neville Chamberlain in May 1937 following the successful resolution of the crisis caused by the abdication of Edward VIII. Despite the continued presence of former Labour and Liberal politicians in senior posts, the government and its supporters were united in broadly conservative policies: seeking economic recovery through orthodox economic measures, the avoidance of war through the 'appeasement' of Europe, and the defence of the Empire as a prime strategic and economic asset. Ministers paid lip-service to the League of Nations in order to win the 1935 election, but had little respect for it and preferred to trust in the strength of Britain and its empire to secure peace.

Although the government was alert to changes in public opinion, it was relatively free from domestic constraints in its Spanish policy. It held an overwhelming majority in the House of Commons over Labour and the opposition Liberals, and it was not troubled by extra-Parliamentary pressures. It is significant that the only occasion when it was admitted in Cabinet that the Civil War was 'getting troublesome from a domestic point of view' was when demonstrations were directed at the German Embassy.[2] Despite the belief of left-wingers at the time, moreover, the government was not in thrall to business interests, even though these were considerable. In January 1937 it was estimated that British investments in Spain were at least £40 million (40 per cent of all foreign capital invested in the country), although this was a tiny proportion of British capital invested worldwide.[3] Concern for the safety of this capital was undoubtedly a consideration for the government. However, business interests lacked decisive influence, and did not work to the sole benefit of one side or the other. Franco's attempt to blockade the north coast of Spain was, for instance, resented by the South Wales steel industry which relied on Basque ore.

Of greater significance in the formation of policy was division within the government, especially under the prime ministership of Stanley Baldwin, who took little interest in foreign affairs. In the absence of leadership from Baldwin, control over Spanish policy rested with the Foreign Office and with Anthony Eden, a glamorous and often impulsive foreign secretary who stood on the liberal wing of the Conservative Party and became increasingly isolated within the Cabinet. Eden's policy on Spain evolved considerably during the Civil War, although primarily in response to the actions of Germany and Italy rather than as a consequence of personal sympathy for the Spanish Republic. As his suspicion of the two dictators deepened, so too did his reluctance to contemplate a Franco victory and his will-ingness to countenance the use of British power to enforce inter-national agreements. In this he was successfully resisted by the majority of the Cabinet, and especially by the Conservative right wing, represented most vociferously by Sir Samuel Hoare. Hoare, as First Lord of the Admiralty, was well placed to undermine Eden, not least because the upper echelons of the Admiralty shared his antipathy towards the Spanish Republic. First Sea Lord Ernle Chatfield, for instance, once confided that Franco's was a 'much nobler cause than the Reds''.[4] The political balance within Cabinet moved against Eden when Neville Chamberlain became prime minister in May 1937. Not only did Chamberlain have better-formed views on foreign policy than Baldwin, but he was also willing to intervene directly to implement them. After prolonged tension between Chamberlain and his foreign secretary, Eden resigned in February 1938 and was replaced by the less combative Lord Halifax.

In Whitehall, government policy towards the Civil War was influenced primarily by the Foreign Office, where Sir Robert Vansittart was the permanent under-secretary until January 1938. After a difficult working relationship, Eden was able to engineer Vansittart's removal to the new and less influential post of chief diplomatic adviser, and replaced him with the more pliant Sir Alexander Cadogan. An official of independent views and great suspicion of Germany, Vansittart voiced his disquiet over non-intervention only once he had been sidelined. In January 1939 he pointed out to Lord Halifax that Britain's

1 *Anthony Eden (left) and Sir Robert Vansittart (right) leave the Foreign Office, 1937*

policy had been one-sided and certain to make Britain's position 'well nigh untenable'.[5]

More than any other department of state, the Foreign Office remained a self-consciously elite institution, recruited from Oxbridge and the public schools, with a strongly male culture. (Following one of the Duchess of Atholl's many interventions on the Civil War a senior official minuted that 'I still feel rather sorry for the Duke of Atholl.')[6] Not surprisingly, anti-communism was rife in these circles, as, to a lesser degree, was sympathy for Franco's Nationalists.[7] The main exception was Laurence Collier of the Northern Department who was the only leading Foreign Office official to identify fascism as a greater threat to British interests than communism. Indeed, in one spirited outburst he would attack his colleagues for acting as 'Conservatives first and Englishmen afterwards' in appearing to connive at Italian intervention in Spain.[8]

This balance of sentiment was even more visible amongst British officials and diplomats within Spain itself. The ambassador, Sir Henry

2 Neville Chamberlain (centre) and Lord Halifax (right) (with Prime Minister Van Zeeland of Belgium), 1936

Chilton, was a leading critic of the Republic. He removed himself to Hendaye on the French side of the border at the start of the war and remained there until his retirement in 1938. His views were shared by many British consuls around Spain, most notably the courageous but splenetically 'anti-Red' consul Norman King in Barcelona. Most felt that the outrages of the early phase of the Civil War had vindicated their warnings, seemingly alarmist, of the pre-war period. Moreover, they felt more comfortable socially with Nationalists, and many assisted in the escape of suspected Franco supporters (often with the help of the Royal Navy). Accusations of pro-rebel bias were particularly directed against the British authorities in Gibraltar. A local left-wing politician drew up a detailed list of unproven allegations which included the toleration of rebel spies in the colony and the official harassment of Republican refugees and British journalists. Pro-Republican meetings were banned, while the Catholic bishop of Gibraltar poured out anti-Republic tirades from his pulpit.[9] Despite their prejudices, however, most British diplomats gave even-handed service in Spain and struggled to offer humanitarian assistance in an environment rendered extremely dangerous by warfare and political intrigue. George Ogilvie-Forbes, the British chargé d'affaires in Chilton's absence, saved the lives of many suspected anti-Republicans by keeping the Madrid Embassy open until January 1937, and Consul Stevenson in Bilbao became closely identified with the Basque cause until the fall of the city. Another diplomat, Geoffrey Thompson, found his political sympathies shifting as a result of being bombed by the Italians in Valencia (the British mission having moved there after leaving Madrid).[10]

Apart from the Foreign Office, other ministries had substantial interests of their own in the Civil War. For instance, the War Office was anxious to monitor the military performance of the two sides and their new tanks and aeroplanes, while the Home Office dealt with the many political and humanitarian issues that affected Britain directly. These interests were not always compatible. For instance, the Admiralty was anxious not to take on extra commitments and was hostile to the Republic, while the Board of Trade wished to safeguard British commerce by keeping trade routes open. In particular, the tensions between the Admiralty and the Foreign Office were central to many of the debates within government over its response to the conflict.

The outbreak of the Civil War in Spain coincided with a period of relative international quiet (and, indeed, a time when most politicians were dispersing on holiday) following the crises precipitated by the Italian invasion of Abyssinia in October 1935 and the German remilitarisation of the Rhineland in March 1936. Despite the blows that both actions dealt to the prospects for European peace, the Foreign Office had remained relatively optimistic. Italian de facto conquest of Abyssinia resulted in the withdrawal of sanctions in May 1936, and appeared to create new opportunities for reducing British–Italian friction in the Mediterranean and Middle East. Similarly, Hitler's coup in reoccupying what was, after all, German territory in the Rhineland was followed by diplomatic initiatives aimed at a new five-power conference to guarantee the security of the French and Belgian borders. The Foreign Office did not lose sight of this prize during the early months of the Spanish Civil War, and regarded the non-intervention agreement as helpful not least because it cleared the agenda for further progress on this question. Eden had written privately in August 1936 that 'I am very unhappy that this terrible Spanish question should now come to complicate our troubles in Europe', especially at a time when Germany and Italy had accepted an invitation to the five-power conference.[11] However, the chimera of a 'new Locarno' (referring to the successful west European treaty of 1925) had to be abandoned in 1937 due to German unwillingness to negotiate.

Despite the equanimity of the Foreign Office in the face of these two crises, Britain's strategic and diplomatic position was perceived to be increasingly perilous. While German revanchism was a cause for concern, more direct threats to British interests were posed by a fully mobilised Italy which was inflaming Arab resentment against British rule in Palestine, and by Japanese militarism in the Far East. More worrying still was the possible conjunction of all three threats and, consequently, the danger of overextending the resources of the British Empire. Reducing the number of Britain's potential enemies thus became a prime objective of government. Increasing concern on this score coincided with the perception that France, racked by internal political divisions, was no longer a dependable ally. This was the context for the policy of appeasement as pursued by Neville Chamberlain, which had the aim not only of resolving disputes in Europe, but also of preventing Fascist Italy from becoming too closely allied with Nazi Germany. The desire to conciliate Italy, coinciding with the massive Italian intervention in Spain, ensured that for the British government the Spanish Civil War would be inextricably bound up with appeasement.[12]

The early weeks of the Civil War demonstrated the degree to which some government ministers and civil servants saw communism as the main threat to European stability and viewed the Spanish conflict accordingly. Sir Maurice Hankey, the long-serving Cabinet secretary, had even pondered on 20 July 1936 whether 'before long it might pay us to throw in our lot with Germany and Italy' as Bolshevism was 'menacing' France and Spain.[13] Sir Samuel Hoare's definition of neutrality in early August was 'a situation in which the Russians neither officially or unofficially give help to the Communists. On no account must we do anything to bolster up Communism in Spain' (as it might spread to Portugal and threaten British imperial interests).[14] Soon afterwards Orme Sargent, assistant under-secretary at the Foreign

Office, minuted that – to avert the danger of Europe dividing on ideological lines – Britain must stop France from 'going Bolshevik' under the influence of the Civil War.[15] Comments of this nature lend credence to the argument that ideological anti-communism primarily determined the British government's response to the Civil War, especially in the early months, and that its official impartiality was a front concealing a 'malevolent neutrality' designed to secure the defeat of the Spanish Republic.[16]

There is no doubt that the British government did not view the survival of the Spanish Republic as a prime national interest, and, indeed, was willing to contemplate an alternative form of government in Spain. Britain's interests were presented very starkly by Anthony Eden in January 1937: 'First, that the conflict shall not spread beyond the boundaries of Spain; and second, that the political independence and the territorial integrity of Spain shall be preserved.'[17] As this formula made clear, the British government was happy with any outcome so long as the resulting regime was stable and independent, and hence did not threaten Britain's strategic position. Given the hostility to the Republic in government circles, and the fears of its slide into revolutionary chaos, there was an initial predilection to see this stability as being provided by a military government. However, it is important to bear in mind that ideological distaste for the Republic was but one of many factors influencing the formation of policy, a blend that changed constantly during the course of the Civil War. For example, the situation in the opening weeks of the Civil War was chaotic, and immediate decisions had to be taken to meet specific requirements. In the longer term, British policy was neither coherent nor determined, and was often deflected by diplomatic, legal, political, and humanitarian considerations. Above all, the rapid inter-nationalisation of the Civil War, the possible threat to British strategic interests, and the danger of a European conflict meant that any preference about the form of government in Spain following the war had to be balanced against wider concerns. Indeed, from the late summer of 1936 onwards British policy towards Spain cannot be abstracted from the question of relations with Germany and Italy.

Immediate British government responses to the outbreak of the Civil War were moulded primarily by three influences. The first was the accumulation of reports in the months preceding July 1936 from official sources in Spain. Led by the ambassador himself, most British officials viewed conditions under the Popular Front government with grave concern. In their opinion, the government could not govern, could not control its extremist element, and could not protect British interests from the mounting anarchy. These reports were supported by unofficial sources – for instance, the historian and Conservative Party official Arthur Bryant, who had the ear of Stanley Baldwin, returned from Spain with a highly pessimistic analysis.[18]

A second influence was the prevailing perception of Spain in Conservative and Foreign Office circles. Throughout the war Spain continued to be seen as a second-rate and unimportant country where representative government was unlikely to flourish. Patronising attitudes were adopted towards the Spanish and their ability to govern themselves efficiently and democratically. For instance, in December 1936 Eden endorsed the view of the Spanish writer and diplomat Salvador de Madariaga that there did not have to be a choice between a fascist and a communist Spain: Primo de Rivera's dictatorial government of the 1920s, 'though far from being a democracy in our sense of the word, could hardly be described as Fascist'.[19] Others in the Foreign Office spoke hopefully of a 'liberal' Franco dictatorship winning the support of the masses with social reforms.[20] This belief in an authoritarian middle ground, between the extremes of Right and Left and appropriate to Spain's stage of political development, underpinned the British government's numerous abortive attempts to secure a mediated settlement.

Thirdly, it is important to emphasise the degree of confusion in early British analyses of the situation in Spain. It was far from clear who (if anyone) was in charge in Madrid as Republican governments came and went; the arming of the workers to defeat the rebels suggested that the Republican authorities had lost control;[21] and the atrocities (especially on the Republican side) caused revulsion. In the absence of any direct threat to British interests, especially Gibraltar, and as the British government was willing to consider a military regime as an acceptable solution to Spain's turbulence, its initial response was to wait and see what transpired. The strongest measure taken was to send the Royal Navy to Spanish waters – officially to offer humanitarian assistance, unofficially to project British power into a potentially dangerous conflict.

Almost immediately, however, the government was confronted with important choices that could affect the course of the war. The first of these occurred on 21 July when the Spanish Republican authorities requested the right for its navy to take on oil in Gibraltar. Although the government could not forbid the supply of oil, private contractors appear to have been informally discouraged from doing so and the fleet departed unfuelled. This action was influenced by antipathy to the Republican fleet which had massacred its officers, but also by concern that refuelling the fleet would be treated as a hostile act by the Nationalists – a fear brought home by the bombing of some vessels sheltering at Gibraltar.

A second and much more significant issue was that of the supplying of arms to the Republic, initially raised by the Spanish ambassador Julio Lopez Oliván in conversation with Eden on 28 July. On 29 July the Cabinet agreed that it was unable to prevent the sale of private aeroplanes for 'civil' use (some were indeed already being sent to the rebels), and Eden was permitted to proceed as usual with processing requests for arms sales. Privately, Eden was adamant that no weapons would be sold, and had already minuted on 28 July that 'I hope that we shall be able to avoid supplying [arms] by some means or other.'[22] Eden's caution was reinforced by the fact that the Spanish ambassador was sabotaging his own instructions, imploring Eden not to accede to his government's requests.

These early episodes gave a clear indication of how British policy would develop. Diplomatic norms would be respected, and there would be no official neutrality between a recognised government and the rebels. However, nothing would be done to assist the Republican government against its attackers, and in practice an attitude of impartiality would be adopted. This policy, displeasing to the Republicans, had the advantage of maintaining the possibility of good relations with both sides. Moreover, the government kept in step with the evolution of British public and political opinion which saw little to choose between the two sides and, for differing reasons, favoured non-intervention by all the powers. It was only in the autumn, when evidence of fascist infringement of non-intervention began to change public sentiment, that the government had to work harder to justify its policy.

By the late summer the strategic and diplomatic context of the war had been fundamentally altered by many countries' formal adoption of the non-intervention agreement, and by the internationalisation of the Civil War. The British government was aware of the military support that was reaching the Nationalists, but did not see any immediate dangers to the strategic balance in the western Mediterranean. When Admiral Darlan of France was sent on 5 August to present his government's fears of an Italian threat to occupy the Balearic Islands, he was given short shrift by Sir Ernle Chatfield, who could perceive no such danger. Darlan's visit was taken as evidence of French 'panic' and an attempt to drag Britain into the Spanish conflict.[23] Opinions were soon to be revised. On 19 August Owen St Clair O'Malley's Foreign Office memorandum warned of the danger of Italy using the war to weaken Britain's position in the western Mediterranean,[24] and on 24 August a sub-committee of the Chiefs of Staff reported very precisely on Britain's security interests in the Iberian peninsula. Identifying Gibraltar as the key strategic and commercial interest, and Italy as the main threat to regional stability, the committee saw the goals of British policy as:

> (a) the maintenance of the Territorial integrity of Spain and her possessions (Balearics, Morocco, Canaries, and Rio del Oro);
> (b) the maintenance of such relations with any Spanish government that may emerge from this conflict as will ensure benevolent neutrality in the event of our being engaged in European war.[25]

Thus within a month of the outbreak of the Civil War, British policy formers had had to come to terms not only with the struggle for power within Spain, but also its implications for Britain's imperial security.

The making of the non-intervention agreement dominated diplomatic activity in the first months of the Civil War. The initiative was taken by the French prime minister Léon Blum, whose administration was sympathetic to the Spanish government and was permitted by an agreement signed in 1935 to supply it with arms to the value of 20 million francs. Pierre Cot at the Air Ministry immediately began to organise the dispatch of military assistance. Blum, however, changed his mind and, at a Cabinet meeting on 25 July, it was agreed to prohibit the export of French arms and aircraft to Spain. The change in policy was partly the result of pressure from British government ministers whom Blum had met at a previously arranged conference in London on 23–4 July. Baldwin, in particular, warned that Britain might not take sides if French intervention provoked war with Italy, while Eden had apparently warned Blum to 'be careful'.[26] Blum was, however, also influenced by divisions within his own Cabinet (where the Radicals were mainly opposed to intervention) and by the danger that the Civil War would further inflame French politics.

The British government, which had already decided not to intervene in the Civil War, welcomed Blum's adoption of non-intervention as a means of preventing the polarisation of Europe and diminishing the danger of war. It was feared that precipitate French action in support of the Spanish Republic would endanger the projected five-power talks and result in a Europe divided into two blocs, with the unwelcome prospect of Britain being forced to side with the Soviet Union against the fascist powers. Indeed, Baldwin's only known instruction to Eden at the start of the Civil War was that, 'on no account, French or other, must he bring us in to fight on the side of the Russians'.[27] It is fair to add, however, that both in government and in the country at large there was no support for war over Spain in any circumstances.

The tension between British caution and French domestic political pressures created a situation in which Britain could achieve its diplomatic objectives, but at the price of appearing to bully the French government. Evidence of fascist intervention in Spain made it very difficult for Blum to maintain support for French non-intervention, and on 1 August he gave notice that the policy would be abandoned unless Italy agreed to join the embargo. On 7 August the British ambassador, Sir George Clerk, paid a visit to the French foreign minister, Yvon Delbos. Ostensibly acting on his own initiative, Clerk warned of the 'danger of any action which might definitely commit the French Government to one side of the conflict and make more difficult the close co-operation between our two countries which was called for by this crisis'.[28] Whatever the reason for Clerk's intervention, it must have contributed to the subsequent French decision to suspend once more the supply of arms to Spain. However, while doing nothing to dispel the suspicion of British interference in French internal affairs, Clerk was probably acting in order to help Blum and moderates in his government against pressure from the French Left and the trade unions to supply arms to the Republic.[29]

It was soon realised that non-intervention would be politically acceptable in Britain and France only if other countries (especially those sympathetic to the rebels) made similar declarations. However, there was disagreement over the form that this wider embargo should take. The Foreign Office resisted the French idea of an agreement limited to Britain, France, and Italy. As Sir George Mounsey pointed out on 3 August:

> the French government would no doubt like to draw us into some commitment to support, even if only morally, the present Spanish Government, and then deter other foreign Governments from sending arms to the rebels in the face of Anglo-French opposition.[30]

Instead, the Foreign Office insisted on an impartial non-intervention that would be 'practically universal': the formula that was eventually adopted. By mid-August British officials approached non-intervention with genuine enthusiasm, and had come round to seeing it as a useful tool in achieving their broader aims.

The British government's mood of self-congratulation on the establishment of both the non-intervention agreement and, from September, the Non-Intervention Committee is understandable. Here was a forum in which all of the European powers could meet as the basis for future co-operation at a time when both Germany and Italy were outside the League of Nations. Moreover, it was a policy that carried with it the still non-interventionist British public opinion of the first weeks of the war. Many in the labour movement saw non-intervention as a victory that would prevent the British government from helping Franco and, if observed, would promote a Republican victory. Labour leaders were more concerned by the Italian claim that there should be '100 per cent non-intervention', covering humanitarian and political assistance as well as arms. Even the Communist *Daily Worker* initially welcomed non-intervention, to which the Soviet Union had adhered, on these grounds. Thus, for British opposition opinion the extension of non-intervention to include all of the foreign powers was the condition for accepting Britain's own impartiality in the conflict.

What was not made clear at this point was that Spain was not the true focus of the British government's endeavours. These were almost wholly concerned with the question of European peace, and would remain so until the end of the Civil War. Within the Foreign Office it was soon accepted that non-intervention was being consistently broken, initially by the fascist powers and, after 23 October, by the Soviet Union as well. It was also accepted that non-intervention was, in the words of one official, a 'piece of humbug', the alternative to which was war;[31] it was more important that it should exist than that it should achieve its stated objectives. Plans for non-intervention control were grudgingly endorsed by the Foreign Office, at considerable expense to the taxpayer, in the knowledge that they would have no real impact. This sense of cynicism was reinforced by the record of the Non-Intervention Committee which met in London under the chairmanship of the British junior minister Lord Plymouth. The rules of the Committee seemed designed to obstruct the investigation of illicit arms supply through bureaucratic delay, and to avoid giving offence to Germany and Italy. The desire to conciliate the fascist powers, combined with their own determination to intervene in Spain, turned non-intervention from a diplomatic victory into a humiliating trap. In May 1937 one Foreign Office official, presented with evidence of German bombing of the Basques, would minute that 'I do not think we are under any illusions about the German share in these air atrocities; but there is nothing we can do about it short of breaking up the non-intervention agreement.'[32]

The non-intervention agreement, while primarily concerned with international relations, also had significant implications for domestic politics. The police carefully monitored the activities of Republican agents alleged to be buying arms and recruiting pilots, and this extended into a more general surveillance of pro-Republican activity in Britain. Even more controversially, non-intervention was, in effect, extended to cover the flow of information between Britain and Spain. In October 1936 Julián Gorkín, a senior figure from the POUM who had been invited to address a meeting of the Independent Labour Party, was turned back at Croydon airport. The Home Office exclusion order was queried by the Foreign Office, which pointed out that Nationalist agents resident in Britain such as the Duke of Alba were quite free to propagandise their views. The revealing response from the Home Office was that no one would be refused entry unless:

(a) they are dangerous to us – some communist agents are, (b) they are going to address public meetings, thereby disturbing public order and an already over-taxed police. (This is quite different from talking privately to one's friends.)[33]

This policy clearly counted against the Republicans who had much more to lose from being excluded from mass audiences in Britain. The Nationalists operated within established circles of supporters and had little popular support. The Republic also suffered from government policy on the granting of visas to Spain, which were often withheld unless a visit could be justified on non-political grounds. The Communist journalist Claud Cockburn was prevented from returning to Spain because he had briefly joined a militia at the start of the Civil War. Subsequently, journalists and politicians were forced to sign a declaration that 'nothing will take place in the course of my visit that could be construed as implying any intervention by me'.[34] The Labour leader Clement Attlee, who signed such a declaration, was criticised by Conservatives on his return for his pro-Republican statements in Spain and forced to make a 'personal explanation' to Parliament. However, the government was aware of the limitations on its legal powers in this area. In December 1937 the leading Labour politician Sir Stafford Cripps objected to Foreign Office attempts to restrict a humanitarian delegation with which he was involved. Civil servants backed down from becoming embroiled in legal argument with a lawyer of Cripps' reputation, and contented themselves with the thought that

> if, as seems probable, [the delegation] either misbehave or cast an intolerable burden on the British representatives in Spain, we should in future be on strong ground, from the practical if not the legal point of view, in being stricter in future, even in the case of MPs.[35]

With the consolidation of the machinery of non-intervention, British government attention in the autumn of 1936 turned to relations with the Nationalists, and the pressing question of what would happen if (and when) they won the war. Relations were plagued by a number of difficulties. The rebels' grievances were forcefully conveyed to the Foreign Office on 2 September by Juan de la Cierva, the aviation pioneer and Nationalist sympathiser, who had just returned from a meeting with Generals Franco and Mola. He summarised their complaints as follows: Britain had initially failed to keep Tangier neutral, had given facilities to Spanish government ships in Gibraltar and had interrupted cable services to rebel territory. Most importantly, Britain had hindered exports from Nationalist Spain by maintaining the pre-war payments agreement whereby any foreign currency earned would be accorded to the Republican government.[36] These problems stemmed primarily from the continuing recognition of the Republican government as the legal government of Spain. While Britain had downgraded these relations by keeping its ambassador across the French border in Hendaye (as did many other countries), this situation was greatly resented by Franco. In order to improve relations without actually recognising Franco's regime, the British government embarked on a series of pragmatic measures, which included the suspension of the payments agreement in November 1936 and the formal exchange of agents (a step that was short of full diplomatic recognition) with the Nationalists in November 1937.

Relations were further complicated by the fraught question of belligerent rights. Under international law, one option open to the British government would have been to declare itself formally neutral in the Civil War, and to have conferred belligerent rights on both parties. In 1861, for instance, Britain had declared neutrality during the American Civil War. Such a declaration generally occurs when three conditions are met: the insurgents must possess a certain amount of territory of the legal government; they must have established their own government; and they should be conducting the conflict according to the laws of war. Although not affecting the question of diplomatic recognition, the conferring of such rights places both parties on the same footing in terms of the conduct of the war, and grants them certain privileges and obligations.[37]

The question of belligerent rights had significant practical ramifications during the Spanish Civil War because one of the main benefits of belligerent status is the right to blockade enemy ports. In the opening phase of the Spanish Civil War this would have helped the Republic, which inherited the greater share of the fleet. However, the British government was unwilling to sanction a step which would potentially extend the war to the high seas in a vital trading area, while the Admiralty in particular did not see the Republican fleet as deserving of such rights. In any case, the Republican government resented being accorded the same status as the rebels under international law, and did not request belligerent rights. Thus, in August 1936 non-intervention was preferred by the British government to a formal declaration of neutrality.

As the Nationalists rapidly gained the upper hand at sea, however, the question of belligerent rights again became a pressing one. Now, however, it was understood that a state of belligerency would hasten a Nationalist victory against a Republic dependent on supply by sea. In October 1936 Franco's forces appeared poised to take Madrid, and, on Eden's advice, the Cabinet agreed on 21 October to grant belligerent rights once Madrid had fallen. The successful defence of Madrid derailed this strategy, and, under French pressure, Eden soon changed his mind and came to see belligerent rights as the only leverage that Britain could exercise over Franco. Eden's reluctance deepened in 1937 on the realisation that so long as Franco was dependent on foreign support there would be a danger that a Nationalist blockade against Soviet ships, supported by Germany or Italy, could spark an international war. Belligerent rights became the focus of pressure from right-wingers within the Cabinet (such as Hoare) and in Parliament, as well as the major grievance of the Franco regime. The British agent Sir Robert Hodgson wrote that, on his arrival in Salamanca, the British stance on this issue was particularly resented: by denying Franco the right to blockade, British policy 'was responsible for the demolition of many Spanish towns [through bombing], the needless prolongation of the Civil War, and the loss of many Spanish lives'.[38] It is important to note that the Nationalists had a genuine grievance. J. L. Brierly, professor of international law at Oxford and a Republican sympathiser, confided that 'I do not think that most opponents of belligerent rights for Franco realise the strength of his claim on purely legal grounds.' It was, he added, most unusual to withhold rights in this situation and if it were not for intervention by the fascist powers Franco's claim would be 'irresistible'.[39]

Franco sought to force the issue by declaring a blockade of Barcelona in November 1936. This directly affected Britain, as much of the Soviet war materiel was being brought to Spain in British merchant ships, at a time when the British merchant marine was the largest in the world. Confronted with this challenge, the Admiralty issued provisional orders that the navy should no longer protect British merchant ships trading with Spain from being stopped and searched by Spanish warships. Though this order was soon rescinded, the Admiralty still took the opportunity to call for the conferring of belligerent rights even prior to the fall of Madrid. This was resisted by Eden who was already concerned at the implications of a Franco victory facilitated by Germany and Italy. While he was prepared to take steps to prevent British vessels carrying arms to Spain, he was not willing to grant the Nationalists the wider advantages of belligerent rights. His diary entry for 21 November makes clear that he took this stance 'for international rather than Spanish reasons. I do not want even to appear to follow Hitler and Mussolini at the moment, but would prefer to "show a tooth" in the Mediterranean. Still less do I want to facilitate a blockade that is maybe intended to starve Madrid.'[40] A compromise was reached whereby legislation was rushed through Parliament (the Merchant Shipping Bill) which prohibited all British ships from carrying arms to Spain. Accordingly, it was believed that the rationale for Franco's claim to belligerency had been met, and Soviet weapons would have to find other avenues for reaching Spain. However, frictions remained, as in the later stages of the war food imports became almost as vital for the Republic as weapons, and Franco's navy would again seek to impose the right to blockade.

During 1937 Anthony Eden was increasingly forceful in demanding a modification in British policy towards the Civil War. He was influenced by pressure from the parliamentary opposition for non-intervention to function effectively and, more significantly, by evidence of intensified Italian and German intervention. In the autumn of 1936 he had not appeared very concerned about this, and had made a much-derided comment in Parliament that there were 'other governments more to blame' than those of Germany and Italy for breaches in non-intervention.[41] Eden was particularly concerned at the prospect of Italy establishing a base in the Balearic Islands, and in late 1936 he stipulated that a commitment to maintain the national territory of Spain should be included in the proposed British–Italian 'Gentleman's Agreement' to secure stability in the western Mediterranean region. Although the Italians cavilled at such a specific reference, they did permit simultaneous publication of notes which proclaimed the Italian desire to see Spanish territory remain 'intact and unmodified'. British satisfaction at this denial of Italian expansionist intention, however, was soured by the immediate departure of many more Italian soldiers for Spain. By the end of the war some 72,000 Italians had served as 'volunteers' in Spain, by far the single largest foreign contingent in the Civil War.

These events convinced Eden of Mussolini's bad faith: he now saw a

Republican victory as preferable to a Franco victory achieved through massive Italian assistance. Eden was particularly concerned by the question of 'volunteers', fearing that an Italian force would remain in Spain to threaten British interests at the end of the war. In a dramatic gesture, Eden brought proposals to Cabinet on 8 January 1937 for a unilateral blockade of Spain by the Royal Navy to prevent the arrival of arms and volunteers. According to Eden, such measures were vital to avoid war with the 'Dictator Powers' and to prevent their conquest of Spain. However, he lacked the support of Baldwin, and his proposal was widely denounced by his colleagues as dangerous and unworkable. Sir Samuel Hoare feared that the proposals, which amounted to an attempt to 'stop Franco from winning', cut across the concerns of those 'who were very anxious that the Soviet [sic] should not win in Spain'.

Despite this reverse, Eden's initiative had two important consequences. The first was that it forced the British government to press for control of non-intervention (rather than the toothless observation scheme already existing), and from March 1937 the British, French, German, and Italian navies shared responsibility for patrol of the Spanish coasts. This broke down following the Republican aerial attack on the German pocket-battleship the *Deutschland* in June, the German revenge shelling of the port of Almería, and an alleged submarine attack on the cruiser *Leipzig*. Secondly, Britain successfully promoted an extension of non-intervention to cover volunteering and, even before this came into effect on 20 February, unilaterally declared that the 1870 Foreign Enlistment Act would apply to the Spanish Civil War. The 1870 Act had dubious legality in the Spanish context, and its revival was designed primarily to give a lead to other states rather than seriously to curb British volunteering. Recruitment and organisation of the International Brigades was simply driven underground and, while eleven cases were referred to the director of public prosecutions, no legal action was taken.[42]

Eden suffered a further rebuff from his Cabinet colleagues in March, on the question of German threats to British economic interests in Nationalist Spain. While attention had been focused at the start of the war on the revolutionary expropriation of British companies in the Republican zone, relations between the Nationalists and the mining companies in southern Spain were also strained. The companies had been no friends of the Republic, which they blamed for promoting labour unrest. In 1931, for instance, Rio Tinto had decided not to invest any new capital in Spain except in cases of 'absolute necessity'.[43] After the start of the Civil War, however, the Nationalist authorities placed new regulations on the mines and demanded to be granted the sterling value of their exports. The chairman of the Rio Tinto Company, Sir Auckland Geddes, was also concerned by the requisition of minerals for export to Germany by the HISMA-ROWAK company, and saw this as an opportunity to alarm the British government about the longer-term threat posed by Germany to Britain's own supply of pyrites. The result was Eden's memorandum, presented to Cabinet on 3 March, which envisaged going as far as using the Royal Navy to intercept the transit of ore to Germany and Italy. The scheme was again heavily criticised by Hoare, who submitted a written statement warning of the danger of war, and by the chancellor Neville Chamberlain, who argued persuasively for a more graduated response. The apparent crisis in relations with the Nationalists soon passed. Rio Tinto was able to persuade them to relax the financial controls imposed on the company, and the British government was soon in a position to improve bilateral relations through the exchange of diplomatic agents, encouraging the Nationalist authorities to restrict the activities of HISMA-ROWAK and not to rely exclusively on Germany and Italy.

Before the arrival of the agents, however, Britain had to endure a period of particularly severe strain in relations with the Nationalists following their offensive against the Basque country in the spring of 1937. In April Franco unexpectedly proclaimed a blockade of the northern coast, intended to prevent British foodships from reaching Bilbao. The British government initially acquiesced in this, following advice from Ambassador Chilton and Royal Navy officers on the spot that a de facto blockade was in place and that Britain did not have the means available to challenge it. Despite the illegality of the Nationalist action, it was agreed on 7 April that British shipowners would be warned of the dangers in Basque waters, and that Royal Navy protection would not apply within the three-mile territorial limit. As interim measures, merchant ships were told to wait at the nearby French port of St Jean de Luz, and the powerful battlecruiser *Hood* was sent to the Basque coast. At an emergency Cabinet meeting on 11 April ministers were aware of the fine line that separated a blow to British prestige in accepting this infringement of the freedom of traffic on the high seas, and the alternative danger of war with the Nationalists. It was agreed that the legality of the blockade would not be recognised, but that ships would be advised not to proceed to Bilbao. Meanwhile, compromise solutions would be sought. For instance, ships engaged in the export of iron ore to South Wales might be permitted to travel to Bilbao with their holds empty of food. Thus, in the first phase of the Bilbao crisis the Admiralty, often on the basis of spurious evidence, was allowed to dominate the British response.

The government's conciliation of the Nationalists soon began to break down. Evidence accumulated to show that the blockade was far from effective: the threat posed to shipping by Nationalist mines was disputed, and it was pointed out that shore-based Basque guns could easily protect vessels within the three-mile limit. Government ministers struggled to defend their position at an emergency Parliamentary debate on 14 April. The matter was conclusively settled on 20 April when the *Seven Seas Spray* was the first of a number of ships to break the blockade from St Jean de Luz. This achievement, combined with the most forceful domestic political opposition of the entire Civil War, now put paid to Franco's blockade. On 22 April Vice-Admiral Blake on the *Hood* escorted three more vessels to Basque territorial waters, warning off a Nationalist cruiser in the process. This episode, while doing little to prolong the war in the North of Spain, soured British relations with the Nationalists. On 26 April Sir Henry Chilton reported a heated interview with the military governor of Irún who conveyed Franco's 'disgust' at the actions of the Royal Navy, and added that 'if we [the British] wanted war we could have it'.[44] Chilton was instructed to make soothing noises to the effect that Britain was merely exercising its right to offer protection on the high seas, and was acting wholly 'impartially'.

The damage to relations was almost immediately compounded by the successful campaign to persuade the British government to accept 4,000 Basque children for safe-keeping during the siege of Bilbao. Despite the public resentment felt by Franco's government at this incident, many of the children stayed in Britain until the end of the war and beyond, even though the British government was increasingly desperate to repatriate them. The case of the Basque children, who were evacuated despite the combined scepticism of the Home Office, the labour movement, and the Save the Children Fund, is a good example of the difficulty that the British government faced in pursuing a coherent policy during the Civil War.[45]

The fall of the Basque country had a further unforeseen consequence for the British government. The Nationalist authorities demanded that the steamers of Bilbao shipowners, formerly in the service of the Spanish government, should be detained in British ports with a view to the legal establishment of rebel ownership. Hearings at the Admiralty Court and the House of Lords eventually found in favour of the Spanish government. This raised the prospect of attempts being made to commandeer the vessels, and Spanish consuls were soon engaged in weeding out pro-Nationalist crew members with a view to guaranteeing control of the ships. In the event, a number of attacks were made on vessels with the assistance of British Fascists. On this occasion, however, the Home Office sided with the Republicans, instructing the police that they should not take sides in the dispute – but should also protect those in de facto possession from violence.[46] Despite ugly confrontations in ports such as Cardiff, Port Talbot, Belfast, and Avonmouth, a combination of Spanish loyalist crew members, the police, and local trades unionists were able to prevent the commandeering of any ships apart from one, the *Rita Garcia*, which was seized and taken from Immingham to Hamburg.

The damaging farce over the blockade of Bilbao, followed by the departure of Hoare to the Home Office, increased Eden's authority on Spanish policy, at least until Neville Chamberlain, as prime minister, began to assert his own dominance over foreign affairs. The foreign secretary's goals were to prevent a victory for Italian and German intervention in Spain whilst protecting British interests and prestige. In the summer of 1937 two distinct threads became apparent in Eden's policy. The first was the need for a diplomatic initiative to control (and if possible to end) the war following the collapse of the naval control scheme. Eden's main priority was to reduce foreign intervention in the conflict, with a view to ensuring that the victor would not be dominated by one of the powers. Accordingly, in July 1937 a British plan was adopted which envisaged the withdrawal of volunteers from both sides in return for the granting of belligerent rights. Such an initiative would help the Nationalists in the long run, but would secure a 'Spanish' solution to the conflict. Despite considerable diplomatic effort into the autumn of 1938, however, the plan met with intransigence from the rebels and made little progress.

Eden's second concern was to promote British influence with Franco's regime through the appointment of an agent. Cabinet had given its permission in principle as early as March 1937, but Eden had to await a convenient moment for what would be a politically very sensitive appointment. Eventually, Sir Robert Hodgson was sent in November with a brief officially limited to commercial issues. This was clearly disingenuous as commercial relations were already being successfully managed through Hendaye, and Hodgson was accorded full diplomatic recognition on his arrival in Salamanca. Hodgson's appointment caused a storm of protest in Parliament. However, the opposition's claim that this de facto recognition of Franco's government represented the 'slippery slope' to full recognition[47] was to miss the point that the whole thrust of this aspect of British policy was pragmatic: to safeguard British economic interests in Nationalist Spain, to curb German and Italian domination at Franco's headquarters, and to maintain the possibility for good relations with a victorious Franco regime. Thus, while the staunchly anti-communist Hodgson proved popular with the Nationalists (their foreign minister joked that an *avenida* would be named after him),[48] he was unable to do anything to reduce Franco's grievances on diplomatic recognition and, above all, belligerent rights. The Duke of Alba, as the Nationalist agent in London, was well received in Conservative circles, but also failed to move British policy on this issue.[49] He became convinced that a Judeo-Masonic conspiracy, involving Eden and Vansittart at the Foreign Office, was dictating Britain's response to the Civil War.

Eden had a further opportunity to demonstrate resolve over Spain in the summer of 1937, when there was a spate of attacks on ships sailing to Republican ports in the Mediterranean by 'pirate submarines', which were known to be Italian vessels acting on Franco's behalf. The British response was unexpectedly strong: the navy was instructed to sink suspected submarines and a conference was convened to determine an international strategy. By the time that these talks began in Nyon, the British, who had cracked the Italian codes, already knew that Mussolini had suspended the submarine campaign from 4 September. Even so, the outcome was a triumph for Eden. An international anti-submarine patrol was established, and was joined in November by Italy (which had refused to attend the conference). Thus, Italy had been brought to heel without being isolated, and Eden was able to report to Cabinet that Nyon had not been the 'anti-fascist' conference that some colleagues had feared. Furthermore, the rapid organisation of the patrols, which began on 20 September, was evidence of the preparedness of the Royal Navy. The patrol was eventually suspended in August 1938 having, apart from an attack on the British vessel *Endymion* in the spring, proved successful in defeating the submarine threat. One of the costs, however, was that the Nationalists and their Italian allies now turned to aerial attacks on shipping to achieve their objectives.

Eden's success at Nyon did nothing to reduce the tension between him and Neville Chamberlain, especially as he followed it up with further stern public warnings against Italian aggression. In a speech at Llandudno in October he stated that the government distinguished between non-intervention and 'indifference': Britain was not indifferent to Spanish territorial integrity, to the foreign policy of future Spanish administrations, or to the problems caused in the Mediterranean by the intervention of other powers.[50] Disagreements over both the style and content of foreign policy (especially towards Italy) resulted in Eden's resignation in February 1938. Freed of this incubus, Chamberlain now wanted to strike a deal with Italy as quickly as possible and was not going to allow the Spanish conflict to stand in his way. Eden had argued that any progress on a wider settlement with Italy must be based on evidence of Italian goodwill, especially on what he regarded as the crucial question of intervention in Spain. In the British–Italian talks that followed Eden's resignation, however, the British government received little in return for conceding the main points at issue, especially recognition of the Italian conquest of Abyssinia. The Earl of Perth (the British ambassador in Rome and chief negotiator) reported that it had been made clear that settlement of the Spanish question 'was a pre-requisite of the entry into force of any agreement'.[51] Discussion then turned to how such a 'settlement' could be defined. The British government was hampered by Chamberlain's more specific pledge to Parliament on 21 February (during the debate on Eden's resignation) that no Anglo–Italian agreement would come into force until there was 'substantial progress' in withdrawal of Italian soldiers from Spain. The agreement (which had been signed on 16 April) was thus not implemented until the autumn, when the distraction caused by the Munich crisis and the token withdrawal of 10,000 Italians (misleadingly presented as 'half' their forces) allowed the British government to claim that its terms had been fulfilled. On 16 November 1938 the Anglo–Italian Agreement came into force with the Spanish war still unresolved and many Italians left on Spanish soil. Chamberlain and his government had finally washed their hands of Spain, although they would find that Italian friendship had not been bought in exchange.

In this final phase of the war British policy came closest to actively promoting a Franco victory when, as Jill Edwards has written, the Cabinet 'connived at the starvation of Barcelona in the hope of hastening the end of the war'.[52] The bombing of British ships during the summer of 1938 in Republican ports created outrage in Parliament but did not elicit the same response as submarine 'piracy' had done in 1937. The Cabinet toyed with various schemes to alleviate the problem, but its anger was turned more at British shipowners engaged in lawful trading than at the Italian bombers. The shipowners, especially Jack Billmeir, whose fleet of vessels trading with Spain had greatly expanded during the war, were described either as profiteers or as the marine equivalent of the International Brigades. Chamberlain's biggest fear was that, if the carnage became too great (if, for instance, one ship per day was sunk), feeling would be so aroused that the government would be forced to take action, dragging Britain into war with Franco and undermining appeasement.[53] In fact, the progress made by the opposition on this issue was dissipated by the Parliamentary recess, and then overtaken by the autumn's more serious crisis over Czechoslovakia.

While the bombing of the merchant ships brought considerable humiliation for the British government, it remained surprisingly sensitive to the possible damage to its international standing. In November 1938 Lord Halifax had described a Nationalist attack on a Republican vessel in the North Sea as 'irregular' but not 'piracy'. However, later in the month Halifax would recommend the possible use of force by the navy in order to release British-chartered Greek ships, carrying wheat bought by Britain from Romania, which had been detained in Palma. Despite the objections of the Admiralty, it was felt that British prestige might be at stake in the incident.[54]

Although Britain had given up any hope of influencing the

outcome of the Civil War by bringing its deal with Italy into force, the war dragged on for some months and the Republic refused to die quietly. With the fall of Barcelona sealing its fate, however, both the British and French governments saw no purpose in antagonising a victorious Franco by withholding recognition. Despite some futile attempts to secure humanitarian guarantees from the Nationalists, recognition was accorded unconditionally on 27 February 1939, arousing fury on the opposition benches in Parliament. Almost immediately, the British cruiser *Devonshire* facilitated the surrender of the island of Minorca and its occupation by Franco's forces in order to pre-empt any Italian interest in the island.

Although ugly and callous, Chamberlain's policy in this latter phase of the war had been conditioned above all by external factors just as Eden's tougher and apparently more pro-Republican policy had been throughout 1937. Eden's prime objective had been to prolong the war in order to weaken the resolve of the fascist powers and make a 'Spanish' solution possible. As one official had noted in October 1937, 'this is a realistic and cold-blooded policy because it seems that we care nothing for the sufferings of the wretched Spanish people through another winter or longer of war'.[55] For Chamberlain the Civil War had become a dangerous irritation to his grand design which still hinged on a reconciliation between Britain and Italy. The sooner the Civil War was ended, the sooner Britain could begin to work at winning the Nationalists away from German and Italian influence.

Chapter 3

POLITICS

Evidence of the disturbance that the Spanish Civil War caused in British politics is not hard to find: there was a plethora of rallies, committees, pamphlets, and debates. There is also the testimony of the many people, especially the young, who were drawn into activism by the Civil War and for whom it represented a powerful, and emotive, element in their political education.[1] Yet, while the war challenged everything, it changed little in British politics. Even the marginalisation of pacifism, a palpable consequence, marked the acceleration of an established trend. The Civil War gave rise to impressive agitations; yet their effect on government policy was minuscule. It offered the Communist Party an opportunity to challenge Labour after years of sectarian isolation, yet the contours of politics on the Left remained largely unaltered. The Civil War caused division, but did not divide cleanly. Although often presented as a battle between Left and Right, the struggle was primarily within the Left and (to a far lesser extent) the Right, while the National Government hid behind the smokescreen of non-intervention.

The most important determinant of the political impact of the Civil War was the continuing supremacy of the National Government which, even after its modest decline in the election of 1935, still enjoyed a daunting Parliamentary majority of 249 seats over Labour and the opposition Liberals. There was little evidence from by-election results to suggest that this dominance would be broken when the next general election was held. The Labour Party with 154 MPs, was still recovering from the trauma of the 1931 crisis, while the Liberal Party (with twenty MPs opposing the government) was divided into factions. This meant that, even had Labour chosen to oppose non-intervention from the start, Parliamentary politics alone were unlikely to alter government policy. Debates, of which there were many, did

3 *A pro-Republican demonstration in Trafalgar Square as the war nears its end, February 1939*

not threaten the government's majority even though Parliamentary questions did chip away at its authority.

The caution of the Labour leadership over Spain and the lack of interest displayed by the Conservatives, combined with the ineffectiveness of Parliament as a forum for opposition, displaced political activity into unorthodox forms. Frustration with the major political parties encouraged those who sympathised with either Republicans or Nationalists to organise outside the existing party structures, creating a series of new and ephemeral committees. In addition, the combination of the government's intransigence and the emotion generated by the Civil War resulted in an upsurge in extra-Parliamentary protest. This came to a head in January 1939 when an 'Arms for Spain' demonstration in London was violently dispersed by police for coming too close to the Palace of Westminster (at least two female protesters escaped a beating by the simple – if expensive – expedient of wearing a fur coat).[2] However, the prospects for successful extra-Parliamentary pressure on the government were restricted by the attitude of the trade

4 British artists paint hoardings in central London to raise funds for Spanish refugees, February 1939

union leaders. Still haunted by the memory of the 1926 general strike and legally constrained by the Trades Disputes Act of 1927, they were unwilling to countenance any attempt to coax their members into industrial action over Spain (or, indeed, any political issue).

These frustrations with conventional politics suggested an alternative basis for political action: individuals and their circles of friends, and specific regions and localities. Many of the newly created movements revolved around a few strong personalities, amongst whom a group of female politicians were particularly prominent. Women such as Ellen Wilkinson, the Duchess of Atholl, and Eleanor Rathbone (an independent MP) had their own various reasons for supporting the Spanish Republic. However, as part of the small band of women MPs in the inter-war House of Commons they were already well used to working together across party lines, and co-operation over Spanish campaigns came more naturally than it would have done to many male colleagues. Nor was co-operation limited to Spain alone. Rathbone and Atholl toured the countries of central and eastern Europe together immediately before they visited Spain with Ellen Wilkinson in April 1937. These women were also leading members of the small all-party Parliamentary Committee for Spain that campaigned on behalf of the Republic.[3]

The relative unimportance of Westminster gave greater weight to regional political activity. The debate over the Civil War was conducted nowhere more fiercely than in the correspondence columns of local newspapers, where the minutiae of the Spanish Popular Front's disputed election victory and the validity of atrocity stories were endlessly discussed. Here, the prominence of Spain as an issue owed much to the relative strength and vitality of the left-wing parties, and often the presence of a Catholic community to put the Nationalist case. In London's East End, for instance, left-wing Jews were particularly keen to oppose a 'fascist' military rebellion that revived memories of Spain's expulsion of the Jews in 1492. Yet East End Catholics – often fellow Labour Party members – were at the same time being expelled from pro-Republican rallies for causing disruption. As one commentator described them: 'Nominally Labour, they were avowedly pro-Franco.'[4] Organised political activity over Spain at this level was, however, almost wholly a pro-Republican phenomenon. Support for the Nationalists was limited to some Catholic urban areas and was otherwise a cause for individual right-wing Parliamentarians and journalists. Frustration felt by many citizens that more had not been done for Spain by the government, combined with a belief that the Civil War had a relevance to even the remotest British constituencies, contributed to local support for the Republic. The Motherwell socialist David Murray addressed a meeting on Spain in the Outer Hebrides, taking the theme that 'the people of Spain are very like the people of Lewis'.[5] Yet, far more typically, activity was at its most intense in urban or industrial areas, such as London, South Wales, and Central Scotland.

The Civil War, therefore, created an unusual set of conditions in British politics. Enthusiasm and sympathy for the Republic briefly corroded party loyalties, and there was considerable spontaneous activity not easily controlled by the established parties. This offered an opportunity for the Communists to challenge Labour for the leadership of the Left. Not only would the unity and energy of the Communist Party contrast favourably with Labour's internal divisions, but the large

number of organisations (both national and local) that were forming
to aid the Republic would have need of the Communist Party's
organisation and discipline. As J. R. Campbell told the Communist
Party Central Committee in January 1937: 'the interest [in Spain]
becomes greater every week that passes . . . This Party has the task of
putting itself at the head of all the diverse movements that are
operating on the question of Spain.'[6] The Communist Party's efforts to
fulfil this ambition and impose leadership on pro-Republican sentiment in Britain formed the most significant political confrontation of
the Civil War years.

Before we turn to study the role of the political parties in detail, it is
first necessary to assess the influence of pacifism on British political
responses to the Civil War. Spain inevitably revived the questions
about the morality of war that had so troubled the conscience of inter-
war Britain. Pacifism had been a particularly powerful force in British
politics since the carnage of the Western Front, although its influence
had begun to wane even before the coming of the Civil War. The
Labour Party, which had been strongly influenced by pacifist ideas,
had already begun to distance itself at its 1935 conference when Ernest
Bevin subjected George Lansbury, the revered party leader and ardent
pacifist, to brutal verbal attack. After Lansbury's subsequent resignation, power passed to leaders such as Hugh Dalton who were far more
ready to support British rearmament against Germany and Italy. Even
so, the Labour Party continued to vote against the military estimates
until 1937, and one of the most frequent Conservative retorts over
Spain was that Labour had endorsed a dangerous policy which might
lead to war (by demanding the ending of non-intervention) while
opposing any concomitant revival in Britain's military strength.

While the mainstream of left-wing politics swung away from
pacifism in the mid-1930s in response to the threat of German and
Italian aggression, the pacifist message was being refined and sharpened by the Peace Pledge Union (PPU), founded in May 1936 by the
Reverend Dick Sheppard. The PPU grew rapidly to a membership of
136,000 in 1940, despite the death of its charismatic leader in October
1937. It took the place of some earlier organisations such as the No
More War Movement which had broken up over how to respond as
pacifists to the Spanish Civil War. The PPU gave pacifism a more

distinctive voice in the later 1930s, although this also emphasised the degree to which pacifists had lost support in the main political parties. The pacifist Labour MP Alfred Salter, for instance, supported non-intervention and refused to distinguish between a civil war and wars between capitalist countries: 'it is just as wrong to kill a Fascist as a Communist, a German as an Englishman'.[7] Yet, although joined by a handful of MPs such as Lansbury, this stance was by now uninfluential within the party.

A further complication was the role of the Communist Party, which equated the campaign for peace with muscular anti-fascism. The Communist-backed International Peace Campaign did much to undermine the broadly based League of Nations Union (LNU). Although supported by prominent figures within the LNU such as Lord Cecil, the campaign alienated the LNU's Catholic and Conservative members. The Communists had also begun to establish a series of local cross-party peace councils, drawing the comment from Gilbert Murray, another prominent member of the LNU, that they were 'an infernal nuisance. They are forming these Peace Councils all over the place and talking about intervention in Spain and opposition to fascism, which is the best way to wreck the peace cause.'[8] The Communists themselves realised the limitation of the councils. It was reported to the party's Central Committee that many of them would be split if the issues of arms for Spain or recruits for the International Brigade were raised. It was agreed that they should mainly help with aid for the civilian population.[9]

For a minority of pacifists the Spanish Civil War confirmed them in their beliefs − a road had opened that would lead them to support the Munich settlement in 1938 and to oppose war in 1939. For a wider group, however, the Civil War forced them to modify their pacifism and to accept that war was a valid response to aggression in certain circumstances. The change was particularly apparent amongst the young. The Duchess of Atholl observed that meetings in support of the Spanish Republic were largely attended by 'young men who, a year or two ago, might have supported the notorious Oxford peace resolution'.[10] At the same time, however, the question of how to avoid war remained central to the debate on the Civil War in Britain. Even those who volunteered to fight in Spain did so in the belief that they were helping to prevent a wider war. When the Labour and Conservative

Parties eventually diverged over the question of non-intervention, each would accuse the other that its policy brought a heightened danger of war.

In Britain, as elsewhere, the Communist Party made the Spanish Civil War uniquely its own. Unlike the other British political parties, the war united the Communists and convinced them not only that their strategy was correct, but also that their cause was just. Through political campaigning, fundraising, and, above all, the organisation of the International Brigades the party established itself by 1939 as the embodiment of 'anti-fascism'. Such commitment and sacrifice transformed the Communists' standing in British politics, and has continued to colour subsequent historical assessment. However, while the party's strength of purpose is beyond dispute, its effectiveness needs to be viewed more critically.

By 1936 the Communist Party was already emerging from the damaging years of sectarian isolation between 1929 and 1933, when other parties on the Left had been vigorously denounced as 'Social fascists'. Belatedly awakening to the rise of Hitler, the Seventh Congress of the Communist International in 1935 approved the new policy of the 'Popular Front' against fascism and war. In Britain, as elsewhere, this freed the Communists to pursue a more creative policy, not only reviving old contacts within the Labour movement, but also reaching out to new supporters in the middle classes and the intelligentsia. In particular, it allowed the party to place itself at the heart of the progressive tradition in British politics. Where the Communists had previously been seen by many as an alien political force, the agents of a foreign power and ideology, the Popular Front allowed them to present themselves as defending traditional British liberties. In September 1936 a London Communist Party demonstration used tableaux derived from English radical history, from Magna Carta and the Peasants' Revolt to Shelley and the Chartists, to show how 'Communism grows from England's soil . . . it is natural to England as the green grass and hedges.'[11]

Despite the greater freedoms of the Popular Front era, however, a number of constraints on Communist policy remained. Firstly, it was a small, if rapidly growing, party: its declared membership rose from 6,500 in February 1935 to over 11,000 in 1936, and 17,750 in July

1939. Even in large cities branches might only consist of a few hundred members, and experienced cadres were scarce. Thus, the leadership had to know how to prioritise objectives and make the most of limited resources. It was also a party still oriented towards the trade unions and the working class. The influx of recruits in the later 1930s from the universities and the middle class was a mixed blessing, appearing to dilute the party's proletarian character and distract it from its main objectives. Secondly, party policy was subservient to Moscow. The analysis of Spanish politics and, in particular, the hostile attitude adopted towards alleged Trotskyists in both Britain and Spain faithfully reproduced the Moscow line. Despite the considerable discussion of Spain within the party, there was little scope for originality. Finally, policy towards Spain could not be seen in isolation from the party's broader political strategy of forging working-class unity in Britain. In the words of the Communist Party's general secretary Harry Pollitt, 'unity represents the single policy we have to face', subsuming issues such as Spain, rearmament, and unemployment.[12] Thus, while many individual Communists came to identify with the Spanish struggle as an end in itself, the leadership could not afford to lose sight of the fact that only progress towards unity made such endeavour ultimately worthwhile. The Political Bureau noted, for instance, that the rank and file's 'preoccupation' with the Spanish campaign resulted in an unsatisfactory response to a petition for affiliation to the Labour Party.[13]

When the Civil War began the Communist Party was campaigning for affiliation to the Labour Party as the basis for a 'United Front' of the working class. The events of July 1936 in Spain were helpful to this campaign as they appeared to offer glowing proof that the armed, united workers could defeat fascism. The Labour Party's support for the Popular Front in Spain, it was argued, made ridiculous its rejection of unity in Britain.[14] The attempt to coax Labour in this direction persisted until the Labour Party conference in October, when Communist affiliation was rejected and non-intervention endorsed. Until this point Communists had been instructed to give money raised for Spain to the Labour movement's own fund: now Harry Pollitt asked for all contributions to be sent to him so that they could be used, he added knowingly, in a 'far more effective way'.[15]

Even before October, however, differences appeared between the two parties. Firstly, unlike Labour, after some initial confusion the Communists came out strongly against non-intervention. This was in spite of the fact that the Soviet Union had adhered to the agreement (on the grounds that it would preserve world peace and help Spanish democracy by cutting supplies to the rebels). This does not mean, however, that there was a rift between Moscow and the European communists. The Soviet Union regarded non-intervention with grave suspicion and, while maintaining diplomatic formalities, sanctioned the foreign communists' pro-Republican campaigns even prior to its own decision to intervene in the Civil War in October. Secondly, the Communist leader, Harry Pollitt, demanded a sustained political campaign which would energise the Labour movement and put pressure on the government to help the Republic, a step that Labour was initially unwilling to contemplate. Thirdly, the decision of the Communist International to organise the International Brigades inevitably distanced the Communist Party from the Labour Party, given that Labour was extremely unlikely to contribute to such a radical (and potentially illegal) measure.

The reverse suffered by the Communists at the autumn's Labour Party conference, although softened by the support that they received amongst rank-and-file delegates, initiated a new phase in which hostility was focused on the Labour leadership. This was heightened by the very personal accusation that leaders such as Ernest Bevin had betrayed Spain, and the fact that non-intervention was not finally abandoned by Labour until June 1937. This phase was dominated by two developments: the creation of the British Battalion of the International Brigades, and the pursuit of working-class unity 'from below'.

The formation of the British Battalion was a tribute to the organisational skills of the Communist Party, especially after the government prohibited recruitment in January 1937. The Battalion united the party, both in pride and in shared loss. It injected a remarkable note of ceremony into the 1938 Congress where a former commanding officer offered a moving address: 'As Fred Copeman concluded, Chopin's "Funeral March" was played on the great organ. As it came to the close, the whole Congress rose to its feet, and after two minutes' silence a far-away trumpet sounded the Last Post.' However, the benefits of enhancing the anti-fascist reputation of the Communist Party had to be balanced against the costs: notably, the death of some of the most promising young party members. Harry Pollitt, who was deeply involved with the enterprise and visited the Battalion five times, was unable to ignore the personal tragedy that volunteering often resulted in for International Brigaders and their families. Moreover, the raising of funds to care for the Battalion's dependants and wounded, while essential, was an additional burden for already stretched resources.

Meanwhile, in January 1937 the launching of the Unity Campaign clearly marked the change in political strategy. This initiative united the Communists with the smaller Independent Labour Party (ILP) and the Socialist League (a left-wing faction within the Labour Party), and was designed to appeal to the Labour movement rank and file. The campaign was, however, crippled by the action of the Labour Party in forcing the disbandment of the Socialist League, and by the rift between the Communists and the ILP over Spain. The ILP identified with the anti-Stalinist POUM in Catalonia, and shared its analysis of the Civil War as a revolutionary struggle for socialism. The Communists in Britain, however, argued that the war was being fought 'for the maintenance of democracy and a free Constitution in a country whose economy is still backward and whose institutions until recently were autocratic and feudal in character'.[16] Harry Pollitt saw Anarchist-backed revolutionary measures such as the collectivisation of hair-dressers and the destruction of money as time-wasting distractions from fighting the war.[17] The problem was exacerbated by the fact that the POUM were the target of Soviet hostility as a 'Trotskyist' party, allegedly bent on collaboration with the Nationalists. The liquidation of the POUM after June 1937 severely damaged relations between the Communists and the ILP in Britain, and the ILP volunteers in Spain were even described by the Communist *Daily Worker* as a 'stain on the honour of the British working class'.[18] The Unity Campaign could not bear such strain, and was swiftly allowed to collapse.

Following this debacle, Communist strategy reverted to trying to shame Labour into taking stronger action. Once Labour had officially abandoned non-intervention at its conference in October 1937, the objective switched to pressing for a mass mobilisation of the Labour movement in support of the new policy. In 1938 Spain retained its significance for the Communists as the key to resolving the threat of war in Europe, under the slogan of 'Save Spain, Save Peace'. In the spring, following the Austrian *Anschluss* with Germany and the successful Nationalist offensive in Spain, the Popular Front campaign appeared to be gathering momentum. In March the Communist Party called for the unity of all 'Labour, democratic, and peace forces'[19] and received support from some Liberal MPs and newspapers such as the *News Chronicle*. A successful cross-party conference on Spain coincided with important fundraising initiatives by two of the largest trade unions (representing the coal miners and the engineers). However, the Labour leadership refused to be drawn, and the endorsement given to the campaign by the Co-operative Party (a constituent of the Labour Party) was overturned at its annual conference in June 1938.

Communist commitment to Spain remained intense, despite the scaling down of Soviet military support after the Munich agreement in September 1938 which had convinced the Soviet leaders that the Republic's cause was hopeless. Communist support was buoyed up by the much-feted return of the International Brigaders in December 1938 who gave new leadership to the campaign. Some volunteers subsequently toured Britain addressing meetings in an International Brigade 'convoy'. In the winter of 1938–9 two new campaigns were launched, to send foodships to Spain and to demand 'Arms for Spain' through mass demonstrations in London. The demonstrations were joined by aircraft workers who walked off their jobs early to be present. This was the closest approximation to industrial action on behalf of the Spanish Republic in Britain, but was too little and too late to affect the attitude of the British government.

Communist policy towards Spain was particularly important for its ramifications on the local level. Wherever the party was strong, it contributed to broad-based organisations campaigning for political and humanitarian support for Republican Spain. Such local committees had numerous objectives. For the activists they were first and foremost to help Spain. In terms of domestic politics, however, they were also intended to put pressure on the Labour movement to mount its own pro-Republican campaign, to demonstrate the vitality and superior organisation of the Communist Party, and to win new recruits. In Manchester, for instance, it was reported that during the Spain campaign in the summer and autumn of 1936 the party 'registered a greater recruitment than we have done for some time'.[20] In Birmingham, the Communist-backed Birmingham Council for Peace and

Liberty gave a much earlier and stronger lead on Spain than the local Labour movement was willing or able to provide, and formed an avenue for many academics and professionals to join the party.[21] In South Wales a Communist-backed regional Council for Spanish Aid was founded from the miners' federation and the Cardiff Trades and Labour Council, but was strongly opposed by the 'official' Labour movement.[22] In Battersea, Communist activists underpinned a vibrant Aid to Spain Committee, officially organised by the local trades council. When the trades council eventually voted to exclude Communist delegates, Communists remained active on the committee by representing other organisations such as the Co-op Women's Guild.[23]

On Spain, as on most political issues in the later 1930s, the Communist Party was undoubtedly the most energetic force on the British Left. It is noteworthy that in mid-1937, when many Communist leaders began to complain that Spain was being made too prominent an issue and that the campaign had 'fallen flat' amongst the members, the leadership did not back away. Instead, it decided to renew its efforts and to make Spain appear more relevant to the British working class.[24] It was Spain, above all, that allowed the Communists to penetrate into new areas of political and intellectual life, away from their working-class strongholds. The reward was a rapidly growing membership and a reputation for active anti-fascism that survived even the appalling setback of the Nazi–Soviet Pact in August 1939. However, Communist policy on Spain was tinged with failure. Not only was the Spanish Republic eventually defeated (not least through the policy of the Soviet Union) but the Communists had also failed to use Spain to force the realignment of British politics for which they had worked so assiduously. At the core of this failure, as we shall see, stood the British Labour movement.

For the Independent Labour Party (ILP), the smallest of the major parties on the Left, the Civil War brought tragedy and decline. Paradoxically, one of the last occasions on which the ILP made a significant contribution to British and international politics was also an episode which demonstrated the weaknesses that would make the ILP suffer political eclipse. Indeed, it is unlikely that the ILP's role in the Spanish Civil War would deserve much attention at all were it not for the fact that it was drawn violently into the poisonous struggle within

Spain between international communism and the anti-Stalinist opposition represented by the ILP's 'brother-party', the POUM. In particular, the ILP's role has been magnified by Orwell's *Homage to Catalonia*, perhaps the most influential book to emerge out of the Civil War.

The ILP, founded in 1893, had for many years been the main political component of the Labour Party. However, the creation of individual Labour Party membership in the 1918 constitution, combined with the disillusioning experience of Labour governments in the 1920s, turned it into a left-wing 'party within a party'. In 1932 the ILP disaffiliated from Labour, presenting itself as a revolutionary socialist party. Membership and organisation rapidly declined, from over 16,000 members in 1932 to a mere 4,392 in 1935. Its residual strength in cities such as Glasgow gave the ILP greater prominence in Parliament than its numbers might justify: four MPs were elected in 1935, including the highly respected party leader James Maxton.[25]

The outbreak of the Spanish Civil War presented the ILP with a unique opportunity to promote itself within Britain. At a time when the Communists had distanced themselves from revolutionary politics, here was a genuine revolution in a fellow European state which the ILP, alone on the Left, was fully able to endorse. Hence, where the Communist Party saw the Civil War as validation for the Popular Front, the ILP saw it as proof of the need for the revolutionary struggle against fascism. The *New Leader* portrayed the situation in the early months, at least in Catalonia, as a revolution in the classic mould – indeed, a re-run of the Russian Revolution. Catalonia, it stated, was run by 'Soviets' and the war was being fought to create 'Soviet Spain' rather than to restore the discredited 'bourgeois' parliamentary regime.[26] Thus, from the very beginning the ILP's support was tied to a particular vision of the Civil War, and it saw itself as aiding one specific party within it, the POUM, the Marxist Unity Party created in 1935. (The ILP had only fleeting contacts with the Spanish Anarchist movement.) This overt support marked the ILP out from the Labour movement and the Communists. The Comintern, of course, did channel aid to the Spanish Communists, but would not admit to doing so. Labour's aid fund, conversely, was aimed at the general relief of distress amongst its Spanish affiliates, but became, in effect, a general fund for humanitarian assistance. The ILP's own fund, however, was intended to go straight to the POUM in order to *'be used by our comrades in the way they think best in their situation'.*[27] The implication that funds placed at the disposal of the POUM might be used for political purposes or even to buy arms showed the ILP as the most honestly partisan of the British left-wing parties.

The ILP had raised £2,272 by May 1937, of which £1,022 had been sent directly to Spain.[28] The rest was spent on medical supplies, an ambulance, the party's military contingent, and on political campaigning. Later the ILP took responsibility for the care of forty Basque refugee children in a home in Street, Somerset. However, the effect of these substantial demands on the party was damaging. The treasurer raised the question of whether the large amount of time given to Spain and other international matters in 1937 had deflected attention from 'socialist propaganda work and efforts to build up the party'. In December 1937 the leadership had to raid its own fund established to aid the Basque children simply to meet the party's running costs.[29]

Because the ILP was so closely connected to the POUM and to what it saw as the Spanish Revolution, its response to the Civil War fell into two distinct phases, corresponding to the rise and fall of the revolutionary forces. Between July 1936 and June 1937, its role was one of furthering the interests of the Spanish revolution. The ILP's demands in December 1936, for instance, were for an end to the embargo on arms to Republican Spain, no recognition for the fascist rebels and a Volunteer Labour Battalion to be sent to Spain.[30] ILP leaders such as John McNair operated freely in Barcelona running the ILP political office, and the military contingent which finally arrived in January 1937 was incorporated into the POUM's own military units. The ILP was inevitably drawn into the tragic struggle between the revolutionary forces and those of the Communist-backed central government which came to a head with the week-long fighting in Barcelona in May 1937 (the ILP unit was on leave at the time and helped to defend the POUM headquarters). Following their defeat, the POUM leaders were arrested and the party was suppressed. ILP and other foreign supporters of the POUM were forced to flee for their lives, and POUM units were absorbed into the Republican army.

This opened a second phase of the war, lasting until its end, in which the ILP's main role lay in mobilising domestic and international pressure for the amnesty of POUM prisoners. A nine-point programme of action for Spain drawn up in December 1937, for instance, dealt almost solely with this issue.[31] Coverage of the Civil War in the *New Leader* (already mainly limited to Catalonia) declined markedly after the suppression of the POUM. Although they remained publicly supportive of the Republic, the hostility of leading ILP figures to what they saw as the Communist-dominated regime in Republican Spain became increasingly useful to the Republic's enemies. John McGovern's 1938 pamphlet *Terror in Spain*, which denounced the Stalinist oppression, was welcomed by the notorious right-wing MP Captain Ramsay.[32]

The main political problem that the ILP faced on this issue was that in Spain it was clearly in conflict with international communism, while in Britain itself it was still eager to construct a working relationship with the Communist Party. The Unity Campaign launched in January 1937 coincided with the murderous build-up of tensions between the Communists and their rivals in Spain. This contradictory policy reflected two essential features of the ILP in the later 1930s. Firstly, there was the growing awareness amongst leaders such as Fenner Brockway of the ILP's dangerous political isolation, forcing them to look for potential allies. Secondly, and equally damaging, the ILP had barely begun to register that its headlong decline since disaffiliation in 1932 had left it, in political terms, unimportant and even irrelevant. While the blow had been cushioned by its continued parliamentary presence, the ILP had become – like the (nearly solely Catalonian) POUM in Spain – a regional (primarily Scottish) political force.

In fact, there was very little space for the kind of revolutionary, anti-war socialist politics that the ILP was promoting in the late 1930s – their natural allies would be tiny groups of Anarchists and pacifists. Mainstream Left politics, and hence the connection with the working-class masses which the ILP leaders hankered after, were moving in a very different direction: the Labour Party towards reformist policies and endorsement for rearmament, and the Communists towards an inclusive Popular Frontism. In this context Brockway, for one, was willing to admit a lack of confidence in the ILP ranks – 'a feeling of weakness compared with Labour Party strength and of disadvantage compared with Communist Party resources'.[33]

Thus, the Spanish Civil War was ultimately a severe setback for the ILP because it followed two separate policies at the same time: a policy of complete independence in Spain, for which it was to pay very heavily; and a policy of seeking common ground with the Communists inside Britain. It is hardly surprising that this ill-starred strategy broke down. What was surprising was that the ILP clung so long to the wreckage of its liaison with the Communist Party after it did so, even as the Communists struck out vengefully at them. The Civil War had served to demonstrate that the ILP no longer had the resources to sustain an independent international policy on such a major issue as the Civil War. However, it would be wrong to lay all of the ILP's problems at the door, as some of the party's historians have, of its theoretical 'dogmatism'.[34] The fault of the ILP in the Spanish Civil War lay not so much in dogmatism, but rather in the unwillingness of a once-great party to accept its decline into irrelevance, and a fatal naivety in dealing with international communism in its most murderous phase.

The Labour movement, more than any force in British politics, was racked with disputes over the Spanish Civil War. At issue was not so much the nature of the conflict – which was seen by all sides as a fascist attack on a democratic government – as the priority which should be given to it, and the manner of Labour's response. The rift in the Labour Party and trade unions has often been described as a struggle between Left and Right. However, it would be more accurate to define it as a struggle between the central institutions of the Labour movement and the radicalised sections of the membership who neither understood nor cared for the way in which those institutions acted on their behalf.[35]

Spain threw into sharp relief the transformation of the Labour movement since its humiliation in the 1931 crisis. In the aftermath, despite an initial tilt to the Left, Labour's new course took the form of closer integration in policy-formation between the party and the trade unions; more pragmatic policies both domestically and internationally; and tighter party discipline, especially towards the Left. Although the trade unions had not captured the party, the concept of Labour as a genuine union of its political and industrial 'wings' was closer to fulfilment in the 1930s than at any point in its history, before or since. The closeness of the new relationship was symbolised in the formation of a National Council of Labour which became the guiding force in Labour movement politics. Despite Clement Attlee's election as party leader in 1935, the most influential figures on the council were the trade unionists Sir Walter Citrine (general secretary of the TUC) and Ernest Bevin (leader of the transport workers), alongside their Labour Party ally Hugh Dalton.

Trade union influence profoundly affected the Labour movement's response to the Civil War. The unions defined their internationalism in bureaucratic terms, relating directly to specified organisations in other countries, perceiving their responsibility to foreign trade unionists and their families in humanitarian terms. This measured response to international crises had little appeal to activists during the Civil War who wanted to see sustained, impassioned action in defence of the Republic. Even so, it is important to challenge the idea that the Labour leadership had no clear policy on the issue, or that their response was primarily conditioned by hostility to the Communist Party. In fact, the reason that there was so much dispute within the Labour movement was precisely because of the leadership's strong support for a policy that was true to the traditions of the Labour movement but did not appear to meet the needs of the moment.

Labour's immediate response to the outbreak of the Civil War was to declare support for the Republic, while the TUC organised a Spanish Workers' Fund for humanitarian relief. Soon, however, the Parliamentary recess and the departure of many leaders on holiday left preponderant influence in the hands of Walter Citrine, already a pivotal figure through his presidency of the International Federation of Trade Unions. In a series of meetings, Citrine succumbed readily to Anthony Eden's arguments in defence of non-intervention. A policy emerged that would last until the next summer, according to which Labour maintained its political and humanitarian support for the Republic, while conceding the need for non-intervention in order to avert European war and defend the position of and offer fraternal support to the Socialist Léon Blum. Citrine, like many at the time, believed that effective non-intervention would help the Spanish Republic. However, he felt that, by securing the right to send humanitarian assistance to Spanish workers, he had discharged Labour's main responsibility in the conflict. Citrine, like other trade union leaders, was also aware that the Civil War might undermine the unions' internal stability by alarming otherwise loyal Catholic trade unionists.[36]

Despite anxiety from the Left, non-intervention was heavily endorsed by delegates at the TUC Congress in September. By the time that the Labour Party met for its annual conference in Edinburgh a month later, however, the situation had been transformed by the mounting evidence of German and Italian support for Franco. Non-intervention was again approved, if half-heartedly, with the backing of the union 'block votes'. Yet two days later the conference was thrown into turmoil by the dramatic intervention of two fraternal delegates from Spain. One, Isabel de Palencia, who had once lived in Scotland and spoke English with a Scottish accent, made a powerful plea for help, conjuring up a harrowing picture of the cruelties inflicted by Franco's 'Moors'. Ironically, when the Spanish delegates had been detained at Croydon airport on their arrival, a Foreign Office official had minuted that neither she nor her colleague were 'in the "Pasionaria" class' of oratory![37] Following her speech a delegation was sent from the conference to Downing Street, and a resolution was adopted calling for the abandonment of non-intervention if it were shown to be ineffective.

The Edinburgh conference did not result in an immediate change of policy, but made one inevitable by illustrating how far the leaders were out of step with their members on this issue. One problem was in formulating an alternative to non-intervention, especially as the French Socialists did not want to see their hands tied while still in government. Moreover, many Labour leaders believed that Edinburgh had been an emotional outburst which had not altered the rationale for supporting non-intervention: namely, the danger of war. Well into 1937 Labour's spokesmen in Parliament continued to call for 'real' non-intervention, with tighter control of Spanish borders and ports.

During 1937 Labour completed the process begun at Edinburgh, in response to both internal and international pressures. Since the start of the war rank-and-file members had become involved in initiatives, such as Spanish Medical Aid (see pp. 100–6), which either had an unclear relationship with the Labour movement or were viewed with disapproval. In March 1937 an unofficial Labour Spain Committee was established to channel the discontent of Labour Party members over Spain. The committee was closely involved with the broader campaign for a greater role for ordinary members within Labour Party decision-making. In the trade unions, the spring of 1937 saw increased pressure over Spain at their conferences, with union leaders running out of excuses for continuing to support non-intervention.

Despite these pressures, however, when the break with non-intervention finally came in June 1937, it was primarily in response to a crisis within the Labour and Socialist International (LSI). The LSI was the successor to the Second International that had collapsed at the start of the First World War. In the 1930s its confidence had been gravely shaken by the destruction of once-proud socialist parties in countries such as Germany and Austria, and the rise of fascism had resulted in ever more power being placed in the hands of the British Labour Party and trade unions. However, the British leaders did not share the intensity of their European counterparts' feelings over Spain. In London in March 1937, Ernest Bevin had dominated a joint gathering of the socialist and trade union internationals on Spain. To the disgust of the Left he had defended non-intervention, and had refused to entertain the Spanish delegate's pleas for more active campaigning, which he saw as synonymous with Communist machinations for a United Front. Soon, however, the worsening situation in Spain following the fall of Bilbao provoked a new crisis. The leaders of the LSI launched discussions for possible joint action with the Communists. The abandonment of non-intervention by all socialist parties was the price demanded to avert the complete collapse of the International, and it was a price that the British were now willing to pay.

The new policy was sealed at the TUC and Labour Party conferences in the autumn of 1937, which called not only for the resumption of the Spanish Republic's right to buy arms, but also for a great campaign to be launched by the Labour Party on behalf of Spain. For a brief moment there was an illusion of unity as the bitter enemies of the previous year joined in supporting the resolutions. In practice, however, little had changed. The Labour leadership remained unwilling to divert resources into a campaign that would, they feared, destabilise the movement. When a Spain Campaign Committee set to work, it was, despite the involvement of left-wingers like Sir Stafford Cripps and Ellen Wilkinson, a disappointment. The high point was a rally at the Albert Hall in December 1937, but thereafter the campaign lapsed into humanitarian fundraising rather than its original objective of placing pressure on the British government.

During 1938, Labour was increasingly mesmerised by the

heightening international crisis and by the Communist-inspired campaign for a Popular Front. While the Popular Front was undeniably supported by many on the Labour Left, the leadership remained deeply suspicious of an alliance of questionable value with unreliable allies. Despite the good showing for Popular Front candidates in the Bridgwater and Oxford by-elections, where Labour stood down in exceptional circumstances after the Munich agreement, Labour was probably justified in believing that such an alliance would not greatly enhance its chances at the next election. However, the Popular Front was never really about electoral politics in Britain: it was a vehicle for challenging Labour's hegemony over politics of the Left, and Labour leaders were adamant that it should not succeed.

Determined attempts were made to force Labour to change its policy over Spain, as the key to a wider reorientation of party policy. On 23 April 1938 many Labour Party and trade union branches were represented at a cross-party National Emergency Conference, boycotted by the Labour leaders. Delegates were particularly excited by the prospect of trade union action to force the National Government to abandon non-intervention. The engineering union had recently threatened not to co-operate with the government's rearmament plans unless it made its foreign policy more acceptable on Spain and other issues. The coal miners' federation held a special conference on 28 April, which called on the TUC to convene its own special conference to review ways of coercing the government. A widely supported movement was also underway in Scotland, co-ordinated by the left-wing Glasgow and Edinburgh trades councils.[38]

The appearance was briefly created of a powerful tide of opinion within the Labour movement. In fact, however, the Left was far less united than it appeared. Even the most radical trade union leaders were unwilling to place their organisations at risk by engaging in political strikes. Thus, the calls for political action were largely transformed into fundraising campaigns which offered little challenge to the Labour leadership or government policy. The demand for a special TUC conference resulted in a secret session of that autumn's TUC Congress devoted to Spain. While Congress adopted a tough resolution on 'Arms for Spain', the initiative was immediately overshadowed by the Munich crisis and came to nothing.

The experience of the Spanish Civil War was exceptionally bitter for many rank-and-file members of the Labour Party. They were profoundly unimpressed by their leaders' response to the Civil War, which appeared uninspired and unimaginative. It was of no relevance to them that Labour's response was consistent with the movement's conception of internationalism: Spain was a unique event which demanded a unique effort from both the leaders and the rank and file. Surprisingly, the only prominent leader who began to bridge this gap was the unemotional Clement Attlee. He was also the only leading figure in the party to visit Spain during the war, heading a Labour Party delegation in December 1937. He returned greatly impressed by the creation of the Republican 'People's Army', which he believed stood comparison to the British 'new Armies' of the spring of 1915.[39] He delighted the Communists by visiting the British Battalion of the International Brigades, and a company was named in his honour. He was attacked by Tory backbenchers on his return for a statement that 'When we return to London, administered by socialists and workers, we shall convene a public meeting to inform the people about the facts of the situation and the unbeaten invincible Republican Spain.'[40] However, even if Attlee was briefly touched by the political emotions generated by the Civil War, it was not sufficient to affect the policy of the Labour movement on his return to Britain.

The Civil War found the Liberal Party, even more than Labour, still recovering from the effects of the 1931 crisis. Most Liberal politicians had initially supported Britain's National Government, but many of them had then gone into opposition under Herbert Samuel following its abandonment of free trade in 1932. From 1935 the leadership passed to Sir Archibald Sinclair, while Sir John Simon took charge of the 'National Liberals' still in government. The situation was further complicated by the existence of a small semi-independent clique of MPs around David Lloyd George, surviving on the strength of the former prime minister's prestige and private funds. Although the Spanish Civil War presented some political opportunities for the Liberals, it ultimately emphasised their weakness and marginality.

The Liberals had been in grave danger of being submerged in the National Government, but had been saved in part by the government's divergence from a foreign policy based on collective security after the 1935 election. Thereafter, the Liberals were able to cultivate a niche as the most committed upholders of the idealism of Versailles: international peace presided over by a strong and respected League of Nations. Unfortunately, the Spanish Civil War gave little hope for attaining this vision, as the League was generally ignored and all of the powers acted with immense hypocrisy. Moreover, the situation inside Spain offered little real encouragement for liberalism. Despite the rebirth of a democratic Republic (under Soviet aegis), prominent Spanish liberals such as President Manuel Azaña spent the war sunk in pessimism and believing that Britain had betrayed the liberal cause.

Like Labour, the opposition Liberals initially supported non-intervention while calling for it to be both more effective and tied to a stronger League. Their belief that Britain should not take sides was only slowly undermined by concern at the level of fascist intervention. The Liberal Assembly in June 1937 called for non-intervention to be made a reality, but it took another year for the Liberals to break with the policy officially. The Liberals played a role in the Parliamentary debates over the Bilbao crisis beyond their numerical strength; the contribution of Lloyd George in particular caused considerable damage to the government's case. However, they overreached themselves when, in return for what they took to be a promise from Eden for the organisation of convoys into the port, they agreed to abstain rather than vote against the government. They subsequently felt betrayed when the convoys failed to materialise.

For Lloyd George the Civil War offered one more chance to hold the attention of Parliament on a great international issue. He lost no opportunity to play this role to the hilt, calling for the bombing of Italian aerodromes in the Balearic Islands in retaliation for attacks on British ships.[41] While his speeches concentrated on the threat to British interests, it is also apparent that he sympathised strongly with the Republicans, saying of the 'class war' in Spain that: 'I have been in the same fight all my life. The landed aristocracy, conservative churchmen, and the vested industrial and financial interests have always fought me. And I them.'[42] Lloyd George's stature as an apostle of liberty was also attractive to some Labour Party pro-Republicans: Philip Noel-Baker attempted unsuccessfully to persuade him to visit Spain as a follow-up to Clement Attlee's recent expedition.[43] Ultimately, however, Lloyd George was already too discredited as a public figure to make any great impact during the Civil War. His adoption of this and other issues was widely seen as shameless self-promotion to revive a moribund career.

More consistently prominent during the Civil War was Wilfred Roberts, Liberal MP for North Cumberland, who threw himself into political and humanitarian campaigning on behalf of the Republic. He visited Spain in November 1936 with the all-party group of MPs, drafted its report, and became one of the leading figures in the National Joint Committee for Spanish Relief that grew out of it. He was adamant that his main objective was to help the Spanish Republic and, while proud of his liberalism, did not object to working with members of any other political party, including the Communists. Although it would be wrong to see him as a Communist 'fellow-traveller', this willingness to co-operate sometimes led him into trouble and, at times, made him appear a catspaw for the Communists.[44] Roberts' heavy involvement in Spain was resented by the Liberal leaders, one of whom complained that he spent nine-tenths of his time on a country over the fate of which he could have 'no influence whatever',[45] neglecting his official portfolio on agricultural policy. He himself admitted that he was seen as a 'fanatic' on the issue by fellow Liberals.

The Civil War raised acutely the question of the degree to which the Liberal Party could aspire to play an independent role in British politics. Wilfred Roberts was brutally realistic about this and would have been happy to accept the leadership of the Labour Party in a Popular Front campaign against the National Government. While this stance was shared by some other Liberals such as Sir Richard Acland and the News Chronicle proprietor Sir Walter Layton, the party leadership was much more circumspect and shared the Labour Party's concerns at the political implications of any such agreement. Thus, the Civil War underlined the fact that many Liberals were only loosely connected to their party, and – at least in the short term – appeared to have had little respect for its independence.

The Conservatives, the dominant political party in the 1930s, were of all the parties the least troubled by the Civil War. Most Conservatives agreed that the Civil War was deplorable, but saw it as a distraction from more important international issues. According to Leo Amery, they 'found little to choose between both sides, either on the merits of the case or in the ferocity of the methods. In any case no national or even party interest was directly affected.'[46] This assessment was somewhat disingenuous, as contemporary diarists such as Harold Nicolson and Henry 'Chips' Channon evoke a Parliamentary Tory party that had no difficulty in siding with the rebels against the 'Reds'.[47] Yet this sentiment was rarely translated into political action. Even those Conservatives who supported Franco strongly, and wished to see the government do more to help his cause, had little incentive to undermine non-intervention when it was already seen to be objectively favouring the Nationalists. Thus, there was little debate over Spain within Tory ranks, with few MPs leaving a record of their views on the subject. Where opinions can be ascertained within the party, they tend to be those either of Cabinet ministers or of the minorities strongly critical of government policy.

Even among leading Conservatives, evidence is limited. Samuel Hoare's anti-Republicanism is well-known. So too is that of the chief whip David Margesson who wrote to Chamberlain soon after the rising that a victory for the rebels 'would be splendid'.[48] On another occasion he confided to an Italian diplomat that: 'Our interests, our desire is that the [military] revolution should triumph and communism be crushed.'[49] Lord Hailsham was a close friend of the Duke of Alba, the Nationalist representative in London.[50] There was, therefore, clearly support – in some cases enthusiasm – for the rebel cause amongst leaders of the Conservative Party. Such sentiments, however, were generally restrained by concern for the implications of a rebel victory for British interests.

The Conservative Party organisation treated the Civil War as a political opportunity, enjoying the confusion that it caused amongst its rivals. In by-election campaigns and in pamphlets Labour was branded as a party that either could not decide on non-intervention, or that was willing to go to war over an unimportant issue. Non-intervention undoubtedly chimed with the unwarlike public sentiments of the day. In the words of one Labour Party activist in Birmingham, following a by-election defeat and poor local election results when Spain had figured prominently: 'You do not find the Tory party making the same blunders by continually ramming the troubles of continental countries down the throats of the electorate.'[51] However, Conservatives had to be careful that their government's policy did not abandon traditional territory to Labour. Attacks on British shipping in 1938, for instance, allowed Labour to play a typically Conservative jingoist card.

The main supporter of the Republic within the Conservative Party was the Duchess of Atholl, MP for Kinross and West Perth. Katharine Atholl was an unlikely pro-Republican: she shared with pro-Franco Tories her anti-communism and passion for the British Empire, and had already resigned the whip once in May 1935 over the Government of India Act. Atholl, however, heeded the danger that Franco's rebellion posed to imperial interests, as well as being moved by the humanitarian plight of the Republicans on her visits to Spain. Her private correspondence suggests a deep personal involvement, telling Lloyd George after her by-election defeat that 'I wish I could feel I was worthy in any way to be compared to the Spanish Republicans.'[52] She became prominently involved in organisations such as the National Joint Committee for Spanish Relief, but initially did so without endangering her own position within the Conservative Party. When the break came in April 1938, when she again resigned the Tory whip, it was partly due to mishandling of her local party, which was unimpressed by her high-profile campaigns and also contained a number of staunchly anti-Republican Catholics. Her decision to force a by-election after the Munich agreement in October 1938 was again ill-judged, and she was beaten by 11,808 votes to 10,495. While assisted by Liberal and Labour activists, she received no support from fellow Conservative dissidents. Her Conservative opponent had the full weight of the party Central Office behind him. The arrival of a group of Spanish experts such as the writer Gerald Brenan to campaign in Atholl's support merely emphasised the distance that she had travelled from the parochial realities of Highland politics.[53]

Other MPs on the government side in the Commons who came to sympathise with the Republicans showed considerably more circum-spection than the 'Red Duchess'. The most prominent was Winston Churchill, who initially supported the Nationalists against what he saw as a perfect example of Communist subversion.[54] When introduced to the newly arrived Spanish ambassador, Pablo de Azcárate, he is said to have refused to shake his hand and turned away muttering 'blood, blood'.[55] But Churchill came slowly to share Atholl's concern for the strategic dangers posed by a Nationalist victory. In October 1937 he confided that he was still 'at heart' for Franco, but frightened that a victorious Franco would ally with Italy and create an 'impossible position for Britain and France in the Mediterranean'.[56] By December 1938 his position was that 'the British Empire would run far less risk from the victory of the Spanish Government than from that of General Franco'.[57] Even so, Churchill continued to see the Civil War as a tragic and futile conflict, and retained an unrealistic hope that reconciliation could arise from the bravery that was common to the soldiers of both sides. Azcárate remained bitter at Churchill's lack of leadership over Spain, and saw his own inability to cultivate him successfully as his greatest failure. It is doubtful, in fact, whether Churchill could have played the central role that Azcárate wished. In the later 1930s, while retaining great oratorical force within Parliament, he was a marginal figure within Conservative politics who had alienated many potential allies. Two other MPs on the government benches, Vyvyan Adams and Harold Nicolson (a member of the small National Labour Party, formed in 1931), called publicly for a Nationalist defeat, but succeeded in maintaining their loyalty to the government.

A larger group of MPs on the Conservative right wing called for the government to adopt a pro-Nationalist policy, demanding, above all, the granting of belligerent rights. Most of them belonged to the clique of imperialist, isolationist Tories who had consistently criticised Baldwin's Conservative Party for being too centrist and conciliatory. At least twelve Conservative MPs regularly spoke out for the rebels in Parliament, the best-known being Sir Henry Page Croft, Sir Arnold Wilson, Captain Victor Cazalet, and Alan Lennox-Boyd. Lennox-Boyd was so closely associated with the Nationalist cause that his subsequent entry into the government was criticised as provocative by Labour. Their repeated Parliamentary interventions on Spain gave them a voice beyond their real strength at a time when the rest of their party had little to say. However, they could at times prove an embarrassment: a leaked letter from the Marquis del Moral, a prominent Francoist in London, during the Bilbao crisis expressed the hope that they would remain quiet.[58]

The Conservative right-wingers were united in seeing Franco's regime as defending their own values. In the words of one, the Catholic Anthony Crossley, on his return from Spain, the Nationalists were 'fighting for their religion against atheism, for the right to hold property against compulsory impoverishment, for a military dictatorship against a communist dictatorship, for their country against Internationalism'.[59] They were at ease with an authoritarian solution to the Spanish problem, and admired the nationalism and religious certainty at the core of Franco's movement. However, they were less united in their hopes for the future. While a monarchist such as Page Croft wished for a restoration of the old order, others would come to see the Nationalists building a New Spain of social reform and classlessness.

Within the Conservative Party strong support for the Nationalists came from Arthur Bryant, educational adviser to the Conservative College at Ashridge. Bryant saw Spain as unfit for democratic government (of the organic English variety which he idealised)[60] and viewed the Popular Front as a mere vehicle for communist subversion. While his influence was limited within the party, he did have the power to influence perceptions of the Civil War in Conservative circles through his contacts in publishing and amongst those who attended the college. For instance, in December 1937 he organised a conference on Spain at Ashridge which was strongly weighted to the Nationalist side. Of the speakers three were pro-Franco (Douglas Jerrold, the businessman Arthur Loveday, and Professor Allison Peers) while only the Duchess of Atholl was pro-Republican.[61] Ironically, on this occasion Bryant's endeavours rebounded against the Nationalists as Atholl's notes for her speech would grow into the widely read book *Searchlight on Spain*.

Outside Parliament, the Conservative Right was involved in the establishment of three organisations that supported the Nationalists. All three provided the opportunity to connect with wider currents of pro-Franco opinion, especially amongst Catholics, whom the Right would previously have found difficult to reach. The most significant was the Friends of National Spain, founded in 1937 and strongly supported by Nationalist circles in London. Chaired by Lord Phillimore, the organisation was intended to promote understanding of the Nationalist cause through propaganda and mass meetings. A similar organisation, the United Christian Front, was established by Sir Arnold Wilson and Sir Henry Lunn, a prominent Methodist, in 1937. It grew out of protests at the pro-Republican stance taken by prominent figures in the Church of England, and sought to use the revulsion at the anti-Catholic atrocities in Spain to challenge communism and to promote the re-Christianisation of Britain. A third, much smaller, organisation was the Basque Children's Repatriation Committee, under the chairmanship of Sir Arnold Wilson and supported by the Duke of Wellington. Its purpose was to put pressure on the British government for the refugees' prompt return to Spain, and to make their continued residence in Britain as difficult as possible. One member, the Tory MP Sir Nairn Stewart Sandeman, urged the public not to contribute any money to the 'little Basque devils'.[62]

The first two groups shared an ambition to develop a mass membership which would cut across existing political divisions and reinvigorate the Right. In particular, it was hoped that religion could provide the basis for this political revival. This made the committees attractive to right-wing Catholics such as Douglas Jerrold and Arnold Lunn who were themselves seeking to build a new social order founded on Catholic corporatism. Some indication of the extent of the Friends of National Spain's ambitions is provided by publicity aimed at trade unionists which claimed that Franco's Spain was pledged to such aims as justice for the workers, abolition of poverty and wealth, and liberty of thought.[63] In practice, however, the pro-Nationalist groups did little more than win over a few Catholic members of the Labour Party in cities such as Glasgow and London. Beyond their success in igniting sectarian divisions within Labour ranks, there is no evidence that the Friends of National Spain evolved into more than a propaganda arm of Franco's unofficial London 'Embassy'.

The religious basis of the Nationalist cause made it highly appealing to the Conservative and Catholic Right, but held little attraction for the more secular-minded British Fascists. Although Oswald Mosley enjoyed some Catholic support for his British Union of Fascists (BUF), he was never a strong sympathiser with Franco's cause. He defended non-intervention and stated that no British blood should be shed on behalf of Spain. The BUF weekly *Action* argued that this was a 'war between the equally sterile forces of communism and reaction', and 'nothing but the old nineteenth-century class war: a war between rich and poor'.[64] BUF speakers were instructed to show that the lesson of Spain was that 'class war leads to civil war' and that only the fascists, combining the classes in 'one great National-Socialist effort of patriotic regeneration' could save Britain from sharing Spain's fate.[65]

On the local level, however, the situation was rather different. BUF groups regularly disrupted meetings expressing solidarity with Spain, and also were willing to act on behalf of the Nationalists. When the *Rita Garcia* was stolen and sailed from Immingham to Hamburg in 1938, its crew had been recruited by BUF headquarters. A number of prominent London Fascists were amongst the crew, including a prospective Parliamentary candidate, a district treasurer, and a 'Team Leader' for Bethnal Green. At least one 21-year-old believed that the boat was sailing to Spain where he could fight for Franco. The operation was initiated by Felix George Sturrup, a British businessman in Spain who had returned to Britain as a Nationalist agent and had also been involved in seeking the return of the Basque refugee children.[66]

The Spanish Civil War, as has been noted, changed little in British politics. Indeed, in certain respects it obstructed political realignment. Not only did the war embitter relations between Labour and the Conservatives, Labour's pro-Republicanism also alienated those Conservatives who opposed appeasement but did not sympathise with the 'Reds'.[67] Spain, therefore, ultimately reinforced divisions between the two main parties and made even less likely a '1931 in reverse',[68] whereby moderate Conservatives would unite with Labour and Liberals to ditch the appeasing National Government. And yet this inter-party bitterness was in certain respects deceptive. While Labour and the Conservatives differed greatly in their sympathies, their leaderships were broadly united at least in their appreciation of the Civil War's importance: both saw it as a distraction from the more fundamental problem of how to contain the ambitions of Germany and Italy. Labour, however, was far more troubled by the presence of those within its ranks who refused to accept this order of priority and, indeed, regarded Spain not as a distraction but as the very key to the future peace of Europe.

It was no coincidence that, when it came to campaigning around Spanish issues, the degree of vigour and commitment tended to increase further away from the centre of British politics. Spain posed difficult questions which many in both the Conservative Party and the Labour movement were unwilling to confront. No such considerations bound the communist and socialist Left or the conservative and

Catholic Right. For such groups, far removed from the levers of power in Britain, the Civil War offered a cause that sustained them through a time of frustration and deadlock in domestic politics. Spain alone could not break the deadlock. Even so, it provided an opportunity for activists to throw themselves into a bout of campaigning unparalleled in inter-war Britain for its intensity and creativity, and not only using traditional forms of political protest such as demonstrations but also exploring the newly politicised field of large-scale humanitarian endeavour.

Chapter 4

AID

In the course of the Spanish Civil War substantial amounts of money were raised in Britain for relief work in Spain, and it was through campaigns of this nature that British people came most directly into contact with the conflict. The many funds and committees established at this time appealed to both humanitarian and political sentiments and the Republic was by far the main beneficiary. This was because the bulk of British political sympathy and of humanitarian suffering in Spain lay with the Republican side. However, while many individual donors were motivated by humanitarian concerns it would be wrong to see these campaigns as purely humanitarian in their objectives. Almost all were an attempt to intervene directly in the course of the Civil War, to favour one side or another. Funds which attempted to be genuinely impartial, giving aid equally to both sides, tended not to flourish. Thus, relief work became an extension of politics. Party politics offered little hope for influencing the British government to change its policy, and the option of joining the International Brigades could only appeal to a few, but fundraising and the organisation of relief was open to all and could make a material difference. A foodship could avert starvation, an ambulance unit could assist on the front-line. The inventor Geoffrey Pyke devised a scheme whereby engineering workers voluntarily reconditioned lorries for use as ambulances, and later advocated the collection of sphagnum moss for field dressings.[1] Ultimately, however, the location of relief work in the political arena ensured that it was affected by the political divisions (especially on the Left) discussed in the previous chapter.

The Civil War gave rise to a vast range of *ad hoc* organisations (both nationally and locally) committed to fundraising and relief. Part of the reason for this diversity was the lack of structures in place to channel the unparalleled degree of interest which the war generated. In the years since 1945 there has been a wide range of international, governmental, and non-governmental humanitarian agencies continually on hand. In 1936 the situation was quite different. The intense philanthropism of the First World War had internationalised relief work, extending assistance to refugee Belgians and wounded Serbs as well as British victims of the war.[2] However, the international institutions that emerged from the war were ill equipped to handle a crisis such as that in Spain. The League of Nations was not strong enough to make a humanitarian intervention in its own right. The two best-known British organisations involved in international relief, the Society of Friends and the Save the Children Fund, did take a strong interest in Spain but were avowedly non-political, and could not meet the demand for supplying aid that would assist one particular side in the war. The British Red Cross was willing to raise funds but would not involve its personnel directly in a civil war.[3] The initiative therefore passed either to the British government or to the new organisations that soon developed.

The British government's contribution to humanitarian work was far from negligible: naval evacuation of refugees alone in 1936 and 1937 cost £73,000.[4] It failed, however, to offer strong leadership. Its formal stance, influenced by the need for impartiality under non-intervention, was that it would not provide financial help for humanitarian work 'except as part of an agreed international scheme previously accepted [by] both parties in the Civil War'.[5] Of course, the extremely hostile relations between Republicans and Nationalists prevented any such scheme from coming into effect. The policy was eventually modified in December 1937 when, at Anthony Eden's suggestion, it was agreed to support the International Commission for Assistance of Child Refugees in Spain. Although many conditions were applied that delayed the release of funds, £25,000 was eventually granted to the scheme. It was suspected that Franco would not approve, but the project was attractive to the Cabinet both as a response to a humanitarian crisis and as a political gesture: in Neville Chamberlain's words, 'we had to get on good terms with the Spain of the future'.[6] A further £50,000 was given to the Red Cross to ease the plight of Republican refugees in France at the end of the war.

Beyond these limited interventions, the government's role was largely a restrictive one. It was strongly opposed to the sending of funds to Spain, on the grounds that they might be used to procure arms. However, given that non-intervention did not preclude humanitarian aid (including motor vehicles) and that the government did not possess powers to prevent the voluntary collection of funds, its ability to influence the development of British aid was limited. Mild attempts were made by the Foreign Office to discourage Spanish Medical Aid from sending a medical unit in August 1936 and MI5 ran a check on the volunteers, but passports were eventually granted and no obstacles were placed in the way of further units. Indeed, it seems likely that the British relief agencies in Spain offered a useful cover for intelligence gathering. A driver with the Scottish ambulance unit, for instance, suspected that a British military attaché in Valencia was hoping to glean information on Republican troop movements in Madrid from the unit's commander.[7] It must be stressed, however, that in many respects the government's attitude was remarkably tolerant. By 1937 both Spanish Medical Aid and the Catholic relief fund were supplying medical units that were, in effect, auxiliary services of the Republican and Nationalist armies.

These two cases raise in acute form the many political issues posed by relief work in the Civil War. Organisations such as Spanish Medical Aid were overtly political both in their support for the Republic and in the nature of their work in Spain. At the other extreme, it was essential that the care of Basque refugee children was perceived as a 'non-political' activity, as any political connotations would have alienated many of those who supported it. The problem was not simply that many who made a donation wanted to contribute in some way to the victory of their own side: political tensions within Republican Spain also meant that relief might be used to favour one faction over another within the same side. The relief funds of both the Labour movement and the ILP were directed specifically at their own sister-organisations in Spain, while Spanish Medical Aid worked primarily with the Communist-led International Brigades. For both political and legal reasons the Labour movement was determined to preserve the integrity of its own activities in Spain, and consistently resisted attempts by the Spanish government to bring it under its control. However, these political intricacies were often lost on ordinary people. Given the diversity of the multitude of funds and committees bidding for aid for 'Spain', it is apparent that many who donated money to them often had only the sketchiest idea of how their donation would be used.

The development of the aid campaigns was partly conditioned by the nature of the donors. While there were wealthy benefactors for both sides, there is no doubt that most of the money donated came either from institutions such as trade unions or from small individual contributions. The campaigns were made possible by great sacrifices: the time of those who ran them, and the contributions (often in kind rather than in money) of those who gave to them. Many of those who gave were themselves poor or unemployed. Douglas Hyde, at this time a Communist organiser in North Wales, wrote that 'often the sacrifices were so huge as almost to appal me'. Poorly paid slate quarrymen paid for Dutch-auctioned militia hats and scarves with unopened pay packets.[8] The Edinburgh socialist Janet Murray addressed a meeting in Dundee and confided that 'there was so much obvious poverty in the audience that I was ashamed to ask for money'.[9] While she was not deterred – and went on to take £12 for Basque refugee children – fundraising among the poor was clearly a political as much as a humanitarian act. The donation of gifts in kind – such as clothes and tinned food – was similarly encouraged for its political rather than its material value. One packer confided that donated clothing was 'so bad that a lot of it is not worth the transport'.[10] Thus, the arrival of the Basque children was both an extra burden and an opportunity. They were seen to appeal to wealthier sections of society not otherwise involved in Spanish causes.

An important question of interpretation is that of how far the various pro-Republican campaigns should be seen as facets of a single movement. It has been argued that there was an 'Aid Spain Movement' in Britain which brought together supporters of the Republic from across the parties in relief work, and which was the closest approximation to a Popular Front in this country.[11] Undoubtedly, many individuals did work together, irrespective of party, in local 'Aid Spain' committees, Spanish Medical Aid committees, foodship committees, youth committees, and many others, and these were given a semblance of order by the formation of the National Joint Committee for Spanish Relief. However, it must be borne in mind that the idea of an 'Aid Spain Movement' is one imposed with hindsight. No such body existed at the time. Moreover, the term clearly has a political connotation. It was first coined by the Communist *Daily Worker* (which listed 'Aid Spain' donations) and cannot be isolated from the broader Communist project of seeking to establish a position of leadership in solidarity with the Spanish Republic. The myth has persisted that 'Aid Spain', however defined, was the only legitimate avenue for supporting the Spanish Republicans: in practice there were myriad avenues, all equally legitimate. All of the various institutions involved in helping the Spanish Republic – political, religious, and humanitarian – had their own interests and objectives. In the case of the Labour movement this precluded any co-operation with other organisations apart from in certain restricted circumstances. But, as will be seen, even where co-operation between organisations was attempted these differences often laid the basis for conflict. Thus, the idea of an 'Aid Spain Movement' is of little help other than indicating the general preponderance of support in Britain for the Republic over the Nationalists.

British campaigns for relief in Spain evolved considerably over time. In the chaotic opening months of the war the emphasis was very much on responding to specific needs: for instance, providing medical services for the Republicans bereft of many trained professionals, or the care of refugees both within Spain and in Britain. There were, however, two common features. Firstly, all of these initial responses were united in the desire to respond immediately to a war that did not seem likely to last long. Secondly, while the Labour movement's Spanish Workers' Fund claimed hegemony over fundraising within the Labour and trade union movement, no single campaign asserted any general authority over relief work.

This changed at the end of 1936 with the almost simultaneous establishment of two new organisations. The better-known National Joint Committee for Spanish Relief was formed in November 1936 in response to a visit to Spain by a cross-party group of MPs. Following a series of meetings bringing together interested organisations, the committee was established as 'an all-party, non-political, non-sectarian body to co-ordinate relief work and to undertake certain specific pieces of work not being done by other organisations'.[12] In practice, however, the committee was never intended as anything other than a means of supporting the Republic, and its officers, such as the Duchess of Atholl and Wilfred Roberts, were committed pro-Republicans.

Non-political organisations such as the Society of Friends and Save the Children were represented, but were adamant that they would retain complete independence of action. The Friends stated firmly that the new committee should be based on 'co-operation rather than co-ordination', supporting existing appeals rather than initiating new ones.[13] The 'political' character of the National Joint Committee alarmed both of these organisations, so much so that they forced it to agree to a statement of impartiality being read out before all of its public meetings.[14]

The National Joint Committee divided its resources between relief work in Spain and campaigning in Britain. The Spanish operations, administered by G. T. Garratt, consisted primarily of the evacuation of children from Madrid, the establishment of a children's colony at Puigcerdá, and the sending of foodships. By the end of the war the committee was helping to care for 8,000 children in central Spain. Even before its work was fully established, however, it was confronted with the unexpected arrival in Britain of 4,000 Basque refugee children in May 1937. Until the end of the war the children would absorb much of its human and financial resources: of the £71,042 raised in its first year, for instance, it was estimated that over 65 per cent was spent on their care.[15]

Within Britain, the National Joint Committee lacked the power to 'co-ordinate' relief work as had originally been envisaged. The Labour movement refused to consider any formal association, not only because of the presence of Communists such as Isabel Brown on the committee, but also because it jealously guarded the integrity of its own activities. Thus, while the committee was eventually composed of some 150 organisations, it acted primarily as an umbrella for them. The real importance of its work was threefold: it provided a focus for solidarity with Republican Spain; where possible, it sought to initiate new campaigns; and it established new local bodies where there had formerly been none. Its leadership was most evident in the autumn of 1938 when, despite the distraction of the Munich crisis, the committee launched a powerful campaign to send foodships to the starving people of eastern Spain.

At the same time as the establishment of the National Joint Committee, a very different initiative known as the General Relief Fund for the Distressed Women and Children of Spain was launched.

This was formed by the Infanta Beatrice, cousin of the exiled Spanish king Alfonso XIII, who had also been present at the early meetings of the National Joint Committee. She was assisted by Kendall Park, a British businessman who had been resident in Barcelona for many years. The General Relief Fund differed from the National Joint Committee in its political orientation, its composition, and its methods. It was intended to be completely impartial – delivering aid to both sides – and did not aspire to run its own relief operations inside Spain. Instead, it would appeal for funds with the support of prominent figures in business and the Churches. The committee's membership was described, even by conservative observers, as representing those on the Right, although its appeal was also backed by those who could not be deemed right-wing such as Lord Cecil and Professor Gilbert Murray. Its constituent organisations included the Red Cross, the Catholic Bishops' Committee, Save the Children, and the Society of Friends. The latter two agreed to co-operate in the hope of obtaining a slice of what they believed would be a lucrative appeal, and shared the running of a canteen in Barcelona with Kendall Park. However, while the initial appeal raised £2,000, and despite favourable treatment by the British government,[16] the Fund never lived up to expectations. By 1938 it was described as 'moribund' and its work in Barcelona was taken over by the Friends.[17]

The lack of any surviving archives of the General Relief Fund makes it difficult to reach a judgement on its record. However, it is tempting to see it as an attempt, possibly backed by the government, to channel humanitarian sentiment away from the pro-Republicanism of the National Joint Committee. It certainly helped Anthony Eden in Parliament to proclaim that the Royal Navy had recently supplied food from the Relief Fund to both Republican and rebel ports.[18] The Fund's failure reflected the lack of appeal that 'impartial' relief work held for the public when both sides in Spain were not seen as equally deserving. Moreover, it demonstrated the inability of a few wealthy individuals to generate a sustained campaign by sending an occasional appeal to The Times. On the only occasion when something slightly more innovative was attempted, when Kendall Park's son took a Spanish dance troupe round Britain's resorts, the initiative barely covered its costs.[19]

The greatest obstacle preventing an *ad hoc* body such as the National

Joint Committee from achieving greater success was the stance of the leaders of the Labour movement, who were determined that they alone should control relief work amongst the organised working class. Soon after the outbreak of the war the National Council of Labour established a Spanish Workers' Fund which was part of the International Solidarity Fund run jointly by the socialist and trade union Internationals. From September 1936 a Madrid-based committee representing the Spanish Socialist Party and the socialists' trade union federation administered incoming relief from this fund, and made recommendations for future aid shipments. From 1937 the Internationals invested heavily in a large base hospital at Onteniente, partly as a means of competing visibly with the large amounts of help (including arms) being supplied by international communism. The Spanish Workers' Fund raised some £200,000 in the course of the Civil War, although over £70,000 of that sum was raised by the miners' federation in 1938. Money came primarily from grants from trade unions and Labour Party branches – a form of fundraising that did nothing to involve or excite grass-roots members. Even the coal miners' massive contribution, nominally a 'levy' of the members, was largely paid for out of the reserves of the various regional mining unions. As in so many other areas of Labour's response to the Civil War, this represented the logic of trade union bureaucratism extended to the movement as a whole. The trade unions were aware of the dangers of being challenged in the courts if they used their members' funds in a 'political' manner, yet were unwilling to motivate their members to raise funds themselves. Consequently, many ordinary members became involved in local committees and organisations which might have been deemed 'unofficial', but which gave far more opportunity for individual enthusiasm and initiative. A leader of the Birmingham Labour Party bewailed the fact that: 'Some of our folk have spent most of their time with the Spanish Medical Aid Fund; that being more left I suppose makes it more worthy.'[20] It was notable that on the rare occasions when alternative methods of fundraising were employed they were often highly successful. For instance, a scheme for buying 3d milk tokens in Co-op stores quickly raised £32,000.

Ultimately, the greatest contribution of the Labour movement's aid campaign was not the amount of money raised but the efficiency and professionalism with which aid was purchased in Britain, shipped to

Spain, and distributed to where it was most needed. The leaders were correct to see this work as highly effective – if neither as glamorous nor as politically eye-catching as the activities of their rivals. However, they failed to grasp the degree to which this cautious approach failed to meet the aspirations of rank-and-file trade unionists and members of the Labour Party.

The difference between these two worlds was nicely captured by Dr Hyacinth Morgan, who wore two very different hats as the medical adviser to the TUC as well as the chairman of the Spanish Medical Aid Committee. Reporting to the TUC on his visit to the Belgian-staffed Onteniente hospital, Morgan was delighted by the quality of the facility but doubtful that any British surgeon could be found to serve in it: 'I have personally never yet regarded any doctor sent out to Spain [from Britain] as being of the type that would be regarded as appropriate according to British standards.' The best remedy, he claimed, would be for the Spanish government to decorate its surgeons – many more high-quality British doctors would go if a decoration equivalent to the DSO or MC were available that would help them professionally![21] The gulf could not have been greater between this overly professional attitude and that of Spanish Medical Aid, which was willing to rely on the enthusiasm and ingenuity rather than the qualifications of its staff.

The Spanish Medical Aid Committee, created in July 1936, was the first organisation specifically intended for humanitarian intervention in the Civil War. It was in many respects the quintessential British relief organisation of the period, not only in its great success as a fundraising body, but also in the beguiling simplicity with which it channelled the humanitarian impulse in a political direction. The initiative was taken by medical workers on the left wing of the Labour movement in association with Isabel Brown, a Communist with great experience in organisations such as the Relief Committee for the Victims of Fascism. The lead was taken by Dr Charles Brook, secretary of the Socialist Medical Association, in forming a committee to send a medical unit to Spain. An influential body of supporters was gathered with strong links to the health profession. The highly respected Christopher Addison, a former Liberal minister of health now in the Labour Party, became the committee's president. Dr Morgan, the TUC's medical adviser and a Catholic, was its chairman. In order to maximise the committee's appeal its work was defined as non-political. According to Brook their first public statement made no reference 'to fascism and dictatorship – they were making their appeal to the medical profession solely on humanitarian grounds'.[22]

The committee's initial objectives were to make a contribution to the Republic's medical needs and to galvanise support within the Labour movement. Despite some reservations amongst its leaders, the Labour movement granted £1,000 to help the departure of the first unit on 23 August. The committee had received a flood of volunteers after advertisements were placed in the medical press, and a team of four doctors, four medical students, four nurses, and six drivers was soon assembled. Kenneth Sinclair-Loutit, a 23-year-old medical student with a background in both the Territorial Army and the Cambridge Socialist Society, was placed in charge of the unit; he had, it was reported, disregarded a threat of disinheritance from his father in order to volunteer.[23] The unit was accompanied by Viscount Peter Churchill, a cousin of Winston Churchill, who was one of the committee's treasurers and acted as its Spanish representative during the first year. Churchill was an enigmatic figure with no previous record of political activity. His subsequent comment that 'there were fewer disguises and more frequent moments of truth' in Spain did not correspond to his own role.[24] He appears to have been drawn to the Civil War by a love of intrigue and relished the intensity of the conflict that he found there.

On arriving in Spain in early September the unit was based at the village of Grañen, 18 kilometres behind the front-line in Aragon. Despite the success in establishing a small hospital on the site, aided by reinforcements in September, the experience at Grañen was unhappy. The volunteers regretted being stationed on a relatively inactive sector of the front, at a time when the centre of the war was shifting to Madrid, and found that most of their work involved treating sickness amongst local people. Criticism of Sinclair-Loutit's management of the unit by the staff was compounded by bitter personal and political differences. In particular, the role of the Communist Party caused resentment: not only did party members within the unit meet in a caucus, but Communists based in Spain such as Ralph Bates and Tom Wintringham were regular (and proprietorial) visitors. A mutinous

round-robin signed by seventeen members of the unit listed allegations of inefficiency and political bias.[25] The unit's secretary, Aileen
Palmer, reported her disillusionment with the work at Grañen at the
end of November. She sadly noted that Spanish Medical Aid's spectacularly successful London rally had coincided with a miserable night of
feuding at the hospital.[26]

Sinclair-Loutit was eventually replaced as administrator, and in
January 1937 most of the unit departed for Albacete to work with the
newly formed XIV International Brigade. (One criticism made by
members of the British Battalion in the XV Brigade was that they
should have been treated by the British unit.)[27] The Grañen hospital
was given over to the Republican government. The new commander
of the British unit was Dr Alexander Tudor Hart, a committed
Communist whose wife (an Austrian photographer) was responsible
for initiating Kim Philby into the world of Soviet espionage.[28]

After the departure from Grañen it was no longer possible to speak
of a single 'British unit'. The work of the Spanish Medical Aid
Committee in Spain became more diffuse. British medical staff now
worked not only with the International Brigades, but also in hospitals
throughout the Republican zone. By July 1938 they were working in
nineteen hospitals (not including those on the front-line) and the
committee had sent out seventy-two vehicles.[29] British staff served at
all of the major battles after January 1937, most notably at Brunete in
July 1937. There the unit's dead included Dr Randall Sollenberger, an
American communist, and Julian Bell, son of Vanessa Bell and nephew
of Virginia Woolf. In the middle of 1937 the staff serving with the
International Brigades were incorporated (with military rank) into the
Republican army. This often disconcerted the volunteers, as well as
redefining the British unit rather uncomfortably as an arm of the
Republican war effort – very different from the initial idea of a
humanitarian mission. Sir Richard Rees, who objected both to the
change in status and to being a 'communist stooge', eventually left to
join the Quaker relief effort in Barcelona, but most of the staff voted to
agree to the new conditions.[30] Under the new arrangement Spanish
Medical Aid would simply act as the 'channel' for Spanish government
requests. The position of go-between was entrusted to Rosita Davson
as the committee's representative in Barcelona. She replaced Peter
Churchill, who had opposed the unit joining the army on the grounds

that such a step broke an undertaking given to the British government. His departure under a cloud may also have been connected to his involvement in the shady work of arms procurement for the Republican government.[31]

Domestically, the work of the committee suffered a setback in November 1936 when the Labour movement suspended its co-operation (holding back a further £1,000 that had been promised). The ostensible reason was that Communists were involved in the work of the committee, although, given the prominence of Isabel Brown, it could reasonably be asked why this issue had not been raised when support was first agreed. The underlying reason was concern at the manner in which the committee had given over responsibility for the hospital at Grañen to the Spanish authorities, coinciding with a decision to send out a new unit composed of unstaffed vehicles and equipment which would be given to the Republicans. The Labour leaders feared that the neutrality of their own relief work would have been embarrassed by further association with the British unit. However, while releasing no more funds, the Labour movement did not wholly disown the committee.

The loss of support at the highest level did nothing to damage the committee's appeal amongst the rank and file of the Labour movement – and more widely in British society. Of the £54,000 that had been raised by the middle of 1938,[32] most had come from relatively small donations – either from individuals or from local collections. Isabel Brown's emotive and highly effective fundraising speeches became legendary. The work of the committee was also helped by the creation of many local related bodies. The Battersea 'Aid to Spain' committee, over a twenty-month period, raised £750 to pay for an ambulance.[33] The success of Spanish Medical Aid was particularly impressive in the context of the problems of not only creating a fundraising body almost overnight, but also one that would have to administer supplies and the movement of personnel in a war zone made more complex by acute political problems. It is, thus, not surprising that there were tensions within the committee which were rarely visible to the public. These tensions were threefold: organisational, strategic, and political.

Following the resignation of Charles Brook in December 1936, the organisation of the committee's work was entrusted to two people, Leah Manning and George Jeger, a young Labour Party candidate and mayor of Shoreditch. His brother Santo, an East End doctor, was also active in the committee, and both would subsequently become Labour MPs. George Jeger was appalled by the chaotic conditions that he inherited in the office, and believed that his typist's main function was to spy on him for Isabel Brown! The relationship between the two main officers was complicated by Leah Manning's almost complete involvement from May 1937 in the evacuation of the Basque refugee children. She took a dislike to Jeger and refused to speak to him or come to the office, dealing only through a go-between.[34] Matters came to a head when, in September 1937, an internal report heavily criticised all aspects of the way in which the committee was run, including the lack of formal record-keeping, poor contact with local committees, and failure to check the political reliability of medical personnel.[35]

As with the organisational problems, the strategic issues that the committee had to face cut across simple political divisions. There was an inherent tension between the need to follow the wishes of the Spanish government, without losing so much control over the work in Spain that efficiency was sacrificed. Following the decision to allow the unit to join the Republican army, Dr Tudor Hart, now an officer, appeared to be acting to supply the Republican army as much as the British units in his ordering of drugs and equipment from London. Jeger commented that 'it is doubtful how far our jurisdiction extends' over Hart and the other personnel.[36] The question of control was posed even more forcefully in 1938 when the Spanish government decided to establish a new committee, with its main agent in Paris, to control and co-ordinate all foreign aid. In July Spanish Medical Aid agreed that, while anxious to secure maximum co-operation, 'we also desire the maximum of independence, and . . . we are not willing to subordinate ourselves entirely to Paris'.[37] Hostility within the unit towards Rosita Davson in Barcelona centred on the belief that she was too willing to give British equipment away to the Spanish authorities.

The main political problem within the committee was the relationship between Communists and members of the Labour Party. While Isabel Brown was the only committee member openly in the Communist Party, she was consistently supported by allies such as Lady Selina Hastings and Professor Marrack, a Cambridge biochemist. Morgan reported privately to the TUC on the internal politics of the

5 *An ambulance donated by the Artists International Association following a sale of pictures, January 1937*

committee, and was saddened that those he believed should have supported him did not always do so. He was particularly annoyed at the appointment of the left-wing trade unionist Leah Manning as honorary secretary. Morgan actually resigned at one point, provoking fears of a tide of resignations that would cripple the committee. Although he decided to stay on, the decision of the Labour movement not to appoint formal representatives meant that it could not expect to exercise any real influence. Even so, the decision to set up a hospital at Ucles in mid-1937, intended to care only for Spanish wounded, appears to have been a sop to those in the committee who did not like the close relationship between the British unit and the Communist-led International Brigades.[38] Thus, while the objectives of Spanish Medical Aid were above all humanitarian, it was never possible to lose sight of the fact that it was also a political campaign that straddled the contentious divide between the Labour leadership and the Left both within and outside the Labour Party.

6 Volunteers of the Scottish Ambulance Unit prepare to leave Glasgow,
January 1937

Spanish Medical Aid is often compared to the Scottish Ambulance Unit Committee that was formed in September 1936, and, indeed, the two felt themselves to be rivals. In practice, however, the two organisations were in most respects dissimilar. The Scottish unit was founded by Sir Daniel Stevenson, a wealthy businessman and chancellor of Glasgow University, who was extremely well connected in Scottish public life. Although his actions during the Civil War identified him as a supporter of the Spanish Republic, he had also been a strong advocate of British–German friendship and was, accordingly, treated with some suspicion on the Left. Stevenson formed a committee of well-respected people, and was supported by the general secretary of the Scottish TUC. However, the committee never had the popular appeal of Spanish Medical Aid, relying more on large donations from Stevenson's wealthy acquaintances (and from Stevenson himself) for its income. By the end of the war the committee had spent over £20,000, with Stevenson incurring a personal debt of £3,000.[39] Relations between the two medical aid committees were strained as the London-based organisation saw its Scottish counterpart as undermining its own efforts and, in particular, claimed that it had broken an agreement not to raise funds in England.

Stevenson's committee sent its first unit to Spain in September 1936, under the command of Fernanda Jacobsen, like Stevenson an active member of the Liberal Party. Operating on the front-lines to the south and west of Madrid, the unit pulled back to the capital as the rebels advanced. These early months were not short of controversy: five men were sent home for indiscipline and looting, and were joined by a sixth who complained that the unit only helped the government side. Two drivers were captured by the Nationalists and freed on the personal intervention of Anthony Eden. At the end of the year the surviving volunteers came home briefly to Scotland, until a reequipped unit returned to Spain with new volunteers in January.

In November 1936 Stevenson was able to secure the backing of the Labour movement, which over the next two years donated £3,000. This was despite the reservations of one leader of the Labour Party in Scotland who commented that the unit was 'well intentioned but badly planned . . . my opinion is that the wealthy people of Scotland who organised the show ought to provide the finance. This is the only thing they have done on behalf of Democracy in Spain.'[40] Likewise, Spanish Medical Aid denounced a 'Liberal' ambulance unit which would offend the Labour workers of Glasgow and, through 'local provincial pride',[41] refused any co-operation. However, by this stage Labour was about to cut its ties with Spanish Medical Aid, and came close to adopting the less politically controversial Scottish unit as its own.

The Scottish unit was again troubled on its return to Spain. In March 1937 four members left to join the International Brigades. Their public grievances were that other members were circulating anti-government atrocity stories; that Jacobsen refused to work with the authorities in the use of ambulances and the distribution of food; and that she had made provisional arrangements to stay in Madrid if the city should fall.[42] (This latter point contravened her instructions from Stevenson.) In addition, the men were concerned at the unit's involvement in helping Nationalists escape from Madrid to the coast. This operation was supervised by Captain Edwin Lance, an honorary British attaché who was eventually imprisoned for his activities by the Republicans. The allegation that Jacobsen was in any sense pro-fascist is misleading. However, her attempt at even-handedness in such a politically charged situation was certainly dangerous; for instance, she told the dissidents that 'there have been atrocities committed on both sides, and in any case one Spaniard is as good as another'. Her insistence on providing humanitarian relief independent of the Spanish government made her many enemies.

After another period in Scotland the unit returned to Spain for a third time between September 1937 and July 1938. Fundraising, however, was collapsing. Stevenson chose to blame this on the establishment of a centralised committee for Spanish relief in Scotland, preventing him from appealing to the trade unions. The reality was that his committee had never won the depth of support that Spanish Medical Aid had achieved in England. In September 1938 the unit was withdrawn, leaving its ambulances to the Spanish army medical service. Jacobsen, who received an OBE in 1937 for her relief work,[43] remained active in Spain, accompanying shiploads of food from Scotland and staying on in the country even after the end of the war.

In May 1937 the course of British humanitarian involvement in the Civil War was dramatically altered by the arrival of almost 4,000 children evacuated from the Basque country. The need to look after these refugees for an indefinite period placed even greater pressure on the fundraising capacity of the political, religious, and humanitarian agencies committed to their care. At the same time, however, the children achieved more than any pamphlet or public meeting in bringing home the harsh realities of the war to the British people. The campaign to care for the Basque children attracted support far beyond the organisations that had previously taken an interest in the conflict. It was, moreover, the only occasion when, however reluctantly, all of the many strands of humanitarian assistance came together to achieve a brief but effective consensus.

The occasion for the evacuation was the successful Nationalist offensive against the Basque Republic in April 1937. As rebel forces closed in on the capital Bilbao, concern grew for the fate of the children in a city which was short of food and exposed to aerial attack. Large numbers had already been evacuated, primarily to France. The

British evacuation was largely the result of a frenetic campaign by Leah Manning, an agent of the National Joint Committee in Bilbao, who successfully – surprisingly so given the diplomatic ramifications – petitioned the British government to allow a small number of children to enter Britain. This decision, opposed by the Foreign Office, was probably influenced by the furore over the bombing of Guernica on 26 April, and by the example set by the recent French evacuations.

Leah Manning's success was a rare triumph for emotive political pressure over expert opinion. The British government's permission was granted in the face of opposition not only from the Foreign Office, but from all of the agencies with a recognised expertise in the subject. Lewis Golden, secretary of the Save the Children Fund, maintained that his organisation always advised against the removal of young children from their native country, predicting that they would deteriorate 'physically, morally, and mentally' in Britain. He was also concerned that the evacuation was a political stunt.[44] Similarly, the Spain Committee of the Friends' Service Council, the Quaker aid organisation, saw the evacuation to Britain as unsuitable unless 'absolutely necessary', suggesting instead that the children be cared for in France or Catalonia. While both organisations felt that they had no alternative other than to help with the children's care on their arrival, they were careful to deny any financial responsibility.[45] The Catholic Church was also hostile to the initiative, which it saw not only as politically motivated but also as a dangerously open-ended financial commitment. Archbishop Hinsley grudgingly agreed to support the Catholics amongst the evacuees. He was influenced by an appeal from Bishop Mugica of Vitoria, although he also believed that he had received a private undertaking from the home secretary that the children 'would not be disembarked' in Britain.[46]

Supported by the advice of two British doctors, who arrived to check the health of the children, further concessions were won from the government. The number of children to be accepted was doubled to 4,000, and the upper age limit was raised from twelve to fifteen (older children being considered at most risk). In return Sir John Simon, the home secretary, imposed a series of conditions, the most important of which were that the children must be the financial responsibility solely of those who had brought them, and that repatriation should commence 'as soon as conditions permitted'.[47]

It was recognised from the start that it was both undesirable and impracticable for the National Joint Committee to attempt to carry this burden on its own. Even before the arrival of the children a new organisation, which became known as the Basque Children's Committee, was formed to take responsibility for their care. This had the advantage of allowing the participation of the Labour movement and the Catholic Church, neither of which would work directly with the National Joint Committee. The TUC was represented by Vincent Tewson, the assistant general secretary, and Canon Craven represented Archbishop Hinsley. Also on the committee were the Friends, Save the Children, the Salvation Army, and Spanish Medical Aid. While the new body was avowedly 'not a sub-committee' of the National Joint Committee,[48] in practice the links between the two were strong. Many of the leading figures were the same, including the ubiquitous Isabel Brown, the Duchess of Atholl, and Wilfred Roberts – the latter two serving respectively as chairman and secretary. Roberts was later joined by two other MPs, Labour's David Grenfell and the Conservative Captain Macnamara, to provide cross-party balance. Given this overlap, it was understandable that meetings of the two committees were often held consecutively. Inevitably, this emphasised the preponderant influence of the National Joint Committee when crucial decisions had to be taken on issues such as repatriation of the children.

Aided by a grant of £5,000 from the Labour movement, and with other donations building to £22,000 in the first month, the scene was set for the arrival of the children. On 23 May the *Habana* docked in Southampton carrying 3,861 children (who had been chosen by a quota system from amongst the Basque political parties), 95 women teachers, 120 young female helpers (the 'señoritas'), and 15 priests.[49] They went initially to a camp at North Stoneham near Southampton, which had been prepared with remarkable speed by a volunteer workforce. Not surprisingly, the first days at the camp were somewhat chaotic, with serious problems of health and sanitation. All of the children suffered profound stress at being plucked from a war zone, leaving their families behind and being expected to adapt to British customs. In particular, older children – many of whom may until recently have been digging trenches and who saw themselves as grown-up – chafed at camp discipline and took to wandering off the site. The most traumatic moment for the children came with the news,

7 The first of the Basque refugee children arrive in Southampton on the liner Habana

on 19 June 1937, of the fall of Bilbao. The announcement, relayed over loudspeakers, caused great distress and some children even temporarily broke out of the camp. Thus, despite the immense goodwill of many local people, the camp generated bad publicity in right-wing national newspapers. Following official expressions of concern, order was restored through the appointment of Major Irwin as camp commandant. He, in turn, hired twelve unemployed ex-servicemen to patrol the perimeter at night. In July twenty-three boys on a 'black list' of troublemakers were sent to France.

Major Irwin's main task was to oversee the emptying of the camp into smaller homes around the country, and North Stoneham was finally closed in mid-September. Some of the accommodation was provided from within the committee; for instance, the Catholics took the 1,200 children of their own faith. On the whole, however, the committee had to rely on the initiative of local groups which had

8 *Some of the fifty Basque children being cared for at Watermillock, Bolton*

volunteered their services. In order to maximise support these were encouraged to be as broadly based and as non-political as possible, and were often centred on leading figures in the local community who would not have wished to be associated directly with Civil War relief work. Although the committee itself ran a small number of homes for the more difficult children, henceforth much of its work would involve fundraising and monitoring the local homes.

The fall of Bilbao had great bearing on the fate of the children. Not only were their families likely to be dispersed in the face of the rebel advance, but also the new Nationalist authorities in the city were determined to engineer their prompt return. This punctured the tenuous alliance that had formed in support of the children. The Catholics, in particular, could ill-afford the estimated £500–600 per month to look after the children in their care and were quick to call for repatriation. The British government now defined the speedy return of the children as a 'clear British interest',[50] although awareness of the problems involved muted the pressure that it could apply. While the bulk of the committee accepted the need for repatriation in the long term, they believed that this should occur only when safe conditions in Bilbao could be guaranteed, and when any requests from parents had been fully validated.

Pressure was directed from two sources. Felix George Sturrup, a pro-Nationalist businessman and correspondent for the Catholic *Universe*, arrived in August 1937 with a list of some 900 children whose return was requested by their parents. He was dismissed as a 'nuisance' by the Foreign Office and even antagonised the Catholic authorities by rushing into print without their permission. A wholly more formidable opponent was Father Gabana, former chaplain to English-speaking Catholics in Barcelona, who arrived in September with another list of 800 names. Gabana was the representative of the Apostolic Delegate Monsignor Antoniutti, sent by the Pope to Bilbao to facilitate the repatriation of all of the Basque children. He was closely supported by Canon Craven and Captain Macnamara, who was keen to begin the process of returning the children without breaking up the committee. Initially Captain Macnamara's colleagues were highly suspicious of Gabana, openly doubting the validity of many of the parents' requests and seeking permission to send a delegation to the Basque country to interview them in private. Given the Nationalists' hostility to what they regarded as a left-wing body, this request was never likely to be met and smacked of prevarication. The sense that the children had become a political football was reinforced when Gabana met the committee on 4 October. Wilfred Roberts told him that 'The position from a business standpoint was that Franco wanted the children and we have them. He should therefore accept our terms.'[51]

The committee's intransigence had forced a crisis. At the close of the meeting it was agreed to establish an independent commission of lawyers to review Gabana's demands. Outraged at the exclusion of Gabana from the commission, Canon Craven resigned and promptly joined the new right-wing Repatriation Committee chaired by Sir Arnold Wilson. In fact, however, the commission headed by Sir Holman Gregory vindicated Gabana's position. It concluded that conditions were now safe for the children's return as soon as could be arranged, and that repatriation, initially of small groups, should be carried out by co-operation between all of the interested parties. Many members of the Basque Children's Committee regretted the report, fearing that it would undermine fundraising. Even so, they acted quickly to comply with the findings, sending the first cohort of 152 children home on 12 November in the care of Fr Gabana and two of its own representatives. When they reported favourably on the children's reception the return accelerated, with 500 more departing in January 1938.

By early 1938, however, new problems had become evident. Gabana's list dealt with only the most straightforward cases, where both parents were living in Bilbao and had requested their children's return (even if sometimes under coercion). Yet by the summer of 1938 it was clear that there was a core of some 1,800 children whose parents were separated, could not be traced, or were not in a position to look after them. This included 1,000 whose parents were in Catalonia. The intractability of this problem coincided with a decline in public subscriptions in 1938, as well as the perception amongst some committee members that money could be more gainfully spent on supplying food to the hard-pressed Republicans of eastern Spain. Indeed, during the year the committee's policy changed markedly. Regulations were relaxed to force more children to return, the 'adoption' of children by British families was encouraged, and a limited right for the older children to work was secured from the government. Strenuous efforts were also made to generate revenue through Basque concerts and other events. The committee's advocacy of the children's repatriation where at all possible divided its supporters along political lines. While some argued that the need of eastern Spain was now greater than that of the evacuees, others refused to countenance surrendering the children. One outraged London teacher went so far as to claim that some of the committee's officials behaved as if they were 'the agents of Franco' and had discouraged efforts to raise money.[52]

Despite all of these measures, over 1,000 children remained in Britain at the end of the Civil War. At the start of the Second World War in September 1939 the British government immediately intensified the pressure on the committee for repatriation, not only in order to improve relations with the Nationalists, but also because wartime Britain was now less safe than Spain. Even with the rapid return of half of these children, a sizeable number remained who had been effectively adopted or who were old enough to exercise a choice in the matter. In 1945, 410 were still living in Britain, mainly those without any family in Spain, and many of these settled permanently.[53]

The case of the Basque children in Britain has become part of the romance of the Civil War, but it must be kept in perspective. The fact that their arrival was treated as such a remarkable event was due, in part, to the unwillingness of British governments since the First World War to accept refugees – especially those without private means. In comparison, by October 1937 France had taken 70,000 Spanish refugees, and by the end of the war this had risen to some 440,000.[54] Nor did the success of the National Joint Committee in this case open the door for more Spanish refugees to come: following the defeat of the Republic only a trickle of refugees – often senior political and military figures – was allowed to enter Britain.

Two organisations involved in Spanish relief work, the Friends Service Council and the Save the Children Fund, already had well-established reputations for international work of this nature, as well as a firm commitment to complete political impartiality. Despite these similarities and the closeness of their co-operation in Spain, however, there were substantial differences between them.

The Friends (the Quakers), with their impressive history of international relief work, were extremely well placed to intervene in the Civil War. However, it is important to bear in mind that they were not simply a charitable institution, but also a body with specific religious objectives. Throughout the Civil War, leading Friends were concerned that they should not be seen to be offering 'mere' relief, but that they should exercise their specific vocation for reconciliation. They lacked any self-consciousness in this regard, at one point approaching the Duke of Alba (the Nationalist agent in London) with a view to arranging an interview with Franco himself.[55] The Friends were always concerned that they should not be seen to take sides in the Civil War, and, although not allowed to operate in Nationalist Spain, maintained a tenuous presence there through their relationship with Save the Children and the American Friends.

The inception of the Friends' Civil War mission in Spain is particularly instructive. The Eckroyds, a couple who had been living there for almost forty years, hoped to encourage a Quaker presence in Spain and permission was granted for the American-born Alfred Jacob and his English wife Norma to visit Madrid. The outbreak of the Civil War changed the nature of Jacob's visit into a reconnaissance for a future relief operation. However, he did not lose sight of his 'early wish to do something towards keeping Spain from becoming a secular state entirely', and his initial correspondence from Barcelona is imbued with the belief that the suppression of the Catholic Church in Spain might well create an opening for religious evangelism. On 3 October 1936 he urged the Friends to help keep open a Protestant centre at the Barcelona YMCA because: 'Later on, if there is to be a formal vehicle for the expression of religious consciousness in Spain, it will probably have to be non-Catholic, and a rightly constituted Protestant Church is bound to awaken new interest.' Most controversially, he argued that such a centre would encourage conscientious objection. He concluded that 'I need not mention the possible connection of our Quaker service with this. I do not think that we ought to be too separate in Spain, and a right co-operation here may give just the right opening for us.'[56] This sense of optimism for the religious possibilities in Spain did not last long. Within a few months Jacob was warning that there should be no sense of 'ulterior motives' behind their relief work. Even so, the commonly held belief amongst Quakers working in Spain that there was no anti-God (as opposed to anti-Catholic) movement in the Republic suggested a lingering hope for spiritual renewal if the Republic were to succeed.[57]

Jacob's first suggestion was that the Friends should establish sanctuaries for right-wing Spaniards stranded in Catalonia by the Civil War.[58] However, with the support of the Catalan president, Luis Companys, he soon settled on the idea of providing milk for child refugees arriving in Catalonia from central Spain. Canteens were established in Barcelona and a successful joint appeal was launched with the Save the Children Fund. Less successful was the agreement that was reached between the Friends and the Geneva-based Save the Children International Union (SCIU), according to which the Friends would be primarily responsible for fundraising while the SCIU would provide the expertise to run the operation. In practice, Jacob and his wife were already established in Barcelona and resented being treated as employees by the SCIU's abrasive Dr Pictet. Personality clashes were compounded by differences of organisational culture: the Friends saw themselves as egalitarian, democratic, and reliant on local volunteers, and perceived the SCIU as autocratic.[59] The agreement was abandoned in November 1937, although the two organisations continued to co-operate.

These differences were deep-rooted. As early as November 1936 Lewis Golden, secretary of the Save the Children Fund, had admitted that he was personally opposed to the Friends' 'political and religious tendencies'. Eventually he was to resign in July 1937, in part over his organisation's policy on Spain which he considered to be 'wrong and almost criminal' as regards the Basque children.[60] The Fund's own contacts with the International Committee of the Red Cross, which allowed it to work in Nationalist Spain, were valued much more highly than those with the Friends. Thus, two very different conceptions of impartiality were in operation. The Save the Children Fund viewed itself as a primarily professional organisation. The Friends did not allow those who spoke on their behalf to express opinions on the political situation in Spain other than in a personal capacity: however, their personal views were predominantly pro-Republican.

These differences did not disrupt the development of the Friends' relief work in Spain. Buoyed up by intensive campaigning around the country, the British Friends raised the remarkable sum of £87,000 for relief work in Spain (including the post-war care of refugees). This allowed some forty Quakers to be based in Spain (no more than twenty at any one time) and the expansion of operations from Jacob's original Barcelona canteens. Not only were children's colonies established in Catalonia, but Francesca Wilson, a highly experienced relief worker, developed a series of initiatives for refugees in Murcia. She was helped in this by Sir George Young whose hospital in Almería was eventually taken over by the American Friends. Most significant was the role of Edith Pye in the formation of the International Commission for Assistance of Child Refugees, supported by a number of governments, including the British. When the Commission was established, the Friends became its agent for the distribution of relief in Spain.

Humanitarian assistance for the Nationalists was dominated, almost exclusively, by the Catholic Church. The only exception was Sir Edward Bellingham's short-lived and aggressively anti-communist, but non-sectarian, Spanish Relief Fund for Sufferers from Red Atrocities.[61] Catholic fundraising was initiated by two newspapers, the Universe and the Catholic Times. The Universe fund was started at the suggestion of the Nationalist agent Merry del Val with a view to sending medical supplies to the rebels, and £3,574 was raised in twenty days.[62]

Although this level was not sustained, by the end of 1937 £12,503 had been raised, plus £1,463 for the care of the Basque children. The *Catholic Times's* appeal was intended to assist Catholic refugees arriving in Britain, who were often from well-heeled backgrounds and were only given very limited state support. In September 1936 this was absorbed into a new committee established by Archbishop Hinsley, which was intended to co-ordinate all of the Catholic funds. The *Universe* appeal remained separate because its proprietor, Sir Martin Melvin, had wrongly predicted that its support would not last longer than a few weeks.[63]

The new Bishops' Committee for the Relief of Spanish Distress was presided over by Hinsley, with Lord Howard of Penrith (a former ambassador to Madrid) as general chairman. The committee was composed of some of the best-known Catholic laity, including Christopher Dawson, Frank Sheed, and Evelyn Waugh. Some Catholic politicians, however, such as Arthur Hope (son of Lord Rankeillour and a junior government minister) and the Earl of Iddesleigh, refused to serve for fear of embarrassing the government.[64] These reservations were appropriate given that the Bishops' Committee made no pretence to impartiality. While the immediate objectives were listed as 'the relief of the sick, wounded, refugees, and destitute children of Spain', the underlying motive was to provide moral support to those fighting 'atheistic communism' and to dispel the widespread belief in Nationalist Spain that the 'Reds' monopolised public sentiment in Britain.[65] At a fundraising meeting in the Dorchester Hotel, Major General Fuller described Franco as a modern crusader fighting a 'foreign Black Death'.[66] In the course of the Civil War the Bishops' Committee raised £14,500, much coming in donations from wealthy individuals (including £700 from Lady Houston alone). In the autumn of 1936 two ambulances were supplied to the rebel forces, forming the basis of the Equipo Anglo-Español which served initially on the northern front. The Nationalists did not suffer from the same acute shortage of medical personnel as the Republicans and, apart from Gabriel Herbert, who represented the committee, the unit was staffed by Spaniards.

Catholic aid for the Nationalists was not very substantial when seen in relation to the amounts raised for the Republicans. This may have been due in part to a reluctance by working-class Catholics to aid Franco, and may also have been a product of administrative disorganisation. Campaigning for the Bishops' Committee, for instance, appears to have been primarily directed at the 'more prosperous laity', to the neglect of the Catholic workers. Moreover, there were tensions within the Catholic hierarchy. Archbishop Amigo of Southwark, a forceful and profoundly anti-communist Gibraltarian who had made life difficult for Hinsley's predecessor, was not even formally notified of the appeal until December 1936.[67] Nevertheless, it is clear that the cause of medical aid for Nationalist Spain never had the same sense of urgency or emotional appeal as aid to the Republican side. There were several reasons for this. The British public was less well informed about conditions within Nationalist territory, and rebel medical services were more self-reliant than those of the Republicans. Above all, the image of Nationalist Spain was not one which combined easily with humanitarian aid. Where the Republicans were seen as civilian victims of the modern horrors of war, the Nationalists were martial and aggressively self-reliant. However much one sympathised with them, they did not seem in need of help.

Chapter 5

VOLUNTEERS

In December 1936 the eighty-year-old Henry Nevinson spent a sleepless night on hearing that his friend H. N. Brailsford had announced that he was going to fight in Spain 'and so martyr himself: not much good as he is well over fifty and far more useful here, but the thought that I am now too old and feeble to go myself kept me awake for many hours'.[1] This was more than an old man's fancy: both Nevinson and Brailsford had been involved with the volunteer British Legion fighting for Greece in the war of 1896–7 against Turkey. Forty years later, Brailsford (who was sixty-three) was to be turned down by the International Brigades on grounds of age. However, he continued to appeal to younger men to volunteer because 'in my youth I did this sort of thing',[2] and he was to be the first chairman of the fund established for the dependants of volunteers.

While this direct continuity was unique, nowhere did the Communist Party draw more clearly on Britain's radical traditions to legitimise the new politics of the 1930s than in the case of the British volunteers. The International Brigades represented a dramatic new departure: it was the only time during this century in which a British political party has sustained a significant military contingent in a foreign war. Yet it was presented as a continuation of the long-standing British tradition of volunteering to defend liberty wherever it was threatened or suppressed, beginning with Lord Byron's doomed expedition to Greece in 1823–4. The Communist leader Harry Pollitt's language, in particular, was steeped in references to Byron and to the Britons who fought with Garibaldi in Italy in 1859–60 (although never to the more dubious case of the volunteers in Spain of 1835–7). In the words of his eulogy for Ralph Fox, the British Battalion had

> upheld the fine democratic traditions that have characterised the fight on behalf
> of liberty. The great poet Byron went to Greece to fight for liberty; in a later

121

period comrade Brailsford fought for liberty in Greece; these are the examples that our British comrades are following today in the conditions of our time.[3]

Pollitt's protestations deserve to be taken seriously. There had, indeed, been a romantic and libertarian British tradition of volunteering in the nineteenth century which had made going to fight in other people's wars a right – even a duty – of free-born Britons. In the 1930s the Communist Party breathed new life into that tradition, organising the dispatch of more than 2,000 volunteers to fight in the International Brigades. The International Brigades represent the successful merger between the romance of the volunteering tradition and the organisational and propagandistic powers of international communism. But the Brigades, while reviving the volunteering tradition in Spain, would also eventually kill it.

Because of their numerical and political importance the British members of the International Brigades form the main focus of this chapter. However, there were other groups of volunteers from the British Isles to be found on both sides of the lines. The handful of volunteers for the ILP contingent are discussed separately. An even smaller number of Britons also fought for the Nationalists, most notably Peter Kemp, who became an officer in the Foreign Legion. Four seminarists from the English College at Valladolid joined the Nationalist army and one, Paddy Dalton, was killed. Finally, a much more substantial volunteer force was raised to fight with the Nationalists in the Irish Free State by Eoin O'Duffy, leader of the right-wing Blueshirts.

The formal origins of the British Battalion lie with the decision of the Executive Committee of the Communist International in late September 1936 to begin the organisation of the International Brigades. Individual communist parties around the world were charged with recruitment, while a core of professional Comintern administrators and soldiers, presided over by the volatile French revolutionary André Marty, oversaw the Brigades' formation in Spain. The first contingents arrived at the base at Albacete in mid-October, and before the end of the month the XI Brigade of French, German, and Polish Battalions had been created and rushed to the defence of Madrid. It formed the first of what would become five brigades, numbered from XI to XV, comprising members drawn from over fifty nationalities. The exact number of volunteers remains unclear, but there were probably between 30,000 and 40,000, with the French providing the single largest contingent.[4]

As the creation of the international communist movement, the Brigades were undoubtedly a 'Comintern Army'.[5] However, they have to be understood in the context of the largely spontaneous involvement of many individuals in the first months of the Civil War, and of the lessons learnt during that time. British participation in this phase was limited, in part for geographical reasons, but also because many of these earliest volunteers were German and Italian anti-fascist exiles who saw the Civil War as a chance to hit back at the oppressive regimes in their own countries.

Of the early British volunteers, some happened to be in the vicinity by chance. Two East End Jewish tailors were on a cycling holiday in the south of France and established the (mainly Spanish) Tom Mann Centuria[6] in Catalonia which took part in an abortive attack on Majorca. A number of Britons were in Barcelona for the Workers' Olympiad (an alternative to the Olympics in Hitler's Berlin) and were caught up in the fighting. A woman, the artist Felicia Browne, joined a militia column and became the first British fatality on 25 August while taking part in an attempt to blow up a railway station. John Cornford, a brilliant young Marxist who had recently graduated from Cambridge, arrived in Spain in early August with a press card from the *News Chronicle*. Visiting the front-line in Aragon he made a sudden decision to join one of the militias.

In the absence of any formal structures for recruitment these were all genuine volunteers, many of whom decided to fight on impulse. However, at this stage there was no sense of them joining a formal army. In the confusion of the early months of the Civil War foreigners drifted in and out of militias until they discovered a group that they found congenial, or went home with no fear of being treated as deserters. For similar reasons there was a considerable political innocence in this initial phase. Most volunteers came first to Catalonia where they naturally encountered the revolutionaries: the POUM and the Anarchists. John Cornford, an ardent Communist, found himself in the militia of the anti-Stalinist POUM. He then gravitated to a group of German ex-communists who, despite their denunciation of the Communist International for betraying the revolution, he described as the 'finest people' he had met.[7] Thus, political differences were tempered by shared experience, and there was little of the bitterness within the Left that would mar the later years of the war.

For these early volunteers admiration for the passion of the Spanish militias was mingled with frustration at their indiscipline. Both Cornford and Tom Wintringham argued the need for a disciplined international presence that would instruct the militias in 'real' warfare. In Wintringham's words: 'How could these incredibly gallant Spaniards get hold of the art, the science, the discipline of war? By example and by training, given them by foreigners.'[8] As one of the British Communist leaders in Barcelona, Wintringham quickly realised both the military and political advantage of a British unit, on the lines of the Tom Mann Centuria, although he also recognised the need for more than the fifty Britons he estimated to be present in early September.[9]

The British Communist Party reacted more slowly to the formation of the International Brigades than many other European parties. This was partly because it was a small organisation, with its human resources already stretched by campaigns against unemployment and Mosley's Fascists. There were few Welshmen, for example, amongst the initial volunteers because of the effort being put into the Hunger March in the autumn of 1936.[10] Moreover, the Communist Party was initially more concerned with sending men with specialist skills rather than potential soldiers. From early September 1936 the British party's Political Bureau had been calling, without much success, for skilled craftsmen to go to Spain. Eventually in November eight air mechanics were sent to work at reconditioning aeroplanes in the Barcelona Hispano-Suizo factory. The mission was a failure: some of the men fell foul of inter-union rivalries and were expelled; others left when the promise of high wages failed to materialise.[11] The party also sent out a number of seamen and a twenty-year-old pilot, Peter Elstob, who was promptly arrested as a suspected spy and deported.[12] Another limitation was that the British Communist representatives in Spain were based in Barcelona. They appeared aloof from the developments in Albacete and were more concerned with the problems of the British Medical Unit at nearby Grañen. As late as December 1936 Ralph Bates reported to London with an air of detachment that the Brigades in Madrid were reputed to be the most formidable of the militia forces, and recommended a British Battalion within them.[13] While some men were referred on to Albacete, these were not always of high quality – including one man described as one of the most troublesome members of the Tom Mann Centuria.

Eventually the British volunteers coalesced, often by chance, into a number of small units attached to the International Brigades which fought in the early battles in and around Madrid. One group attached themselves to the German Thaelmann Battalion. They were lead by Lorrimer Birch, a 'seven days a week' Communist,[14] and joined by two young non-communists, Esmond Romilly and Keith Scott Watson. This group was almost wiped out at the battle of Boadilla on 20 December opposing a rebel offensive – Romilly lived to commemorate his comrades in his powerful memoir *Boadilla* (1937). At the same time twelve more volunteers had formed a machine-gun company in a French Battalion of the XI Brigade. Amongst their number was Jock Cunningham, a future leader of the British Battalion, and John Cornford who, after visiting Britain briefly in October, had returned with six new recruits. This group, which also fought at Boadilla, formed the basis for 'Number 1 Company' under the former British officer Captain George Nathan. Attached to the French Battalion of the XIV Brigade, the company took part in a failed offensive at Lopera on the Cordoba front. Both Cornford and Ralph Fox, an assistant commissar and leading Communist intellectual, were killed on 28 December. The commanding officer, Lassale, was held responsible and shot on André Marty's orders for treason. George Nathan, an insouciant and reassuring figure with his officer's cane, rose to be chief of operations of XV Brigade, although his application for Communist Party membership in early 1937 was rejected.[15]

By this stage, the British Communist Party had laid the foundations for a recruitment campaign which would allow it to meet its quota of volunteers. The central figure was R. W. Robson of the party's Control Commission. Until February 1937 Robson worked openly from the Communist headquarters at King Street, interviewing potential recruits sent by agents throughout Britain. Initially a profile of age, family commitments, and, above all, military experience was strictly adhered to, although these criteria were subsequently relaxed. Political affiliation was not important amongst volunteers, so long as they subscribed to the broad principle of 'anti-fascism'.

Selected volunteers were then sent in groups across the Channel on the first stage of their journey to Spain. Despite the presence of these large and noticeable contingents, the British authorities were unable to do much to stop them, especially as no passport was required for a weekend excursion to Boulogne. From March 1937 Charlotte Haldane, whose sixteen-year-old son Ronnie had volunteered, was employed in Paris to receive the men and to send home the few deemed unsuitable. Arrangements for the men's travel through France was then entrusted to the French Communists. Despite non-intervention, there was considerable complicity from the authorities with only occasional crack-downs. Entry into Spain became more difficult after February 1937 when the border was closed to volunteers, but other routes across the Pyrenees were soon established.

The question of why men chose to volunteer, and of who they were, has long been debated. The argument has been unduly influenced by the belief that they were mainly intellectuals. The idea that this was, in Stephen Spender's words, a 'poets' war'[16] has been a persistent one. It reflects the high proportion of intellectuals amongst the early volunteers, the temptation of the Communist Party to memorialise these men when they died, and the fact that they were much more likely to write memoirs of their time in Spain. The balance has shifted only in recent decades with the spate of oral histories of the surviving (and previously largely voiceless) members of the Battalion.

The salient characteristics of the British volunteers are, in fact, well established. Despite the high profile of the intellectuals, volunteers came overwhelmingly from the working class. They were likely to be members of a trade union or unemployed (many of the latter being members of the Communist-led National Unemployed Workers' Union). Volunteering was concentrated on the urban and industrial areas. Although exact figures are disputed, the following figures have been calculated on the basis of the British Battalion's archives and appear authoritative: Scotland 437; Wales 122; the North-East of England 86; Lancashire–Cheshire 308; Yorkshire 69; Midlands 71; London 514; Ireland 104 (of whom 29 were from Northern Ireland). Between 150 and 200 were probably Jewish.[17] Recruitment was directed at those between the ages of twenty-five and thirty-five, without family commitments. Inevitably, many both older and younger than this participated, although after February 1937 no more under the age of eighteen were accepted. A persistent demand amongst the Battalion's organisers was for trained men, especially officers. Many had some degree of military experience, especially in the early stages when this was a major criterion for recruitment. Tom Wintringham estimated that 30 per cent of the Battalion were ex-servicemen.[18] Others might have participated in Officer Training Corps at school, although Esmond Romilly had, as a schoolboy pacifist, refused to join it.

Many different reasons have been given for volunteering. To their right-wing critics the men were mercenaries, receiving up to £1 per day for their services.[19] While this charge is easily rebutted (pay was minimal and erratic), an explanation based on social conditions rather than political beliefs is more compelling. A deserter who presented himself in Gibraltar left intelligence officers with the view that his was a case of 'unemployment, communist propaganda, and the intriguing prospect, seen from Bradford, of well-paid employment in company with his friends in glamorous Spain'.[20] Charlotte Haldane, who met many of the volunteers in Paris, later wrote that most were 'unemployed lads . . . Years of depression and the dole had forced them into enlistment.'[21] Charles Morgan recalled that 'I knew why I was there, to get the hell out of the dole.'[22] Undoubtedly a group of men, often unemployed, volunteered because they sought adventure and may have been misled about what they were letting themselves in for. The large numbers of deserters who began to make their way home in the spring of 1937 were drawn primarily from this group for whom the adventure had turned predictably sour.

Yet for the great majority, including the unemployed, volunteering came as a conscious political decision. For those who had been involved in radical and anti-fascist politics for some time before the Civil War, joining the International Brigades was a logical, if immensely more challenging and dangerous, continuation of their earlier activities. Such men had observed the rise of fascist movements in both Britain and the rest of Europe, perceived the connections between them and felt the need to respond in some way. In the words of the young scientist David Haden Guest, one of the later volunteers, it was impossible to 'concentrate on pure mathematics when the world seem[ed] on fire'.[23] Thus, fascism was for the first time fully incarnated in Franco's rebellion and his foreign allies.

It is easier to define what the volunteers were fighting against than what they were fighting for. Given that few had any direct knowledge of Spain, anti-fascism – mingled with sympathy for the underdog – was clearly uppermost in their minds. Moreover they were indoctrinated on arrival with the Communist Party's interpretation of the war as a struggle to defend a democratic Republic against fascist revolt. However, once in Spain many volunteers developed a deep admiration for the Spanish people, and for the new society that they were constructing. One wrote to a friend that 'the poor class of Spain are 500 years behind time . . . they been kept under like dogs but the people have risen now George'.[24] Another, forgetful of the official line, wrote that 'Spain is going to be a wonderful Socialist country in a few short years.'[25]

Even amongst the most committed volunteers, however, political motivations sometimes jostled with more subjective ones; John Cornford himself admitted to having felt 'tied down' since the age of seventeen and now, in Spain, feeling 'for the first time independent'.[26] Tom Wintringham saw his involvement in the Civil War as a way of reconciling his communist beliefs with the Nonconformist and liberal politics of his family: 'I was here because of all I was and would be.'[27] Amongst the intellectuals in particular there was also a tendency to self-romanticisation. The writer John Sommerfield, who took part in the defence of Madrid, saw it as a victory of civilisation over barbarism comparable to Charles Martel's victory over the Moors in 732.[28]

Despite the good political case that could be made for volunteering, it could never, however, be an easy decision. For all those who joined up 'because they wanted to get away from their wives or families',[29] many more faced (or dodged) difficult personal decisions. Walter Gregory from Nottingham was elated at being asked by the local Communist organiser to leave his job in a brewery and 'do something important'. At the same time he was aware that his widowed mother would now have to live on a few shillings a week from the Brigades' relief fund.[30] Jack Roberts gave no word of his intention to volunteer to his mother or teenage daughter.[31] Hywel Francis, who published the definitive history of the Welsh contingent in 1984, later wrote of the need to take into account the 'personal and family traumas, emotions and sacrifices' inherent in volunteering as well as the 'courage and principled heroism'.[32]

In December 1936 and January 1937 the foundations of a British Battalion of the XV International Brigade were laid in the base at Madrigueras near Albacete. It was no different from the other units in the Brigades in that a clear political and military structure was imposed from the start. Parallel to the military command there was also a political command based on political commissars at brigade, battalion, and company level. This imitated the Soviet model that had already been established through much of the Republican army. Officially the role of the commissars was defined as one of building morale and political consciousness, so that discipline would be maintained by mutual consent rather than by brute force. Unlike in a traditional army, the commissar would ensure that the soldiers understood the war that they were fighting as well as catering for their 'comfort, leisure, rest, and recreation'.[33] At the same time, however, they were also the guarantors of Communist control over the brigades, and the point of contact between the Battalion and the Communist leadership in Britain. Thus, while the military commanding officer might not be a Communist (but increasingly was), the commissars had to be. Although this arrangement appears to have worked well, there was always the possibility of tensions. For instance, although the commissars often lacked military experience, they participated in military decisions in an 'advisory capacity', countersigned all orders, and had to be ready to take command if necessary. The senior British commissars tended to be district officers of the Communist Party or, in the case of Will Paynter, a trade union official.

Two men played the leading role in the military formation of the unit. Wilfred McCartney, the first commander, was a former army officer who had recently been released from a prison sentence for espionage. He made few concessions to the differences between the Brigades and a more conventional army, and is said to have referred to the Battalion as 'Harry's anarchists' – for which he received a ticking off from Harry Pollitt. He was denied the opportunity to lead the Battalion in battle, as shortly before the first action he was accidentally shot and wounded by the political commissar Peter Kerrigan. Despite persistent allegations that McCartney had been deliberately removed for political reasons there is no evidence that this was anything other than a mistake by Kerrigan, whose first reaction was to tender his

9 Spanish Medical Aid ambulances and their crews prepare to leave London,
March 1938

10 Volunteers of the British Battalion are inspected by Lt.-Col. Copic, commander of
the XV International Brigade in Mondejar. The Battalion commander Bill Alexander
(wearing a beret) faces the camera

resignation.[34] Indeed, McCartney had already been summoned home for legal reasons. Even so, the accident did follow mounting concern amongst the commissars at McCartney's temperament and political ineptitude, and the Communist Party would not allow him to return to his command in the spring of 1937.[35]

Command passed to Tom Wintringham, a wartime member of the Royal Flying Corps who had become a Communist and was jailed in 1925 for sedition. He saw himself as both a military theorist and as the architect of the Battalion, boasting in 1938 that he had created in only six weeks 'second-rate but useful infantry' out of civilians and ex-servicemen.[36] (Some survivors were less complimentary about the standard of training that he provided.) Wintringham dreamed of leading an army of sturdy yeomen like an 'English captain' of old. His command was cut short by wounds on the Jarama, although he remained with the Brigades and was wounded a second time at Belchite.

With the departure of McCartney and Wintringham, control over the Battalion passed to Jock Cunningham and Fred Copeman. Cunningham had been a soldier in the Argyll and Sutherland Highlanders, and rose rapidly to command the Battalion and then, at Brunete, a regiment of the XV Brigade. Favoured by Pollitt, he was placed on the Central Committee of the Communist Party and, during Pollitt's second visit to Spain, named as the British political leader in the Brigades.[37] Cunningham never recovered from being stripped of his command after the battle of Brunete and ended his days as a vagrant. Copeman was a former sailor in the Royal Navy who had led the 1931 Invergordon mutiny. A working-class Communist, his claim to leadership rested on a charismatic, bullying personality and a sound knowledge of weapons. Unlike many, including Wintringham, he thrived in the terrifying chaos of the Battalion's first battle, and in May 1937 became its leader.

Aside from the military leaders, the British Battalion was moulded by the political commissars Peter Kerrigan and David Springhall, both prominent Communists. Like many commissars after them, they constantly attempted to raise both the rate of recruitment and the quality of the recruits. Their reports to Pollitt reflect their unease at the human material that they were being sent, with too many of the early volunteers having no connection with the working-class movement and little political education. One well-known name, the speedway champion Clem Beckett who would die at the battle at the Jarama, was privately denounced as politically confused and a man who gave voice to dissident elements against the leadership.[38]

The commissars were concerned with the shaping of the Battalion not only as a military unit, but also as a political symbol. At one stage Kerrigan had to remind Pollitt of the need to maintain the war's Popular Front character: there should, for instance, be no hammer and sickle on the Battalion's banner or use of party slogans.[39] (The Soviet emblem had been prominent on the banner of the Tom Mann Centuria.) The issue was also raised in connection with the Battalion's name. The British unit had been named the 'Saklatvala Battalion' in honour of the Indian nationalist and former Communist MP for Battersea. However, concern was expressed that this would not appeal to non-communists: Ralph Fox suggested a 'Chartist Battalion' as it was imperative to emphasise the unit's Popular Front character. The title 'Saklatvala Battalion' never caught the imagination of the volunteers and was quietly abandoned, although there was a wall newspaper called *Sak's Own*.[40]

In the early stages it was far from clear, at least to many volunteers, what the exact nature of the Brigades would be. Just as the state that they were serving was defined by the Communists as a 'democratic and parliamentary republic of a new type', so the International Brigades were intended to be a new type of fighting force, and the vanguard of a new type of army. However, once the decision had been taken that they would be more than a militia-style 'International Column' and would have a fairly rigid command structure, the question could then be posed of how they differed from a conventional army.

Tensions arose primarily over the fundamental question of discipline. The surviving early volunteers had developed a highly democratic form of self-government. Not only were officers and political representatives elected, group meetings were held after every engagement at which the commanders were open to criticism. Discipline had come, in small units, from passionate commitment and the pressures of shared experience, and this was unlikely to work as a bond in the large Brigades that were now being formed. Moreover, many of the volunteers had not come in order to fight in a conventional army.

Terms of service were unclear and some of those who had served in the British armed forces (including Copeman and Cunningham) had been involved in mutinies against military authority. Such tensions were exacerbated by the arrival of adventurers and heavy drinkers, creating problems of indiscipline at base camp. These issues were soon overtaken by the traumatic experience of action in February 1937, and the tightening of military discipline that came later in the year. Even so, the problem of how to create a coherent military unit and punish wrongdoing without alienating the volunteers remained a fraught one.

Before the Battalion went into action, the contingent organised by the ILP arrived in Spain. The ILP had advertised openly in December 1936 for volunteers for a 'British Labour Battalion'. Despite hopes of recruiting 200–300 men, in fact only twenty set off under the command of Bob Edwards. They left London in a comic taxi chase with the police just before the application of the Foreign Enlistment Act. Arriving in Barcelona on 15 January, they were joined by two others: George Orwell, who had made his own way to Spain, and Bob Smillie, the 21-year-old grandson of a famous trade union leader who had been working there in the ILP office. The British commissars with the International Brigade appear to have half-expected the ILP contingent to join them, and, given the opening of the Unity Campaign between the ILP and the Communists at this time, this was not as implausible as it would later seem.[41] Instead, the unit joined the third regiment of the Lenin Division, under the control of the POUM, and set off for the front-line above Huesca in Aragon. As Orwell records in Homage to Catalonia, this section of the line was extremely quiet: occasional sniping was punctuated with incidents such as the night attack on 13 April in which both Orwell and Smillie distinguished themselves. Returning to Barcelona on leave at the end of April, the volunteers had the misfortune to be caught up in the street fighting in early May when they helped to defend the POUM headquarters in the Hotel Falcon. Although after the clashes they went back into the line, where Orwell was shot through the throat by a sniper, the political crackdown on the POUM in June resulted in the contingent's collapse.

Quite apart from the disparity in size, there were significant differences between the ILP unit and the British Battalion. This was a British rather than an international initiative, and was intended above all to display political solidarity with the POUM. Too small to form an independent unit, the ILP volunteers were absorbed into the amicable but chaotic world of the militia columns. The ILP volunteers were also politically heterodox. Orwell himself, who was not at this point an ILP member, joined the column only because he had been rejected by Harry Pollitt for the International Brigades. He was critical of the policy of the POUM and, until the May fighting in Barcelona, his ambition was to go on to Madrid to join the Brigades. Another ILP volunteer, Frank Frankford, made damaging allegations about the collusion between the Republicans and Nationalists on this sector of the line that were enthusiastically carried by the Communist *Daily Worker*. One of the Welsh volunteers eventually left to join the rival Catalan Communist militia.[42] The tragedy of the ILP contingent was completed when Bob Smillie, who had been arrested while leaving Spain in May, died of appendicitis in Valencia prison a month later. Although there is no doubt as to the cause of his death, the suspicion remains that, perhaps due to political malice, the prison authorities were criminally negligent with his care.[43]

On 12 February 1937 the British Battalion was thrown into battle in the Jarama valley, opposing a Nationalist offensive aimed at cutting off Madrid to the south. On leaving their camp Peter Kerrigan had reported to Pollitt that the volunteers made an excellent impression on him with their enthusiasm and efficiency.[44] Many volunteers, however, would feel that they were ill-prepared and ill-equipped. Faced with some of Franco's best Moorish soldiers the British suffered appalling casualties, especially amongst the leaders. The young sculptor Jason Gurney recalled the terror of that first combat for 'city-bred young men with no experience of war, no idea of how to find cover on an open hillside, and no competence as marksmen'.[45] Half the Battalion became casualties on the first day alone. The worst blow fell on the second day when the Maxim heavy machine guns were captured *en masse*. Remarkably, the Battalion held on until the rebel offensive faltered, inspired by the leadership of Jock Cunningham and Fred Copeman after Wintringham had been wounded. Some thirty of the machine gunners had been taken into captivity by the Nationalists and three were executed on the spot. Most of the rest of these prisoners were released in an exchange in May, and a number returned to the

Battalion. One, James Rutherford, was shot in 1938 after being taken prisoner a second time.

The battle of the Jarama was a triumph for valour and determination in the face of tremendous odds. However, many volunteers were appalled at the poor leadership and organisation, described by one as: 'No stretchers, no food, no water'.[46] One company commander, who had been over-promoted and badly mishandled his command, was subsequently tried and consigned to a labour battalion. After the battle the battalion was kept in line on the Jarama for four months. This prolonged active service placed an immense strain on the unit. The devastating losses, which broke the nerve of many volunteers and created a serious problem of morale and desertion, were followed by months of tedious inactivity. The sense of being a forgotten army was captured in the song by Alex McDade that became widely adopted by the British volunteers. It began:

> There's a valley in Spain called Jarama,
> That's a place that we all know so well,
> For 'tis there that we wasted our manhood,
> and most of our old age as well.[47]

Desertion and demoralisation were the main problems confronting the new political commissars Will Paynter, Bert Williams, and Walter Tapsell, who were sent to Spain in March 1937. Some 298 men deserted back to Britain in the course of the war,[48] and others faced imprisonment in Republican jails or special prison camps near Albacete. A 23-year-old volunteer, John Angus, was appointed as British commissar at one such camp, Camp Lucas, and succeeded in reintegrating many men back into the Battalion.[49] In addition to fear and political disillusionment, deserters were also motivated by the lack of any formal terms of service, and many felt that they should be allowed home. The Communist Party Political Bureau, however, had agreed that leave would be impossible as such men would 'never be able to get back' to Spain.[50] Will Paynter thought that repatriation would be an 'injustice for men still at the front', but recognised that such men were not cowards and deserved to return home after six months.[51] For newcomers the matter was settled in September 1937 when the decree incorporating the International Brigades into the Republican army stated that all volunteers would now remain until the end of the war. For those already in Spain, however, the lack of progress on repatriation, which was consistently blocked by the Spanish government, was a source of demoralisation. This was of particular concern to the commissars as they realised that the men would have to return home at some point, and it was important that they return in the right frame of mind. In practice the Communist Party retained control on this crucial question. In 1938, for instance, Jack Roberts was sent home after officer training in order to contest his local council seat in South Wales.[52]

Stephen Spender had a particular interest in the question of desertion. His lover T. A. R. Hyndman had followed him into the Communist Party and then, after Spender's marriage, joined the International Brigades. Hyndman, a former Guardsman, soon became disillusioned with life in the brigades. His health collapsed at the battle of the Jarama, although in the eyes of Walter Tapsell this was a simple case of cowardice.[53] Spender felt personally responsible for Hyndman's plight, and while visiting Spain sought unsuccessfully to secure his freedom. Soon afterwards Hyndman and another volunteer attempted to make their own way home, but were arrested and imprisoned at Albacete. Spender eventually arranged for Hyndman's release after sustained (and politically embarrassing) pleading with the Communist leadership. However, the episode permanently soured his view of the Brigades, which he now saw as utterly Communist-dominated. In April 1937 he warned Virginia Woolf that her nephew Julian Bell should not volunteer as the qualities required for membership of the Brigades, 'apart from courage, are terrific narrowness and a religious dogmatism about the Communist Party line, or else toughness, cynicism, and insensibility'.[54]

In July 1937 the Battalion went into battle again, this time as shock troops in the Republican offensive at Brunete to the north-west of Madrid. After initial success with the capture of the village of Villanueva de la Cañada, the Battalion was ultimately defeated by its main objective, the 'Mosquito Crest' near the old battlefield at Boadilla. The terrible butchery at Brunete was compounded by the burning heat and the lack of defence against air attack. When finally withdrawn from their positions the handful of survivors (only 42 out of 600 were still fit for action) then faced the trauma of receiving the order to return to the line, an order that was challenged by some of the leaders. Although the men were ready to return to action, the order was rescinded. Brunete brought many criticisms from within the unit. A common claim was that the Battalion had been consistently placed in the most dangerous positions – hence the astounding casualty rate.[55] The losses were so heavy that some of the leaders briefly considered liquidating the British unit into a joint battalion with the Americans.

Defeat at Brunete brought to a head a crisis within the Battalion leadership that had both personal and military dimensions. The main protagonists were the military officers Fred Copeman (Battalion commander) and Jock Cunningham (at Brigade level), and the political commissars George Aitken (Brigade) and Walter Tapsell (Battalion). In part the crisis represented a clash between strong personalities, as well as a failure of political control. The Communist Party was to some extent at fault in building up men like Copeman and Cunningham for propaganda purposes as proletarian heroes. In 1937 the party's Central Committee reported that Cunningham had 'revealed on the field of battle those supreme qualities that are the distinguishing marks of a great revolutionary leader'. With reference to a prominent Soviet guerrilla leader, Cunningham was dubbed 'the British "Chapayev"'.[56] This hyperbole did not make such men any easier to control, although Copeman, unlike Cunningham, continued to enjoy Pollitt's support after Brunete. George Aitken became the scapegoat for failing to hold the political and military leadership together.

Also at issue was the apportioning of blame for military failure. The Communist leaders in Britain were very critical of Cunningham's handling of his units at Brunete – he may have been an able 'guerrilla' leader, but he was too 'individualistic' to command an increasingly sophisticated and conventional military force. Soon after Brunete the party acted to end the infighting within the Brigade when all of the leading figures were recalled on 'extended leave' and summoned to a meeting of the Political Bureau. As a result Cunningham and Aitken were not allowed to return to Spain, while Copeman and Tapsell were (but only in the face of disapproval from leading Communists, and not until October). Aitken was disgusted by this outcome, which sent him back to Communist Party work in the North-East of England. He condemned the decision to allow Tapsell and Copeman to return as mistaken and potentially disastrous. However, in practice, neither was to play much further role. Copeman soon succumbed to appendicitis and was invalided home, and Tapsell was killed in action in March

1938. Will Paynter who, as commissar, had taken effective command, would have been happy for none of the old leaders to return. Even so, his final reports to Pollitt in September 1937 were optimistic: 'I can assure you Harry that once we can get rid of the deadweight of repatriations with increased volunteers we shall have a really fine position here. There is now no political strife in our ranks that hinders constructive work.'[57] Paynter set to work to create, in effect, a new battalion.

The leadership crisis within the Battalion may have been precipitated by unique clashes of personality, but should also be seen in the context of the changes taking place in the status and organisation of the Brigades at this time. In September 1937, under pressure from Prieto (minister of national defence) the Brigades were brought within the structure of the Republican army, primarily as an attempt to reduce Communist influence. One consequence was, officially at least, a much greater emphasis on military hierarchy and formality. The Brigade journal *Our Fight* now defended saluting as polite (it would be 'insulting' not to) and gave a number of reasons why the practice should not be seen as 'undemocratic':

> A salute is a sign that a comrade who has been an egocentric individualist in private life has adjusted himself to the collective way of getting things done.
>
> A salute is proof that our Brigade is on its way from being a collection of well-meaning amateurs to a steel precision instrument for eliminating fascists.[58]

Although this admonition was widely ignored in practice, it could be said that in the final phase of the Brigades' existence, from September 1937 to September 1938, they came closest to institutionalisation as a military force. Will Paynter in his farewell letter to the Battalion pointed out that, in this 'army of an entirely new character', discipline must be based on absolute obedience to commanders.[59] The British Battalion was now no longer dependent on charismatic and mercurial leaders: it had a promotion system within its own ranks and a number of British volunteers were sent to officer school. This was also, however, a response to the high casualty rate amongst officers and commissars that afflicted all of the Brigades.

Yet, in other respects, the Brigades remained very different from a conventional army. In this final phase the Communist Party played an increasingly prominent role. Political organisation was officially banned within the Brigades, and, indeed, one cause for concern amongst the commissars was that volunteers had tended to leave all political activism and education to them. Tapsell complained that many Communist Party members had lost their party consciousness and were not debating with the disruptive elements.[60] In practice, however, party activity had never ceased, and it emerged clearly when the calamities of the final year and the rapid turnover of volunteers emphasised the need for continuity and experience. Moreover, the increasing reliance on conscript Spanish troops to fill the gaps in the Brigades' ranks created an opportunity for Communist leadership. One example of this was the 'activist' movement, established by a group of British volunteers in the summer of 1938. Adopting the slogan 'Every soldier an activist – every activist a hero', they sought to raise the levels of morale and competence within the unit while transmitting skills to the new recruits.[61]

The Battalion's first action after Brunete came in September 1937 during the Aragon offensive, on a front where the Anarchist militias had failed to make any progress. There was initial success for the British in the taking of Purburrell Hill and the fortified towns of Quinto and Belchite, although two battalion commanders, Peter Daly and Harold Fry, were killed in action. However, the great prize of Saragossa remained elusive, and a novel tank attack with Spanish soldiers clinging to the backs appeared to be primarily for the benefit of the Soviet military observers.

At Teruel in December 1937 the Brigades were initially left out, to allow victory to be claimed solely by the new People's Army. With the success of the Nationalist counterattack, however, the British Battalion was called into action and won distinction in holding up the rebel advance. The new commander Bill Alexander was promoted captain on the battlefield. But Teruel was also the occasion for the attempted desertion by two Scottish volunteers, carrying details of the Battalion's position to the enemy. Although the facts of their case remain as unclear as the reasons for this unique case of treachery, it has been alleged by Bob Cooney, a former political commissar, that one was shot and the other sent to a labour battalion where he died in a bombardment.[62] The British involvement at Teruel ended with a brief and unsuccessful counterattack at Segura de los Baños in February 1938.

Soon after the collapse of the Teruel offensive, the British found themselves back on the Aragon battlefields. This time they were retreating before the powerful Nationalist thrust in March 1938 that cut the Republic in two. In the chaos the precious anti-tank guns, which had formed an important unit in their own right, were abandoned. After a desperate but successful fighting retreat the Battalion regrouped on the river Ebro. On 31 March it suffered its worst disaster of the war when it ran into an Italian tank column at Calaceite. Out of 650 men, 150 became casualties and 140 were captured. The dead included the commissar Walter Tapsell. The survivors were eventually able to reunite across the Ebro in Catalonia.

Despite this terrible blow, new reinforcements were found and the unit was reconstituted for one last time. In July 1938 Bill Rust paid tribute to the 'resurrection' of the Battalion following the retreat. Unlike after Brunete, there was no 'break-up', and men straggling in after eight or nine days in Nationalist territory still possessed very high morale. Although he was entertained with a rendition of the 'Repatriation Blues', he was convinced that such 'weak elements' could be 'beaten down'.[63]

On 25 July 1938 the battalion took part in the crossing of the Ebro, but failed to take the Nationalist stronghold on 'Hill 481'. The British were pulled out on 26 August and, given the imminence of the withdrawal of the International Brigades for diplomatic reasons, it was supposed that they would play no further role. In fact, they were briefly sent back into battle, before finally being withdrawn on 24 September. In these final two days alone, the unit's strength had been cut from 377 to 173 men, of whom 58 of the 106 Britons survived (the bulk of the battalion being by now made up of Spaniards).[64] The survivors did not return home immediately: the farewell parade was held in Barcelona on 29 October and 305 men were finally repatriated on 6 December.

The Battalion could not have been sustained for so long without a campaign of recruitment and fundraising in Britain. Initially recruitment was carried out relatively overtly by the Communist Party, as it was not thought to contravene any law. In fact, as early as September 1936, Foreign Office officials believed that volunteers could be prosecuted on their return home under the 1870 Foreign Enlistment

Act, long before it was formally applied to the Civil War in January 1937. As has already been noted,[65] the government's action was largely symbolic – the Home Office was aware that it would be very difficult to prove the actual intention of any potential volunteers to fight, and realised that its main chance of success lay in the families of volunteers giving information against recruiting agents. Instead, the act had the effect of driving recruitment underground, and also made the Communist Party more wary about whom it recruited. According to a police agent's report on a London district Communist Party meeting in January 1937, recruitment had been temporarily suspended, and only '100 per cent communist' volunteers would now be accepted. Throughout the war, however, the party was confronted with the problem that, while its members were the best pool for recruits, as a small party it could not afford to squander its slender resources. Unlike in countries which had larger communist parties, it was important to draw in suitable non-communists, as well as preserving the best Communist cadres from the death that might well await them in Spain.

This early period saw the bulk of the recruitment. The International Brigades were being rapidly built up at a point of crisis in the war, standards were fairly relaxed, and the political net was spread wide (indeed, many Communists were not allowed to volunteer at this time by their party as they were more valuable in Britain). Moreover, the Brigades could still appear at this time as a great adventure – after the horrific casualties at the Jarama those who volunteered did so in the knowledge that death or injury was very likely. The Jarama probably did more than British government policy to alter the character of recruitment in the spring of 1937. Increasingly, volunteers were likely to be Communists, and, with the creation of a fundraising organisation for the dependants, older men with family commitments were now being considered. In October 1937 Harry Pollitt admitted to the Central Committee that recruitment was faltering as 'the romanticism is now gone and so many know the sufferings and difficulties'. He also feared the loss of 'the cream of our Party', and hoped for more non-communist volunteers.[66] Even so, by the winter of 1937/8 recruitment was increasingly taking place through 'inner party conscription',[67] as volunteering was now equated with party duty. This created considerable dissension in Welsh Communist circles. There was a last wave of recruitment in Wales in mid-February 1938, but there were few takers. The appeal by the Communist leader of the Welsh miners that Communists should 'die for the party' tried party loyalty to the hilt.[68] In these circumstances, the reconstitution of the battalion after the disastrous retreat of March 1938 was a considerable triumph for the Communist Party.

As men with dependants were recruited and as the number of casualties mounted steeply, the creation of an effective fundraising campaign became a paramount consideration. Initially payments to dependants were made through the Communist Party's own funds. In addition, while the TUC refused to take any responsibility for the volunteers, many individual trade unions were willing to help their members – if only by keeping their union cards clear so that the men could resume full membership on their return. In June 1937 fundraising was formalised with the creation of the International Brigades' Dependants and Wounded Aid Committee. Chaired by Charlotte Haldane and sponsored by, amongst others, the Duchess of Atholl and Eleanor Rathbone, the committee was charged with raising £700 per month and proved an effective fundraiser. By the time of the battalion's withdrawal in October 1938, £41,847 had been raised. However, allegations were also made in Parliament that its offices were being used as a front for recruitment.[69] While this charge was publicly denied, it caused great alarm in private. The leading Communist Bill Rust acknowledged that such recruitment had occurred and warned his comrades that the Communist Party's Popular Front strategy would be jeopardised if it became known that the names of prominent non-communist politicians had been misused in this way.[70]

In addition to raising money, the creation of a fundraising network also offered an opportunity for the Communist Party to draw the wives of volunteers into political action. In January 1937 Harry Pollitt had noted his astonishment at the number of party members' wives who were 'getting very vehement' against their husbands' departure for Spain. For Pollitt this highlighted the party's neglect of women, although the only solution that he could offer was for them to read the Communist *Woman To-day*. J. R. Campbell saw the creation of a national campaign in support of the volunteers as the best way to involve the wives, who might well be subjected to local gossip about the 'Communists who have taken your husband away'.[71]

In spite of its financial support for volunteers' families, the Communist Party had overstretched its resources and did not always deal sensitively with the needs of relatives. There were often complaints that the party failed to communicate news of the fate of volunteers quickly or efficiently. While delays were understandable in such a confused situation, the party's position was vulnerable. One mother complained about the party's 'indifference' – it promoted the Brigade in the *Daily Worker* but did not 'seem to bother much what becomes of [the volunteers] after'.[72] A father believed that he received no compensation from the dependants' fund because his son, who had died on the Ebro, was not a Communist.[73] Relatives of those who had deserted were also concerned that any news that they might glean from other sources could find their way to the Communist Party and be used against their loved ones – for them, Pollitt and his local agents were figures of dread.[74] The Communist Party followed a policy of not notifying relatives until it had confirmation of a volunteer's death, and Pollitt himself was the recipient of abusive letters from relatives who had heard news through other means.

The record of the International Brigades, and of the British contribution to them, shifts uneasily between opposite poles of idealism and cynicism. That so many young (and not so young) men were willing to fight and die in a foreign land has given the volunteers a status which they did not necessarily seek: in the words of the Spanish Communist leader, La Pasionaria, bidding them farewell, 'You are Legend.' The Brigades won praise not only from the Labour movement, but also from Anthony Eden who hailed their defence of Madrid as a 'truly remarkable military feat'.[75] The diplomat Geoffrey Thompson paid a back-handed compliment to the 'very fine men' who were 'fighting in fact for British imperial interests in the Mediterranean'.[76]

Yet, despite their military achievements, the Brigades can never be divorced from their political role as a valuable weapon for the Communist Party within the Spanish Civil War. The Communist Party at the time made every effort to conceal its role in the Brigades, presenting them instead as a spontaneous international movement against fascism. In Stalin's words, the liberation of Spain was 'the common cause of all advanced and progressive mankind'.[77]

Subsequently, however, even communist historians have not been so shy to recognise the central fact that the Brigades were the creation of the world communist movement. Without Communist organisational expertise they would not have existed – at least not in such a form and in such numbers. For this reason, unless one accepts uncritically that what was right for communism was right for Spain, the role of the Brigades will always be a somewhat compromised one. Although no British members of the Brigades took part, as German ones did, in the assassination of the POUM leader Andrés Nin, British volunteers arriving in Spain were asked whether they would help in the suppression of the Barcelona revolutionaries.[78] Both then and since members of the Brigades have been leading advocates of the Communist Party's interpretation of the Civil War.

And yet the extreme cynicism and anti-communism of some commentators needs to be tempered. The very idea of Stalin's Communists leading a crusade for liberty at the same time as the Moscow show-trials is preposterous, and the commitment of Harry Pollitt and the other British Communist leaders to democracy was a highly qualified one. Even so, their political achievement with the British Battalion was enormous. It was nonsense to claim, as Pollitt did, that the battalion had retrieved the 'honourable tradition of the British Labour Movement',[79] because it stood completely outside any such tradition. Instead, what had been achieved was the most successful connection in the history of the British Communist Party between communism and British radicalism. At least in the eyes of the wider Left the British Battalion made the Communists appear not subversive but patriotic.

While reviving the volunteering tradition, however, the Brigades also marked its end. There is one footnote. In the winter of 1939/40, following the Soviet Union's invasion of Finland, the British government permitted a party of 225 men to volunteer for the Finnish side. In a bizarre twist, the unit was organised by a former officer with the Non-Intervention Committee who equipped the unit with belts originally intended for the non-intervention patrols: the buckles' 'NI' was inverted to read 'IN' (for 'International')! Beyond this peculiarity, however, there is no connection between these volunteers and the British Battalion, beyond the fact that together they represent the last occasion on which British volunteers went abroad to fight for liberty in any significant numbers. As the Spanish Civil War recedes, the British Battalion will appear more and more as a thunderous final salute to the idea that it is right that Britons should fight, and die, for their political beliefs in foreign wars.

Chapter 6

INTELLECTUALS

In *L'Espoir*, André Malraux's novel of the Spanish Civil War, an Italian airman who has volunteered for the Republic is asked to interrogate a captured compatriot who has been flying for the rebels. Communication fails because of the ideological gulf separating the two men: 'He and the man before him, each had *chosen*.'[1] This sense of a binding choice was nowhere more apparent than in the response of many left-wing and liberal British intellectuals to the Civil War. The fact that in July 1936 most, with notable exceptions, knew little of Spain and Spanish politics did nothing to prevent their mobilisation behind the Republic, a movement that reached its peak in the June 1937 pamphlet *Authors Take Sides on the Spanish War*. Indeed, their ignorance positively encouraged intellectuals to commit themselves. By the mid-1930s many were deeply concerned at the threat to intellectual freedom posed by the rise of fascism, and Spain appeared to provide the perfect battlefield for the defence of liberal and progressive values. Accordingly, intellectuals rallied to what will be termed the 'liberal interpretation' of the Civil War. Here, they believed, was a democratically elected government, committed to reforming a backward society, that had been attacked by 'fascist' forces both from within and outside the country. While such an interpretation was in many respects accurate, at the same time it ensured that, by presenting the war as a crusade for liberalism and glossing over the complexities of Spanish politics, many intellectuals would eventually come to question its validity.

Intellectuals did not need any help in formulating this powerfully simple interpretation of the Civil War. Indeed, it was shared by the political parties of Left and centre (with the exception of the ILP). However, the theoretical framework and propagandistic genius was provided above all by the Communist Party, already hard at work mobilising the intellectuals long before July 1936. There was no comparable mobilisation on the Nationalist side, not least because the rebels often seemed contemptuous of the need to build political support abroad, and were particularly handicapped in winning the support of intellectuals. The writer C. S. Forester was sent to Spain on a visit arranged by British admirers of Franco, ostensibly to obtain some favourable publicity. However, he returned appalled by the upper-class Spaniards whom he had encountered who, he claimed, hoped to restore the Inquisition.[2] He felt unable to put pen to paper on their behalf.

The Spanish Civil War marked the highest point in a decade of rising involvement by intellectuals in British politics, a decade in which the barriers between politics and intellectual life had been progressively eroded. Intellectuals – broadly defined to include not only writers and poets but also academics and journalists – were unprecedentedly vocal in many areas of political debate. This was, of course, primarily a response to the threatening developments in international and domestic politics during the 1930s: in Stephen Spender's words, he had 'felt hounded by external events' from 1931 onwards.[3] The deepening sense of crisis particularly affected the rising generation of writers, too young to have participated in the First World War and coming to maturity at a time of mass unemployment and fear for the future of democracy. After a period of relative quiescence for intellec-tuals in the years immediately after the First World War, the emerging writers of the 1930s were far more open to political engagement and responsive to international affairs. A number of the younger ones (such as Christopher Isherwood, Stephen Spender, and John Lehmann) were to witness at first hand the rise of Nazism in central Europe.

It was this generation, forged by the terrible legacy of the Great War and by the spectre of a new war to come, that would be identified above all with the Spanish Civil War. The poetic imagery of its leading light, W. H. Auden, dealing as it did in challenges, symbolic journeys, heroes, and frontiers, was ideally suited to the belief of many young intellectuals that the Civil War in Spain represented a test of their political commitment that could not be avoided.

However, while their concern at the rise of fascism was spon-taneous, the intellectuals' response was also being shaped and politi-cised – primarily by a Communist Party fast emerging from the sectarianism and anti-intellectualism of the years between 1929–33. Shaken by the rise of Hitler, communism entered a phase in which it was both eager for alliances with other parties on the Left and open to drawing previously neglected social groups into its orbit. Middle-class intellectuals had previously been dismissed as of little value unless they identified wholly with the Communist Party and the working class; now they were actively courted on their own terms. In 1934 the Communist Party directed itself towards the arts, establishing the British section of the Writers' International and the influential journal *Left Review*. The Communists now offered an exalted role to the intellectual, in the belief that there could be unity between intellectual and cultural 'workers' and the working class. Surprisingly little was demanded in return. In the words of Ralph Fox, 'A writer who can influence thousands through his work, if he comes ever so little towards the working class, even if only to understand that fascism and war are evils, is a valuable ally.'[4]

One sign of the remarkable new tolerance for intellectuals and their liberal foibles was that Stephen Spender was allowed to become a Communist Party member while retaining his freedom to criticise the party line.[5] In fact, Spender had been misjudged by Harry Pollitt and his membership was short-lived. Many others, however, such as the poet C. Day Lewis who joined the party in 1935, gave themselves wholeheartedly to the cause.

As well as targeting new and established intellectuals, the Communist Party was also alive to the possibility of mobilising university students. In fact, this initiative predated the Nazi seizure of power. Communist student groups were established at Cambridge and Durham as early as 1931, and Oxford's October Club was formed a year later. However, the new mood after 1933 made communism far more open and appealing. Student activists were no longer expected to abandon their own social milieu, but rather to work within it at converting their peers. In the words of the leading Communist Willie Gallacher: 'We want people who are capable, who are good scientists, historians and teachers . . . We need you as you are . . . We want you to study and become good students.'[6] The results were impressive: the Cambridge Socialist Society expanded from 200 members in 1933 to almost 1,000 in 1938, within a university of fewer than 5,000 undergraduates. John Cornford was a leading figure both in Cambridge and in the new Federation of Student Societies which galvanised students throughout Britain. The lower middle class was also of interest to the Communist Party, not only because it was perceived as vulnerable to fascism, but also because the expansion of the scientific and technical sector of the economy was creating a new social stratum that did not fit easily into orthodox class analysis. For the Communists the 'black-coated' (white-collar) workers were attractive because they were not catered for by the existing parties and could be brought to identify with the working class. Moreover, given the correct lead, they possessed the leisure and the intelligence to grasp the connections between a threatening international situation and the failure of the National Government at home.

These groups were an important focus of Communist attention in the mid-1930s, and became the core constituency for the Left Book Club, launched by the publisher Victor Gollancz in May 1936. Although Gollancz was a member of the Labour Party, he was closely associated with the Communists until the outbreak of the Second World War and a leading proponent of the Popular Front. Communist Party involvement with the project came more directly from John Strachey who, while never formally a party member, was intimately associated with it. These two, together with the academic Harold Laski (another Labour Party member), formed the selection panel for the club, which was intended to serve those 'who desire to play an intelligent part in the struggle for World Peace and a better social and economic order, and against fascism'.[7] For 2s 6d members received a monthly book (often specially commissioned) and the paper Left News. The success of the club far outstripped Gollancz's expectations. Where he had envisaged a slow climb to 5,000 members, there were in fact 6,000 subscribers within a month and 40,000 after one year. Soon the club became a social and political movement in its own right: there were local discussion groups and separate vocational groups for, amongst others, poets and scientists.

Not all the contemporary intellectual initiatives aimed at professionals originated in the Communist Party. 'For Intellectual Liberty' was formed in the autumn of 1935, modelled on the French Vigilance Committee of Anti-Fascist Intellectuals, to campaign for 'united action in defence of peace, liberty, and culture'. It was started by Leonard Woolf at the suggestion of the French committee, and drew support from eminent left-wingers and liberals including E. M. Forster, Aldous Huxley, Virginia Woolf, and J. D. Bernal. By June 1937 it had 500 members and the basis for a regional organisation. While the committee contained some Communists – such as Bernal, a leading scientist – it was heterogeneous in its politics. Leonard Woolf, who was on the Labour Party's Advisory Committee on International Questions, refused to sign an appeal for the Popular Front in response to the Spanish Civil War.[8]

The outbreak of the Spanish Civil War therefore intersected powerfully with the growing alarm and political mobilisation of British intellectuals in response to the rise of fascism and the disintegration of the international order. In the words of John Lehmann recalling the tremendous impact of the Civil War on his generation:

> everything, all our fears, our confused hopes and beliefs, our half-formulated theories and imaginings, veered and converged towards its testing and its opportunity, like steel filings that slide towards a magnet suddenly put near them.[9]

Pro-Republican intellectuals were in no doubt that this was a struggle that pitted the most basic liberties against fascist oppression. A recurring theme for the contributors to *Authors Take Sides* was that the Spanish people had risen up after centuries of repression, and were fighting for freedoms that Britons took for granted. In the words of David Garnett's contribution, the question had been settled centuries before his birth: 'I am an Englishman and a liberal who has always enjoyed personal liberty and been free to think and speak as he likes.' Intellectuals were quick to emphasise the historical continuity of the stand that they were taking on Spain – and its abandonment by the government and the press. A letter from For Intellectual Liberty to *The Times* in August 1936 noted that:

> At any time during the last 150 years of our history the sympathies of practically all classes in this country and of our Government would have been with the Spanish people and its Government in such a struggle of democracy against military despotism and of freedom against fascism.[10]

In similar vein, Stephen Spender commented that:

> I support in Spain exactly such a movement of liberal and liberating nationalism as the English liberals supported in many countries still groaning under feudalism in the nineteenth century.[11]

However, the appeal of the Civil War lay not only in the defence of liberty against fascism, but also in the creation of a new, democratic, and progressive society in Spain. Kingsley Martin, editor of the *New Statesman*, wrote that the choice in Spain was between a government dominated by reaction and one which 'might be inefficient and tempestuous', but which would allow the Spanish people to move towards 'individual happiness and spiritual and economic well-being'.[12] Philip Toynbee, who visited Spain as part of a student delegation in December 1937, claimed that a Republican victory would 'open the gates of a thousand new schools and universities'. Only the Republic could address the 'pathetic ignorance of Spain and . . . educate her to greatness and strength'.[13]

This essentially liberal interpretation of the Civil War was dominant amongst intellectuals, but, as we will see, it was far from un-challenged. It was to be criticised not only by the Right, as would be expected, but also by academic Hispanists, by supporters of the revolutionary cause in Spain and by pacifists. Moreover, even amongst many of those who subscribed to this view disillusionment eventually set in. For most this disillusionment was principally with the war in Spain itself, leaving intact the appeal of the Popular Front that would be revived during the Second World War in wartime campaigns to help the Soviet Union. For others, however, Spain resulted in a profound disillusionment with communism; thus, the Civil War contributed to the idea of a 'totalitarian' communism that would achieve great influence during the Cold War.

There was no shortage of Republican supporters in the academic world. The eminent Oxford classicist Gilbert Murray, to take but one example, was constrained by his leading role in the League of Nations Union but spoke out strongly against German and Italian intervention in Spain. His son, Basil, went to serve the Republic as a journalist and died after contracting pneumonia there. Amongst academic Hispanists, however, there was considerable hostility to the Republic. According to W. J. Enwright, professor of Spanish studies at Oxford, the Republic had degenerated into a left-wing dictatorship. In any case, Spain was unsuited to parliamentary government and Franco's rebellion was 'common enough in Spanish tradition'.[14] The best-known Hispanist of the day, Edgar Allison Peers, laid the blame for the war on the Second

Republic in his book *The Spanish Tragedy*. While he was careful to maintain a formal political neutrality, it is clear from his journalism that Peers, who as a high-church Anglican was appalled at the anti-Catholic outrages in Spain, was sympathetic to the Nationalists. His enthusiasm was fuelled not only by his religious convictions, but also by his admiration for the new order that Franco was creating – which he saw as free of class spirit, and promoting land reform, education, and greater sexual equality.[15] William Atkinson, a professor in Glasgow, initially saw Primo de Rivera's authoritarianism in the 1920s as the best model for Spain's development, although by the end of the war his sympathies had swung marginally behind the Spanish prime minister Juan Negrín.[16]

At least one leading Hispanist sided with the Republic – Professor J. B. Trend of Cambridge – but the Republican cause otherwise drew its expert supporters from those who were only beginning to climb to prominence – or even those with very limited expertise. Charlotte Haldane, who had holidayed in Spain on a number of occasions since 1933 and written an article in the *New Statesman*, found herself in demand at meetings as an authority following the outbreak of the Civil War.[17] The journalist W. Horsfall Carter was sent to Spain by For Intellectual Liberty in the autumn of 1936, and later became an adviser to the Foreign Office on Spanish affairs in the 1940s. Gerald Brenan, who had lived in Andalucía since the end of the First World War, returned to Britain in 1936 and became an unofficial adviser to the Duchess of Atholl. He contributed to the writing of *Searchlight on Spain* and spoke during her unsuccessful by-election campaign. However, his book *The Spanish Labyrinth*, a milestone in the historiography of modern Spain written to distract him from the 'horrors and suspense' of the Civil War, was not published until 1943.

A more direct challenge to the liberal interpretation of the Civil War came from those left-wingers who saw the events of July 1936 as a revolution. According to this view, held primarily by the ILP and Anarchists, after July 1936 there was no going back to a discredited 'bourgeois' Republic: the road to socialism lay through revolutionary war. Any attempt to restore the Second Republic and unravel the radical changes in the organisation of agriculture and industry, as the Communist strategy required, would be counter-revolutionary.

This interpretation has found increasing favour with historians, especially since the 1960s.[18] However, it is important to note how few adhered to it in Britain at the time. As we have seen, the idea of a Spanish socialist revolution was attractive in the opening months of the Civil War, especially to the first intellectuals to arrive in Catalonia, such as John Cornford. Although George Orwell arrived late on the scene, the revolutionary ideal was to be enshrined in his *Homage to Catalonia*. Despite its later enduring success, however, this was one of Orwell's least successful books during his lifetime. It was widely dismissed by reviewers as 'Trotskyist', sold a mere 683 of the first print run, and did not appear in the United States until after his death in 1950. Orwell returned to Britain full of anger against the Communist Party, which he now saw as a counter-revolutionary force in Spain, and against the British left-wing and liberal intelligentsia which he accused of toeing the Communist line. Orwell claimed that there was a 'quite deliberate conspiracy . . . to prevent the Spanish situation from being understood' in Britain by concealing the truth of the divisions on the Republican side.[19]

Orwell's anger was particularly directed at Kingsley Martin of the *New Statesman* who refused to publish one of his book reviews on the grounds that it 'too far controverts the practical policy of the paper . . . [and] implies that our Spanish correspondents are all wrong'.[20] In fact, as Martin pointed out, his journal had published articles that dissented from the Communist 'line' on the Barcelona fighting. H. N. Brailsford, who had been present in the city, contributed an even-handed account which refused to place all of the blame on the Anarchists and POUM:

> It is a tangled tale, this Spanish epic. The heroism of simple men, who have flung their lives away for the joy of battling half-armed against feudalism, blends with the vanity of leaders and the egoism of parties.

Brailsford was a veteran socialist journalist committed to no party line. However, his concluding comments offer an insight into the accommodations that many in his position were making. The Popular Front, he wrote, was ultimately correct because 'to make an end of feudalism seems no small achievement'. It was creating a New Spain of better education, social services, and, 'above all, a new sense of national unity and ambition'.[21]

Brailsford, like many other intellectuals with far less integrity, had come to the conclusion that the real struggle in Spain was for national liberation and immediate material progress: socialist revolution was not a practical possibility. His judgement was certainly driven by considerations of *Realpolitik*, as was that of the Communist Party: a revolutionary socialist regime would be even less likely to receive international support than the moderate Republic that was being projected. There were, however, other factors influencing intellectuals in this direction.

One was that, in so far as intellectuals had taken an interest in Spain before 1936, the language of revolution had been debased in the analysis of Spanish politics. The very different political events of 1931 and 1934 had both been greeted as 'revolutions' in Britain, and the whole of the Second Republic could be seen as a 'revolution' against feudalism. The Communist Ralph Bates, whose novel about Spanish social strife between 1932 and 1934 was published before the Civil War, left readers in no doubt that: 'This is a novel of the Spanish Revolution.'[22] The philosopher R. G. Collingwood visited Spain in 1930–1 and on inquiring about what he took to be an innocuous local religious festival was surprised to be told that: 'That was the Revolution.'[23] In a country in which all change was routinely hailed as 'revolutionary' it is not surprising that the confused events of the summer of 1936 were simply taken as further evidence of routine Spanish turbulence.

Thus, while the term 'revolution' continued to be used by all shades of opinion, it was generally the Communist Party's interpretation of it in the Spanish context that prevailed: 'The "Revolution" was that of democracy against feudalism and a feudalised capitalism; there were no objective conditions present to justify the straight proletarian seizure of power.'[24] This, then, was a revolution for freedom and order, and not for creating socialism. As Auden reported from Valencia in early 1937:

> a revolution is really taking place, not an odd shuffle in cabinet appointments. In the last six months these people have been learning what it is to inherit their own country, and once a man has tasted freedom he will not lightly give it up; freedom to choose for himself and to organise his life, freedom not to depend for good fortune on a clever and outrageous piece of overcharging or a windfall of drunken charity.[25]

In April 1937 Spender wrote that the 'revolution is a very real thing' – and regretted that Cyril Connolly had allowed it to '"go bad" on him as though it were an undergraduate lunch party'.[26]

This conception of revolution was particularly apparent in intellectuals' response to the anti-clerical outrages, especially the burning of churches. Not all succumbed to the excuse that churches had been used as fascist arsenals and strongholds. However, those who chose to look deeper tended to find the Anarchists' arsonism endearing. It was a sign not of revolutionary class conflict, but of a symbolic break with a hated past, akin to the Reformation in Britain. John Langdon-Davies wrote that the burning of the church decorations was good for Spanish art. By destroying an 'incredible weight of foul ugliness' the arsonists would 'leave room for the artists of today and tomorrow to do better with the space cleared for them'.[27] The attitude of intellectuals towards the attacks – they not only justified them, but also downplayed their significance – was particularly offensive to Catholics. In the words of one Left Book Club text, 'it must be remembered that the burning of churches may be the most common and traditional channel of popular resentment in one country while in others it may amount to the most horrible kind of desecration'.[28] Intellectuals' easy acquiescence in the burning of churches and the destruction of their contents sat uneasily with the persistent theme that the Republic represented the defence of culture (including works of art) against fascist barbarity.

Pacifism posed another challenge to the attitude of intellectuals to the Civil War, not least because so many had been – and in many cases still were – closely identified with the pacifist cause. The dilemma was expressed clearly by the philosopher C. E. M. Joad. He found the ambience of pro-Republican rallies disturbingly enthusiastic for a new anti-fascist 'Holy War', and a recent meeting addressed by a wounded member of the International Brigades had reminded him of similarly emotive scenes in 1914 when men had also fought 'for Liberty, for Democracy, and against Militarism'. Yet, he concluded, the pure pacifist position was difficult to sustain: what should a Spanish socialist have done in July 1936?[29]

A riposte defending pacifist non-violent resistance came from the writer Rose MacAuley who argued that, whether this had worked or not in the Spanish case, 'it would at least have been more intelligent and civilised and better worth trying than the brutal, tragically stupid, tragically barren competition in rival barbarities which Spain is staging now'.[30] However, 'AGAINST FRANCO', her response to *Authors Take Sides*, conveniently sidestepped this debate. Other pacifists struggled to formulate a coherent response. H. Runham Brown, secretary of War Resisters' International, wrote that had he been a Spaniard he would not have joined in the fighting. However, he also argued that the Republican government would have been justified in using force to prevent the outbreak of the Civil War, even if some of the plotters had been wounded or killed in the process.[31] Aldous Huxley supported the idea that a non-violent Spanish Republic would have made a rebellion impossible, but, recognising the impracticality of such a retrospective analysis, gave a highly qualified approval to the Republican cause.[32] Other intellectuals such as Vera Brittain remained truer to the pacifist cause, continuing to argue that, while she detested fascism, it could not be defeated by violence. The best interests of Spain would not be served by making it the centre for new 'Wars of Religion'.[33]

While the objections of the 'pure' pacifists were discomforting for pro-Republican intellectuals, their sting was drawn by the over-whelming belief that in this specific case the ends did indeed justify the means. The philosopher and science fiction writer Olaf Stapledon, for instance, had been an absolute pacifist in the First World War, and continued to believe in the value of non-violence as an ideal in international relations. While he could not deny the justice of selling arms to a democratically elected government attacked by military rebels with foreign backing, even so he continued to agonise over the Civil War. In April 1937 he spoke at a memorial rally for the International Brigades in his native Liverpool, his lecture notes conveying the continuing uncertainty of the pacifist's dilemma:

> did they do right in fighting? / honourable motives but misguided policy? / I wish I could believe [the] Pacifists: / violence is always wrong, and futile/ friendliness alone can win /and human appeal alone can work/
> They preach the most important truth of all in the long run.
>
> but they over-simplify / and forget the bitter facts, and emergency / man is still half savage, animal / pacifism not infallible / takes time to work / useless in emergency
>
> I myself am at heart a pacifist / I could not kill? / have seen too much blood / must be true to that inner light? / yet in emergency I ought to kill?
>
> Anyhow I salute these young men
> (and thank God they have won)[34]

During the first year of the conflict, at least, many intellectuals appeared little troubled in accepting the liberal interpretation of the Civil War as a basis for their action. For them, the more important question was not what was happening in Spain, but what was the best way to respond.

Intellectuals were amongst the first to volunteer to fight in Spain – and amongst the first to die. Two of the founders of the British Battalion, Ralph Fox and Tom Wintringham, had also been founders of *Left Review* – which could eventually claim that six of its writers had gone to fight in Spain. Apart from Fox, other eminent and promising intellectuals and writers killed in the Civil War – all Communists – included John Cornford, Christopher Caudwell, the critic and novelist, and David Haden Guest. Their sacrifice left contemporaries such as C. Day Lewis and Jack Lindsay racked with guilt at not volunteering. Not surprisingly, the cost to the Communist Party's slender resources in the cultural field was soon judged too high, and few intellectuals were allowed to volunteer after the battle of the Jarama.

There were other ways for intellectuals to help apart from volunteering. Auden, who went to Spain in January 1937, toyed with joining the International Brigades,[35] was described in the *Daily Worker* as going to drive an ambulance, and in the end did neither. However, his poem 'Spain', with its memorable refrain of 'Today the Struggle', encapsulated the contemporary mood for taking political action without waiting to weigh the moral niceties: the proceeds went to Spanish Medical Aid. Stephen Spender's decision to join the Communist Party was a personal response to its work on behalf of Spain. He was sent to Spain on a number of potentially hazardous errands, such as looking for traces of the crew of the Soviet vessel *Komsomol* which had been seized by the Nationalists. Two Communist women writers, Sylvia Townsend Warner and Valentine Ackland, volunteered to work in the Communist Party office in Barcelona. They were, however, appalled at the inefficiency and political confusion that reigned there and wrote a savage report for Harry Pollitt. Amongst their allegations was that the British Communists in Spain formed an isolated clique, with an almost colonial attitude towards the Spaniards.[36]

Relatively few intellectuals actually visited Spain, and for many their main contribution to the Republic's war effort was to place their own creativity at its disposal. The result was an outpouring of politicised verse (the pre-eminent medium) such as Edgell Rickword's misogynistic 'To the Wife of a Non-Intervention Statesman'. None of this poetry has the simplicity and honesty of the few poems written on active service by John Cornford. Jack Lindsay pioneered a new art form with his poem for mass recitation, 'On Guard for Spain!' British artists painted pro-Republican murals for the National Joint Committee and sold their art to buy an ambulance. Others took more direct action: the 'Arms for Spain' demonstrators of January 1939 included the novelist Rosamond Lehmann and the future playwright Terence Rattigan. The Communist Welsh novelist Lewis Jones campaigned himself to death for the Republican cause: according to one source, he died in January 1939 after addressing thirty meetings in a single day.[37]

The Left Book Club, formed only months before the outbreak of the Civil War, was inevitably closely involved in supporting Republican Spain. A number of books were offered on the Civil War which, primarily written by Communists, supported the standard liberal interpretation. While propagandistic in tone, however, these books were important tools of political education. The best of them, by Frank Jellinek, was mendacious in its treatment of the POUM, but made a serious attempt to place the Civil War in the context of Spanish history.[38] Only one of the club's books on Spain, Geoffrey Cox's eye-witness account of the defence of Madrid, was written by a non-communist. Cox, a News Chronicle journalist, later recalled that Gollancz had made him omit a sentence comparing La Pasionaria's rallying of the Republican troops to Trotsky's exploits in Leningrad. However, he managed to persuade the publisher to retain a chapter on the atrocities in Republican Madrid.[39] The club also devoted whole issues of Left News to Spain and organised rallies, and Gollancz, with an eye for business, offered to pay 2s 6d to Spanish relief work for every new recruit to the club. Within months two members had each recruited twenty-four new members, securing £8 for organisations such as Spanish Medical Aid.[40]

In the spring of 1937 the writer Nancy Cunard undertook a survey of the views of British writers on the Civil War. They were posed the following question:

Are you for or against the legal Government and the People of Republican Spain?

Are you for, or against, Franco and Fascism?
For it is impossible any longer to take no side.

Writers and Poets, we wish to print your answers. We wish the world to know what you, writers and poets, who are amongst the most sensitive instruments of a nation, feel.[41]

The results of this questionnaire were indeed striking. Of those published, 127 were deemed 'For the Government', 16 were placed as 'Neutral?', and only 5 were 'Against the Government'. *Authors Take Sides on the Spanish War* was a testimony to the importance which the British liberal and left-wing intelligentsia (or at least those consulted) attached to the Spanish Civil War. However, the pamphlet was ostentatiously an exercise in propaganda and the picture that it presents of the opinions of British intellectuals as a whole does not stand detailed examination. Indeed, Nancy Cunard later recalled that she had composed the questionnaire in Normandy and then simply sent out batches to friends with instructions for them to pass them on to their acquaintances.[42] It is only the emblematic status that the pamphlet achieved that justifies the very heavy weight of literary and political criticism subsequently brought to bear on it.

The question that Cunard had posed was loaded and deliberately allowed no room for subtlety of answer. As Valentine Cunningham has demonstrated, the categories into which responses were placed were manipulated in order to emphasise the lack of support for Franco and to allow eminent writers such as Ezra Pound and T. S. Eliot to occupy a spurious position of 'Neutral?'[43] Alongside the well-known names in the pro-government ranks, such as Aldous Huxley and Samuel Beckett, were many more of ephemeral fame or little claim to eminence.

In political terms the government supporters were not wholly united. There were two representatives of the ILP: Fenner Brockway (hardly a literary man) urged the Spanish workers and peasants to destroy capitalism, and the novelist Ethel Mannin hoped to see a workers' state on anarcho-syndicalist rather than Soviet lines. Aldous Huxley saw anarchism as more likely to result in 'desirable social change' than dictatorial communism. Another pacifist, Laurence Housman, wrote that the Spanish government had been 'provocative' and should have acted in a 'constructively pacifist' manner from the start. Robert Nichols was for the Republican government 'in so far' as it was non-communist.

In the absence of a listing of those invited to contribute it is impossible to judge how far the pamphlet lived up to its claim to be 'representative'. Orwell, who was invited, famously denounced the exercise as 'bloody rot',[44] while other leading writers were notable by their absence. Liberal journalists in papers such as the News Chronicle were included – the editor of the Manchester Guardian (W. P. Crozier) loftily referring to his leader columns for evidence of his views. However, there is no evidence that the opinion of the press as a whole was canvassed.

Particularly notable is the absence of the Catholic community, represented in the pamphlet only by Evelyn Waugh (who claimed that if he had been a Spaniard he would be fighting for Franco). In fact, Catholic intellectuals were divided over Spain, although even those who questioned Franco's 'crusade' may have preferred not to be seen to 'take sides' against it. Graham Greene later recalled that he did not respond to the questionnaire because, while he was against Franco, he was unhappy with Republican brutality. He felt more comfortable committing himself to the Basques and even contemplated visiting the Basque country.[45] Greene's literary output at the time reflected these ambiguities. His 1938 novel The Confidential Agent had a barely disguised setting during the Civil War and was sympathetic to the plight of the Republicans. Yet Greene was also deeply concerned with the persecution of the Catholic Church in Mexico, writing one of his most powerful books (The Power and the Glory) on the strength of his visit there in 1938.

Only two literary figures of any significance wrote on the side of the Nationalists, Wyndham Lewis and Roy Campbell. Even before the Civil War Lewis had already used Spain as the setting for his novel The Revenge for Love, an attack on what he saw as the fashion for communism amongst intellectuals. Once the war had started he argued that Britain had wrongly aligned itself over Spain with France and the Soviet Union, and that, blinded by anti-German sentiment, it was preparing for war against Germany alongside these unwelcome allies.[46] Roy Campbell was a Catholic who had converted as recently as June 1936. His boisterous verse was designed to infuriate the pro-government intellectuals, taunting the Republican president in 'Hard Lines, Azaña!' with the thought that: 'The Sodomites are on your side,/ The cowards and the cranks.'[47] Campbell was a loudmouth who, despite his claims, does not appear to have fought in the Civil War. The unpleasantness and triumphalism of his Civil War poetry was tempered only by his deep love for Spain, and an essentially religious anti-fascism that caused him to volunteer to fight in the British army during the Second World War.

Campbell was an isolated (and even hated) figure in literary circles, but was far from alone amongst Catholic intellectuals. Amongst those to give their support to Franco were Hilaire Belloc (drifting to the fascist Right after the death of his friend G. K. Chesterton), Arnold Lunn, Douglas Jerrold, and Bernard Wall. *Authors Take Sides*, whatever its reason for omitting them, reinforced the distance between Catholics and mainstream intellectual life. As the publisher Tom Burns recalled, the Civil War placed a barrier between him and his undergraduate friend Auden – Roy Campbell spoke 'more for my sympathies'.[48] The omission is particularly interesting as the Catholic journal *Colosseum* had published a questionnaire of its own in March 1937 on 'War and Peace'. It had asked leading Catholic intellectuals a series of questions, the second of which was:

> Do you consider that a war in defence of our culture as Europeans is justified, and a practical method of defending our culture? The example occurring to mind is Spain.

The replies were far from uniform. The convert sculptor Eric Gill (a pro-Republican) wrote: 'I do not consider that we can be said to have a culture to defend. Where is this culture?' He received a tart editorial reminder: 'Our question referred to Pamplona, Burgos, Seville.'

Authors Take Sides, published in June 1937, marked the height of intellectuals' commitment to the Republican cause. However, by this stage some were already questioning the certainties on which that commitment was built. From this point onwards concern mounted both at the clash between idealism and harsh political reality in Spain itself, and also at the damage that writing in a propagandistic vein (in however noble a cause) was doing to artistic integrity.

Amongst the leading writers, Auden's political disengagement was quiet but determined. In Spain for little more than a month in 1937, he had been unable, or unwilling, to fulfil the role that the Communist Party intended for him. Indeed, he was refused a pass by the British Communist office in Barcelona on the grounds that he had been making contact with Anarchists on the Aragon front.[49] The discomfort evident in his journalism was expressed also in his poem 'Spain', written on his return. Although 'Spain' became the unofficial anthem of pro-Republican campaigners, it is also notable for its sense of detachment and profound pessimism before the laws of historical inevitability.[50] Orwell savagely criticised the poem's amorality and Auden later rewrote some of the offending phrases. Auden had nothing more to offer the Spanish cause, and by the end of the decade was heading into exile in the United States with Isherwood. Although he subsequently had little to say about his Spanish experiences, it is clear that they contributed to his rejection of politics. Writing in the mid-1950s on the subject of his return to religion he was to observe that witnessing the closing of the churches in Barcelona had left him 'shocked and disturbed'. He was forced to acknowledge that, despite having ignored the Church for sixteen years, 'the existence of churches and what went on in them had all the time been very important to me'.[51]

The mingling of personal and political concerns was even more evident in the case of Stephen Spender. Despite his joining the Communist Party, Spender's own politics had altered little. His book Forward from Liberalism (1937) was intended to describe his own 'approach to communism', but merely demonstrated that, in his estimation, communism was simply the proper home for the liberal in a world threatened by fascism. He was profoundly influenced by the experiences of the volunteers for the International Brigades and both his poetry and prose adopted a refreshingly unheroic tone. In an article in May 1937 he wrote that: 'The final horror of war is the complete isolation of a man dying alone in a world whose reality is violence. The dead in wars are not heroes: they are freezing or rotting lumps of insanity.'[52]

Spender's disenchantment with communism intensified in July 1937 when he joined the British delegation for the Second Congress of the International Association of Writers in Madrid and Valencia. Although he gave no hint at the time, with hindsight Spender claimed to have seen the Congress as a circus at which the Soviet delegates, impressive only for their 'arrogance and mental torpidity', were mainly interested in denouncing André Gide for his recent criticisms of the Soviet Union. He was particularly affronted by a novelist-turned-commissar in the International Brigades (presumably Ralph Bates) who, he claimed, flaunted his high military rank: a salutary example of the 'literary man who had tasted a little power'.[53] While Spender broke with communism, however, he remained a strong supporter of the Republic.

Ralph Bates, who had become a leading propagandist during the Civil War and toured the United States to great effect, himself broke with communism and settled in Mexico when the Soviet Union invaded Finland in 1939. Other intellectuals, such as C. Day Lewis and Arthur Koestler left the Communist Party during the Civil War. Hugh Slater, a journalist for Inprecorr and a significant figure within the International Brigades, published a savage attack on communism in his 1946 novel The Heretics. The book, partly set during the Civil War, saw no difference between the 'inhumanity, hate, and intolerance' of communists and fascists in Spain.

Disillusionment took many forms in Spain, but hinged on the realisation that what had appeared from the safety of Britain as a just war – or even a crusade – was more complex, more squalid, and infinitely less heroic when seen at close quarters. Sir Richard Rees, editor of the Adelphi between 1930 and 1936, went to Spain in April 1937 to work for Spanish Medical Aid. He soon rebelled against what he saw as the overbearing Communist influence and went to work for the Quakers in Barcelona. Although he had volunteered in order to 'cut a heroic figure', he soon found the war itself a powerful antidote: Spain, he recalled, was a country in a 'state of disintegration, its people appearing listless as if in shock'. He himself soon became almost incapable of sympathy for the sick.[54]

Laurie Lee experienced similar emotional exhaustion on his return to Spain in December 1937 to join the International Brigades. He arrived independently, crossing the Pyrenees on his own, and he was never able to shake off the suspicions of the security police that he was a fascist spy (his passport was stamped for rebel-held Spanish Morocco from his earlier visit in 1936). Unlike for many volunteers, his journey through Spain to Albacete was far from uplifting: this was the 'gaseous squalor of a country at war, an infection so deep it seemed to rot the earth, drain it of colour, life and sound'. When he finally joined the Brigades he was to realise that he had come to 'a war of antique muskets and jamming machine-guns, to be led by brave but bewildered amateurs'.[55] Lee's war did not last long: after taking part in the desperate fighting at Teruel he suffered a temporary breakdown and was sent home.

For many intellectuals the disillusionment of the Civil War meant a turning away from politics and an attempt to distance their art from their political beliefs. However, for three intellectuals in particular – one British and two exiled in Britain – their Civil War experiences had a significance for European politics that carried into the era of the Cold War. For George Orwell, Franz Borkenau, and Arthur Koestler, the Civil War helped to crystallise the idea of communism as a 'totalitarian' force irreconcilable with either democratic socialism or liberalism.

By the time George Orwell arrived in Spain in January 1937, although he did not realise it, the revolutionary tide was ebbing fast. He was overwhelmed by his first impressions of the egalitarian new society in Barcelona, and believed that he had discovered 'the only community of any size in western Europe where political conscious-ness and disbelief in capitalism were more normal than their oppo-sites'.[56] He relished the classlessness of the Spanish militias, finding in the essential decency and fraternity of the militiamen both 'a crude forecast of what the opening stages of socialism might be like' and a relief from the oppressiveness of the British class system.

Orwell never lost his belief in the basic decency of the Spanish people, but he was ill-prepared for the sectarian realities of political life in Spain. He had come to left-wing politics relatively late, and had no party attachment. In *The Road to Wigan Pier*, the manuscript that he had submitted to Gollancz immediately before his departure, he had reinvented socialism almost from first principles. He was well-disposed towards the Communist Party, seeing it as simply another party on the Left, and had investigated volunteering for the International Brigades. Crucially, however, his contacts with the ILP ensured that he would join that party's contingent fighting with the POUM militia. Ineluc-tably, he and his comrades were drawn into the violent struggle between the Communists and the revolutionary forces in Catalonia. This involvement was very much against Orwell's instincts. As late as 30 April 1937 he had met with the British Communists in Barcelona to negotiate his transfer to the International Brigades. Orwell was described as a 'leading personality' in the ILP unit, but also one who lacked political understanding: 'He is not interested in party politics and came to Spain as an Anti-Fascist to fight Fascism.' He was listed along with nine other members of the unit who wished to leave it.[57] Days later the situation was transformed by the street-fighting in Barcelona. Although Orwell was little more than a bemused onlooker, two months later he was fleeing from Spain in fear of his life. Secret police reports identified him and his wife Eileen (who was working in the ILP office in Barcelona) as 'known Trotskyists [and] linking agents of the ILP and the POUM'.[58]

Orwell was never a strong supporter of the POUM, which he considered both incompetent and wrong in its political analysis. (He subsequently admitted to having been more sympathetic to it in print than he actually felt.)[59] On his return to Britain, however, he gave vent to his anger at the manner of the POUM's suppression by the Communists. His perception of the Communist Party had radically altered. He now saw it as an organisation committed more to the acquisition of power than to the interests of the working class that he so idealised. After the May fighting he rejected the opportunity to join the International Brigades as: 'Sooner or later it might mean being used against the Spanish working class.' He was also shocked at the Communist tactic of blackening the POUM's reputation. Instead of engaging in honest ideological debate they denounced the POUM as fascist agents. For the first time, Orwell confronted what he would come to see as a 'totalitarian' disregard for the truth. Rarely amongst British socialists, he had experienced the Stalinist Terror at first hand: his wife and comrades had been its targets and, while Trotskyism was (in his phrase) 'not extraditable', the harassment continued even after their return to Britain.

For all of the bitterness that Orwell felt – both political and, in the case of a dead comrade such as Bob Smillie, deeply personal – his analysis of the Civil War was not static. Even in *Homage to Catalonia* (published in 1938) he had argued that the Spanish Republic was still worth fighting for. Despite the lack of democracy, it was a regime that, if victorious, would deliver modernisation and land reform for the peasants. In an article published in 1939, shortly before the end of the war, Orwell argued that in spite of the war the foundations of democracy had been laid in Spain. War had acted as an educational force, drawing ordinary people into positions of responsibility and expanding their political consciousness: return to the semi-feudal past was impossible. This article has been described as an abandonment by Orwell of his earlier views, but more plausibly it should be seen as an extrapolation of his previous belief in the possibility for progress within the framework of the Republic.[60] Paradoxically, this emphasis on immediate material advances brought him close to the liberal interpretation of the Civil War that he had so strenuously rejected in 1937.

In 1942 Orwell's essay 'Looking Back on the Spanish War' marked a further evolution in his thought. He reversed many of his earlier views, admitting that the struggle for power within the Republic was of secondary importance, and that the picture presented by the Spanish government had been 'not untruthful'. From this more distant point, Orwell now argued that the real significance of the Civil War was the abandonment of truth by the Nationalists and fascists, rather than by the Republicans. The rewriting of history to meet the political needs of the moment conjured up the nightmare of the leader who could control the past as well as the future. But while the essay looked forward to the bleak satire of Nineteen Eighty-Four, it also drew comfort and inspiration from the struggle of the working class – 'like the growth of a plant . . . blind and stupid, but it knows enough to keep pushing upwards towards the light, and it will do this in the face of endless discouragements'.[61] Sadly, by the time that Nineteen Eighty-Four came to be written in 1947–8 this belief, too, had been corrupted.

Orwell's understanding of the Civil War benefited significantly from his friendship with the Austrian exile Franz Borkenau, whose work on Spain Orwell greatly admired. Borkenau was a former official of the Communist International who, after being expelled from the party in 1929, settled in Britain as an academic. His book The Spanish Cockpit was the result of two visits to Spain in the summer of 1936 and January 1937. Returning for his second visit shortly after Orwell's own arrival, he was much better placed to realise the degree to which the revolution was already in decline. Arrested and jailed for his critical views, he was saved by the inefficiency of the Spanish police who failed to discover the manuscript that he was writing.

Where Orwell's interpretation of Spanish politics had been based on an instinctive belief in the basic decency of the Spanish people, Borkenau placed the Civil War within a theoretical and historical framework. He saw Spain as different from the rest of Europe, an essentially pre-modern society. The lower classes were capable of defeating French occupation in 1808 or military rebellion in 1936, but lacked the leadership to control their own revolution or the resources to defeat Franco's foreign allies. The Republic was forced to turn to the Soviet Union for assistance – which, in return had begun to construct a 'totalitarian' regime through terror in its own image. The main targets of terror were critics on its own side, with the intention of forging 'complete unity of life and thought in every matter concerning the state, and to make every matter concern the state'.[62] Where Orwell and Borkenau were in agreement was in their belief that the Spanish would never succumb to totalitarian rule, either because Spain was insufficiently advanced, or because it was too nationalistic. For Borkenau the study of totalitarianism – either comparing the Nazi and Soviet regimes or, after 1945, analysing the Soviet Union alone – became the central thread in his increasingly rootless life after the Civil War.

The Spanish Civil War deeply affected the life of another central European refugee, Arthur Koestler. Koestler, a Hungarian by birth, grew up in Budapest and Vienna and joined the German Communist Party in 1931. In 1933 he was sent to join the exiled German Communists in Paris. There he began a long and productive partnership with Willi Munzenburg, the mastermind of Comintern propaganda in the West and founder of many Communist anti-fascist 'front' organisations in France and Britain. When the Civil War broke out Koestler travelled to Seville in search of evidence of German intervention, and was fortunate to escape when recognised and denounced. On a third trip, this time as a journalist for the *News Chronicle*, he made his way to the collapsing Málaga front in February 1937 and, for reasons that remain unclear, placed his life in jeopardy by remaining in the city after its fall to the rebels. He was imprisoned in Seville under sentence of death and only escaped thanks to a campaign in Britain orchestrated by his wife. Help was received from pro-rebel politicians such as the Tory MP Anthony Crossley and Lady Astor, anxious that Koestler's execution should not further tarnish the image of Franco's regime.

During his imprisonment Koestler underwent the deep spiritual experience described in *Dialogue With Death*, and came to question the morality of working for the Comintern. On his release in a prisoner exchange he made a speaking tour of Britain. Feeling unable to adopt the Communist 'line' on the POUM he publicly described the charges against them as 'absurd and perfidious'[63] and left the party. As Koestler was in many ways a more complex personality than Orwell and Borkenau, the impact of the Civil War on him was less overtly political than it was on the other two. However, his experiences in Spain were undoubtedly decisive in his relations with international communism. He tired of the inherent dishonesty of life within the Comintern, not only the grand deceits of Munzenburg's propaganda campaigns, but also the constant lying to those who trusted him. He had, for instance, told the Duchess of Atholl that he was not a communist and she had replied that 'Your word is enough for me.'

For all three of these intellectuals the Spanish Civil War represented a personal encounter with what they saw as 'totalitarian' practices and a watershed in their relationship to communism. It was also a personal bond between them. As Orwell wrote in 1942: 'I remember saying once to Arthur Koestler, "History stopped in 1936", at which he nodded in immediate understanding. We were both thinking of totalitarianism in general, but more particularly of the Spanish Civil War.'[64] This intuition may only have been shared by a few isolated individuals in 1939; but this particular legacy of the Civil War matured in the years after 1945 when Borkenau, Koestler, and, less willingly, Orwell were all seen to popularise the idea of a 'Cold War' between a democratic West and a totalitarian communism. In this sense the Civil War proved ultimately counterproductive for the Communists in their policy towards intellectuals. In the short term the results were gratifying, as intellectuals rallied to the Republican cause. In the longer term, however, the Civil War contributed to a generation of intellectuals deeply suspicious of political engagement, or even willing to throw themselves passionately into the anti-communism of the Cold War.

Chapter 7

RELIGION

In the summer of 1937 George Orwell, on returning from Spain to his home in the village of Wallington, Hertfordshire, wrote to one of his former comrades that:

> This afternoon Eileen and I had a visit from the vicar, who doesn't approve at all of our having been on the Government side. Of course we had to own up that it was true about the burning of the churches, but he cheered up a lot on hearing that they were only Roman Catholic churches.[1]

While by no means all Anglicans would have shared these sentiments, the Spanish Civil War undoubtedly aroused religious passions just as strongly as it did political ones. All of the churches were affected, to differing degrees, by the Civil War. Elements within the Church of England, which sought to remain impartial, tried to tug it towards identifying with one side or the other. The Nonconformists had entered a phase of declining political engagement, emphasised by the collapse of their traditional ally, the Liberal Party. In Wales, however, Nonconformist ministers and their congregations were exceedingly active in supporting the Republican cause.[2] Most significantly, the massacres of bishops, priests, and religious clergy at the start of the Civil War, combined with the apparent lack of sympathy displayed by leading Anglicans regarding them, profoundly alienated Britain's Catholic minority.

The Church of England was, inevitably, far less affected than the Catholic Church by the events in Spain. Although there was some concern at the persecution of Protestants in Nationalist territory, there was none of the sense of grievance felt by Catholics at the fate of their co-religionists in Spain. Anglicans were far more concerned about the sufferings of Protestants under Nazism and of the Eastern Orthodox Christians under communism. In any case, the Church of England was in a profoundly conservative mood in the mid-1930s, reinforced by its strong links with the Conservative Party. Cosmo Lang, Archbishop of Canterbury from 1928 until 1942, was a personal friend of Neville Chamberlain and supported the foreign policy of the National Government. Lang's early identification with the poor as Bishop of Stepney had long since given way to upper-class affectation and delight at the high society in which his office allowed him to move. He preferred campaigns for spiritual revival (the 1937 'Recall to Religion') to those for social justice. Lang's stance during the Spanish Civil War did not waver from supporting non-intervention as a means to contain the conflict. There were, he claimed, 'no clear issues of established government against rebels, or of democracy against fascism, or of religion against irreligion'.[3] It was far from clear what Lang, having dismissed all of the standard interpretations of what the war represented, understood to be actually happening in Spain. Even so, his support for non-intervention was undoubtedly acceptable to the majority of the hierarchy, as it was to Anglican newspapers such as the *Church Times*.

The alternative to the dominant conservatism within the Church, displaying both a greater concern for social justice and a knowledgeable interest in foreign affairs, was best represented by William Temple (Archbishop of York, 1929–42). In his earliest pronouncement on the Civil War, Temple said that it was 'ridiculous' to suggest that this was a war between Christianity and atheism; rather it was a rebellion against a legal (if 'weak and ineffective') government. But the future was 'utterly dark': the only choice lay between a socialist government dominated by anti-Christian forces and a military government which would dominate the Church.[4] As for so many others, the bombing of Guernica shifted Temple's sympathies openly behind the Republicans. However, his involvement remained impartial and humanitarian. In September 1937 he joined a number of bishops and the Methodist Scott Lidgett in appealing to both sides for peace,[5] although he did also endorse a number of pro-Republican aid committees, including Spanish Medical Aid. In November 1938 he sponsored the campaign by the exiled German playwright Ernst Toller to launch an international relief effort in Spain. At Temple's request Archbishop Lang met Toller and was charmed by him into writing a letter of recommendation to President Roosevelt: Lang was not amused when he later learnt of Toller's past as a Communist revolutionary.[6] Temple did not, however, give a strong lead to those within the Church of England who actively supported the Spanish government, although his interventions still earned him criticisms in the Catholic press. His energies in the international field at this time were primarily channelled towards ecumenism and the creation of the World Council of Churches.

More outspoken was Cyril Garbett, Bishop of Winchester, who denounced the bombing of Guernica in the House of Lords as 'an appalling outrage against all the laws of civilisation'.[7] He later championed the Basque children who had arrived in England in his diocese. St John Wilson, Bishop of Chelmsford, who described his own politics as 'very pale blue', took part in a rally in solidarity with the Republic in April 1938 and denounced Franco's 'comic-opera' crusade. Like Temple he incurred considerable hostility from Catholics and the Right. The most prominent Anglican spokesman on European affairs at this time – George Bell, Bishop of Chichester – had taken up the cause of Jews in Germany, but refused to be drawn into the Spanish controversy. Bell suffered embarrassment when his old Methodist friend Sir Henry Lunn invited him to join his pro-Franco United Christian Front; he evaded the request by pleading that he was far too involved in the German Church question to allow him to 'add membership of another committee to those responsibilities'.[8]

In the absence of strong leadership from the bishops, the pro-Republican cause was adopted most publicly by a small group of deans, most notably by Hewlett Johnson, the 'Red Dean' of Canterbury. Johnson had been appointed in 1931 and throughout his stormy career aroused fierce passions and antagonisms by his advocacy of radical causes. During the Civil War he was to be described in establishment circles as a tiresome crank and a meddlesome buffoon. He is often dismissed as a perfect example of the simple-minded communist 'fellow-traveller', and this is partly borne out by his eulogy of the Soviet Union published in 1939, The Socialist Sixth of the World. However, it would be wrong to underestimate the innocent originality of Johnson's thought, or the range of his political interests. Before socialism he had been drawn to Major Douglas' Social Credit movement, and as late as 1935 had published a Social Credit pamphlet. His interest in Spain derived from the same source as his interest in the communist experiment in the Soviet Union: the belief that religion had traditionally condoned a 'sub-Christian' social and economic order based on profit that was now being challenged by a new order based on the 'service motive'. In his view it was unfortunate that, in Spain as well as in the Soviet Union, the new order was being created by brutal methods, including attacks on the churches. However, Johnson refused to accept that these deeds were irreligious, but rather, as he told Lang, the basis for a new world 'more fundamentally Christian in essence, however much it repudiates it in name'.[9] Johnson's combination of extreme materialism with spiritual utopianism was unique, but underlay, to some degree, the entire minority current of Anglican enthusiasm for the Spanish Republic.

In the autumn of 1936 the Spanish government became increasingly aware of the damage that the anti-clerical outrages had caused to its reputation in religious circles abroad. Accordingly, a deputation of Anglican and Free Churchmen was invited to visit Spain with a view to reporting on the situation there. The group was assembled and led by Henry Brinton, an Anglican lay activist, Labour candidate, and (in Foreign Office eyes) 'busybody' who was already involved in the National Joint Committee for Spanish Relief. It comprised A. S. Duncan-Jones (Dean of Chichester and a leading critic of Hitler's religious policy), Francis Underhill (Dean of Rochester), the Methodist Revd Henry Carter, Percy Bartlett (a Quaker), and the Revd Philip Usher. While not an 'official' party, it travelled with the support of a number of individual Church leaders, including Temple.

The deputation, which was in Spain between 29 January and 9 February 1937, reported factually on the closure and partial destruction of the churches in Barcelona, Valencia, and Madrid. It supported claims that the churches had been used by the rebels during the insurrection, and more generally placed the blame for the carnage on the Spanish Church for its neglect of social justice: it had come to be seen by many Spaniards – 'rightly or wrongly – as an instrument used by the powerful to keep them both ignorant and poor'. While they did not visit the Basque country, their report contrasted favourably the work of the Basque clergy in identifying closely with the people and attempting to build a society on the principles of Catholic social justice. The deputation was hopeful that religious toleration would resume when the war was over and praised the social advances of the

Republic in education and health. In conclusion, it doubted whether Spain would experience either a fascist or a communist regime, and envisaged a settlement based on a federal system of government.[10]

The report had reached conclusions that were supportive of the Republic and antagonised Catholics; however, some more committed pro-Republicans believed that the deputation's members had not done enough on their return to involve themselves politically on behalf of the Spanish government. One was the Revd E. O. Iredell, an Islington Marxist vicar who closed his services by giving the clenched-fist salute of the Popular Front and organised collections to 'get machine guns' for the Spanish Republic.[11] He had already visited Spain with Hannah Laurie (a Communist) in September 1936, and they now proceeded to form a second Christian delegation. The more radical profile of this new party was symbolised by the presence of the Dean of Canterbury. Other members included D. R. Davies, a left-wing former Congregationalist minister, and Monica Whatley, a Catholic Labour member of the London County Council who was already at odds with the Catholic hierarchy over the Civil War.

Despite futile attempts by the Foreign Office to prevent their departure, the delegates left for Spain on 29 March 1937. Unlike the previous expedition they visited the beleaguered Basque country as well as the Republican heartland: indeed, some would witness the German bombing of the village of Durango. They were deeply impressed by the harmony that they found between the clergy and the Basque government, and by the government's commitment to upholding civilised values (for instance, in its treatment of prisoners). Some of the party also visited Barcelona, Valencia, and Madrid, and conducted interviews with government ministers. They returned as satisfied as their predecessors that the Catholic Church had invited the attacks made on it, and convinced that it had a role in a democratic Spain so long as it could purge itself of 'reactionary influences'.

The delegates were warmly received by the Spanish Embassy in Paris, which issued a pamphlet based on their experiences at Durango and arranged a meeting with French Catholics (including Georges Bernanos). In Britain, however, progress was slower. They launched a campaign as the 'Christian Committee for Food to Spain', and an initial London meeting raised £300 as the basis for a projected £10,000 foodship for the Basque country. In fact, only £1,000 was eventually raised, partly because of the National Joint Committee's much larger Basque campaign. The money was donated to the care of Basque children in France. The delegates were equally unsuccessful in their attempt to build support for the Republic amongst the clergy of London and the Home Counties; 2,500 invitations were sent for the initial meeting and only 12 attended. Iredell blamed this failure on the 'pro-fascist sympathies' of many clergymen. The committee ultimately turned to developing local Christian initiatives for Spain wherever it had supporters, including Norfolk and Westmorland. In Wales D. R. Davies toured tirelessly even though the visit to Spain had brought on a spiritual crisis that destroyed his belief in Marxism and led him ultimately to become an Anglican priest.[12]

The committee failed not only because it was an independent initiative that was unable to carve out a distinctive identity, but also because of the inherent conservatism of many British Christians towards the Spanish conflict. Hewlett Johnson, however, continued to attract controversy on his return to Canterbury. On 19 April he preached in the cathedral that:

> There is a perfect passion for education, knowledge, and culture in Spain today, and to me that is nearer to the mind of Christ . . . The new order for which they are fighting is in line with the purpose of history, and the belief that there is a great brotherly society. What is that but religion?[13]

In June he spoke in Strasburg for the Intellectuals' Anti-Fascist Vigilance Committee, condemning the German bombing of Guernica while standing almost on the German border – much to the embarrassment of Anthony Eden who asked Lang to try to persuade the dean to moderate his tone.[14] The publicity that this meeting generated was the last straw for Lang, who was concerned that many foreigners assumed that Johnson was himself the Archbishop of Canterbury. At the Church Assembly in June he rebuked Johnson for having brought the name of Canterbury into 'the arena of acute public controversy' over Spain.[15] However, while the dean continued to drive conservative churchmen apoplectic with rage, he managed to retain his office until his retirement in 1963.

For the Christian pro-Republicans, who believed that the Republic was worthy of support both on religious and political grounds, the Basques were vital to their case, as they were seen to be building a new society on Catholic principles. In the rest of the Republic, however, the issue was less clear-cut. With the churches closed, it was imperative to believe that the material achievements of the New Spain were also creating a spiritually superior society. The danger here was that harsh criticism of the failings of the Catholic Church in Spain could inflame religious feeling in Britain: in the words of Lang's chaplain A. C. Don, the Dean of Canterbury's interventions were 'ecclesiastically provocative – the R.C.s [sic] regard him as a representative "Protestant" taking sides against the Roman Catholic Church'.[16]

It certainly complicated matters that, ever since the days of George Borrow in the 1830s, Spain had been viewed by British Christians as a field for evangelism. This had thrived in the religious toleration of the Republic, and in 1932 there were 123 British and American missionaries at work in Spain.[17] Thus, it was often difficult for pro-Republican Christians to disentangle their sympathy for the Republic from their religious aspirations for Spain. The Revd Henry Carter, visiting the offices of the British and Foreign Bible Society in Madrid, reported that Protestant pastors 'spoke hopefully of the wider opening for Christ's Gospel which the end of the war might bring'.[18] It has already been noted that the Quaker Alfred Jacob saw the war as the chance for a religious revival. His colleague Barbara Wood remarked that the mood in Spain was anti-Catholic but not anti-religion – and many Catholics would not 'very much mind' if Catholic ritual were not revived.[19] Thus, those who sought to intervene in the war from a religious perspective might well perceive a future for religion in Spain – but at the expense of traditional Catholicism.

The contention that the Republicans were more worthy of support than the more overtly religious Nationalists could not pass unchallenged. Quite apart from the Catholics, many in the Church of England and the Free Churches sided with Franco as a champion of religion at a time when it was felt to be under world-wide attack from 'godless communism'. They were concerned that the two deputations and the Dean of Canterbury might be taken as speaking for English Christians as a whole. Sir Henry Lunn, in his professional life one of the founders of the modern tourist industry, was profoundly shocked at the indifference of 'large numbers of professedly religious Englishmen' to the events in Spain.[20] Like many on the Right, Lunn was particularly perplexed that some were more solicitous for the fate of the German

Jews than that of Catholics. He wrote to Bishop Bell to ask why 'Bishops of the National Church . . . should refuse to say one word of sympathy with the spiritual descendants of missionaries like Xavier, St Teresa, and St John of the Cross', and appealed that he should consider 'how much nearer we are to faithful members of the Roman Church than we are to any Jews who are suffering misery in Germany to-day, and whose lives I would wish to see alleviated'.[21]

Lunn divided the Methodists' Representative Week in 1937 by proposing a resolution that expressed sympathy for the sufferings of both the Methodist Church in Barcelona and the Catholic Church throughout Spain. Lunn was not wholly successful on this occasion, and a bland final text simply deplored the violence of the Civil War and called for its swift resolution. He was, however, instrumental in setting up the United Christian Front in order to combat the 'Red Menace to Christianity' and challenge perceptions of the Civil War.[22] Chaired by the extreme right-wing Conservative Captain Ramsay, the committee attracted an impressive list of sponsors from across the religious spectrum, including two Scottish bishops, the Dean of Durham, and the president of the Free Church Council.

The Front was not a force for mass mobilisation, unlike the Irish Christian Front in southern Ireland which also took its inspiration from the Civil War at this time. The British organisation was primarily concerned with challenging pro-Republicans (such as the Bishop of Chelmsford) in print and represented a movement for Christian anti-communism rather than one for Christian solidarity. However, even the communist menace could not wholly unite right-wing Anglicans and Catholics in alliance. In February 1938 Cardinal Hinsley refused to allow priests to publicise a meeting of the Friends of National Spain because the 'very violent anti-Catholic speaker' Dean Inge of Westminster would be on the platform.[23] The meeting went ahead, with an uncomfortable Inge claiming that he was present not because of his sympathy for the Catholic Church in Spain, but because 'Red Government' always resulted in the persecution of religion.[24]

Despite the efforts of the United Christian Front, many Catholics in Britain remained alienated by the Anglican response to the Civil War. Even those who expressed sympathy for the sufferings of the Spanish Catholics were unable to do so without ambiguity. Cosmo Lang, for instance, while extending his sympathy to the Spanish Church, added cautiously 'whatever its defects might have been',[25] and some Anglicans were far more outspoken in exposing its failings. The *Church Times* was not alone in publicly accusing the Catholics of siding with fascism over Spain. Yet Catholics, for their part, were unable to understand how a Republican regime that had tolerated anti-clerical atrocities, and under which churches remained closed, could be preferred by some Christians to the avowedly Catholic Nationalists. Indeed, the most striking feature of the Catholic response to the Civil War was the degree to which it united the socially disparate Catholic community in Britain – in defence, at least, of the Spanish Church, if not necessarily in support of Franco's regime.

The Catholic response should be understood in the context both of the politics of Catholicism in Britain during the 1930s, and of the considerable challenge that the Civil War appeared to present to the Catholic faith. Catholic political engagement was subject to two very different dynamics. Firstly, there was a pervading sense of menace: Catholicism was perceived to be threatened both internationally and domestically by the rise of communism (and to a lesser extent by secularism and Nazism). Secondly, there was a sense of hope and a belief that Catholicism offered a solution to Europe's social and political malaise. In particular, Pius XI's 1931 encyclical *Quadregesimo Anno* defined a distinctively Catholic corporatist 'Third Way' between the extremes of atheistic communism and exploitative capitalism. Catholics were inspired by examples of triumphant political Catholicism – such as the regimes of Salazar in Portugal and Dollfuss in Austria – that were seen as quite distinct from fascism. Moreover, the laity in Britain, as throughout Europe, were being mobilised by the papal initiative of Catholic Action. Thus, while most British Catholics were supportive of the democratic system in their own country, many – especially intellectual converts – also accepted that parliamentary democracy was not a universally applicable system of government, and were sympathetic to the idea of an authoritarian state based on Catholic social principles.

This combination of apprehension and self-assertion made the Catholic politics of the 1930s uncomfortable to those who sought to draw a clear distinction between fascism and democracy and who argued that a choice had to be made between them. Catholics sought to avoid this distinction: Cardinal Hinsley would state that he was 'sometimes Red and sometimes fascist, but in reality nothing but a Catholic'.[26] At the same time, however, working-class Catholics (numerically preponderant in the Catholic community) were by now, with the permission of the hierarchy, supporters of the Labour Party and members of trade unions. Yet this membership was far from unconditional – Catholics were exhorted to fight hard to exclude communist and secularist influences from the Labour Party. The Spanish Civil War was thus the latest, and most traumatic, in a series of confrontations between the Labour movement and active Catholics in its ranks.

The issues raised by the Civil War were more complex than the Catholic hierarchy and press in Britain usually allowed. While the Spanish bishops who had survived the initial bloodshed were mainly united behind the Nationalists, there were significant exceptions. The exiled Cardinal Vidal of Tarragona refused to sign the bishops' 'collective letter' published in mid-1937 that appealed to foreign Catholics to support the Nationalist cause. Bishop Mugica of Vitoria, whose diocese included the Basque country, was held responsible by the rebels for fomenting Basque nationalism; he went into exile in Rome in October 1936. The Basque country posed a particular problem to Catholic supporters of Franco. Here, as the second Anglican deputation had observed, the Catholic Church was closely allied with the autonomous Basque government, and fourteen priests were executed by the Nationalists in the autumn of 1936. The Basque 'problem' was only eased with the fall of Bilbao in June 1937.

The Civil War also sowed division amongst foreign Catholics. This was most evident in France where some Catholic intellectuals such as Jacques Maritain were greatly disturbed by the Church's support for the rebellion. Maritain criticised the morality of the rebellion and challenged the assertion that this was a religious crusade or holy war with which non-Spaniards were duty-bound to side. Georges Bernanos, a right-wing Catholic, was horrified by his experiences in Majorca during the rebel occupation, and his powerful denunciation was published in Britain as *A Diary of My Times* (1938).

Relations between the Vatican and the Nationalists were also complicated. The Pope, although fulsome in his sympathy for the suffering of the Spanish Catholics, refused to endorse the rebels unconditionally. Papal support was tempered by concern over the fate of the Basques, over the atheistic element within the Falange Party, and over the kind of relationship a victorious but centralising Franco dictatorship would offer to the Catholic Church. Thus, when Pius XI met Spanish refugees in September 1936, he took the opportunity to warn that selfish and party interests may 'enter into, cloud, and change the morality and responsibility for what is being done'.[27] While formal relations were eventually opened with the Nationalists, diplomatic contacts were maintained with the Republic, with a view to ameliorating the condition of Catholics in its territory. Wholehearted support had to await the new Pope Pius XII's radio broadcast following Franco's victory in April 1939.

These reservations were echoed, in muted form, in Britain. During the Second Republic, educated Catholic opinion in Britain, in so far as it had been interested in Spain at all, had either hankered after the restoration of the monarchy or had sympathised with the CEDA party in seeking to transform the Republic from within. The Popular Front's election victory, followed by the military rising, closed that option and offered Catholics a much more hazardous alliance instead – within the Nationalist movement Catholics made common cause with the fascist Falange (containing atheistic elements) as well as Muslim Moroccan soldiers. Accordingly, two leading Catholic newspapers in England, the *Tablet* and the *Catholic Herald*, greeted the military revolt with a combination of concern for what would happen if it should fail as well as unease as to the implications of a rebel victory for the Church.

The *Tablet* felt that Catholics had 'no choice' other than to support the rebellion, but regretted the loss of independence that would inevitably result as a 'tragedy' for the Church in Spain. The *Catholic Herald* was critical of the rebellion and (like many Anglicans) of the Church's failure to distance itself from privileged groups in Spanish society. It warned of the 'widespread picture, and the partial fact, of the black cassock sheltered by the white terror', and condemned the massacre of the Republican defenders of Badajoz.[28] In both cases, the pressure of events, as evidence mounted of the anti-Catholic outrages, led them to move from initial scepticism to support for the rebellion, if only as the lesser of two evils. In a rapidly polarising situation the Spanish Church was seen as having no alternative other than to throw in its lot with the Nationalists and hope that the more secular forces in Franco's coalition would be marginalised.

After this initial uncertainty, therefore, religious leaders and opinion-formers within the Catholic community soon united in supporting the Nationalists. Cardinal Hinsley stated that the terror in Spain was aimed at the 'wreck of Christianity and the ruin of civilisation', and endorsed the view that this was a struggle between Christianity and communism.[29] Subsequently, Hinsley's supportive reply to the Spanish bishops collective letter was warmly welcomed by Cardinal Gomá.[30] Even so, Hinsley was always careful to maintain that the Catholic Church in England was identifying with the persecuted Spanish Catholics rather than with the Nationalist movement. This distinction was strained in his own case, and even more so in that of Bishop Amigo of Southwark who, as a Gibraltarian, had a strong personal interest in the conflict. Amigo called a special day of intercession in August 1936 where he proclaimed that the Nationalists were not rebels: 'they are fighting for the Church of God'.[31] He continued to argue that this was a clear case of justified rebellion against a government that was guilty of injustice and unable to maintain law and order. Although there were differences of emphasis, the hierarchy was united in presenting the Civil War as a struggle in which ordinary Catholics were wholly justified in supporting the rebels. This message, bowdlerised with stories of Red atrocities, was then transmitted to the Catholic faithful from the pulpit and through the Catholic press.

Although some historians have claimed that the English Catholics were divided over the morality of the Civil War,[32] opposition to the view presented by the hierarchy and the Catholic newspapers was extremely limited. The main critical voice was the Dominican monthly *Blackfriars*. While referring to the 'Red Terror' in Spain, the journal also blamed the Spanish Catholics for neglecting the 'rights and just claims of the working class' and warned the Spanish Church against too close an identification with the rebels: communism could be combated 'only by Christianity' and not by alliance with fascism. Francoism, it was argued, might offer short-term protection for Catholics, but could not achieve their longer-held ambitions for social justice. Indeed, it would make them harder to achieve.[33]

Blackfriars was by far the most significant Catholic voice of dissent over Spain, although smaller journals such as the *Sower* and the *Catholic Worker* did occasionally venture criticism. Bob Walsh, editor of the *Catholic Worker*, sought to use his paper to bring out the complexities of the conflict. He showed his independence by refusing an offer from pro-Franco propagandists to run a special edition showing pictures of atrocities even though the newspaper would have benefited financially.[34] One priest, Father Drinkwater from Birmingham, spoke out in July 1937 against coverage of the war in the Catholic press. It had, he argued, abandoned itself to 'war-time propaganda', had presented the Civil War as a 'crusade for God' which all Catholics must join, had made uncritical use of atrocity stories, and had concealed the anti-rebel views of Catholics in France and elsewhere.[35]

The other main source of dissent was the small group of liberal, anti-fascist intellectuals identified with either the pacifist group Pax or with the People and Freedom group. People and Freedom was established in November 1936 around Don Luigi Sturzo, the exiled leader of the Italian People's Party. One of its main concerns was the Spanish Civil War, on which its policy was 'to refuse to be drawn into partisanship of either side', concentrating on working for peace and mitigation of 'the horrors of the conflict'.[36] The group also gave rise to a further organisation, the non-religious British Committee for Civil and Religious Peace in Spain, under the chairmanship of the journalist Wickham Steed. The committee launched a campaign against the bombing of civilian populations which was being carried out primarily by Nationalists.

For the Catholic pacifists, Edward Watkin (founder of Pax) wrote in March 1937 that, even if Franco triumphed, the Church would be 'reduced to a most unhealthy dependence on the government as her bulwark against red atheism'. The 'Red' assault in Spain should have been met with passive resistance and 'an intensive intellectual and spiritual campaign': rebellion was a *pis aller* at a time when the best form of resistance had not even been attempted.[37]

It is true, therefore, that there were dissenting voices that received occasional coverage in the Catholic press. However, they were a small group of articulate, but hardly representative, Catholics and the significance of this division within English Catholicism was minimal. There was no liberal Catholic intellectual milieu, akin to that in France, within which dissent could flourish. In Britain it took considerable courage to go against the will of the hierarchy and the press, to be pilloried as credulous, disloyal, or pro-communist. However, the dissenters' position was seriously undermined by their neutrality which, in a polarised situation such as the Spanish Civil War, appeared more like sitting on the fence. Unwilling to reject the Nationalist movement completely, they settled for criticising its methods; and, unwilling to side with the Republic, they hoped for a political and religious option (for a politically independent social Catholicism) which no longer existed in Spain.

Accordingly, they chose neutrality partly because they had genuine doubts about Francoism, but also because they had no faith in the democratic credentials of the Spanish Republic. Indeed, many dissenters accepted the ultimate logic of the Nationalist cause. The pacifist Edward Watkin hoped that 'Franco's twilight will defeat the black night of his opponents.'[38] *Blackfriars*, too, tried to make its peace with the rebels. In August 1938 it had concluded that the evidence was 'pretty overwhelming' that the insurrection was 'morally unavoidable', and that a just war to preserve 'their religion and their nation' was the 'tragic necessity' of the Spanish people. When Franco had triumphed it noted that all Catholics could rejoice at the restoration of religious freedom – 'for a Catholic such considerations outweigh all others' – although it was relieved at the end of a 'painful conflict of conscience' for millions of Catholics worldwide.[39] In fact, the dissenting voices of English Catholicism were much more significant for the impact that they would make during and after the Second World War than for what they did or said during the Spanish Civil War.

While intellectual criticism may have been limited, how far did the Catholic working class share the hierarchy's view of the Civil War? This question is of particular importance as it informs our understanding of the response of the Labour Party. It has been argued that Catholic workers were out of step with the hierarchy and Catholic press on this issue, and were likely to share the pro-Republican sentiments of many non-Catholic Labour Party and trade union members. There is some contemporary evidence to support this. In October 1936 the intellectual Bernard Wall, founder of the *Catholic Worker*, wrote that 'by far the majority of [Catholic] working-class men and women, as distinct from their Catholic religious leaders, are pro-Caballero [the Republican prime minister]'.[40] A memorandum by Bob

Walsh, a leading social Catholic activist, in September 1936 claimed that 'Catholic workers are very tempted to support the Madrid authorities in the present conflict.' He argued that some prominent Catholics in the Labour movement, such as Monica Whatley, had caused Catholic workers to doubt the lurid atrocity stories in the press. Accordingly, Catholics were now tending to think either that the Madrid government was in the right, or that both sides were in the wrong.[41]

However, most evidence suggests that these assessments were unrepresentative. Working-class Catholic hostility to Republican Spain was both widespread and durable, persisting until the end of the war. Labour Party and trade union organisers were fully aware that Catholic areas were less likely to support campaigns for Republican Spain, and that the feelings aroused over this particular issue might well exacerbate other unresolved tensions. In addition, the Civil War drove a wedge between Catholic social activists working within the unions and their colleagues. One, a former pupil of the Catholic Workers' College in Oxford campaigning within the transport workers' union, wrote that his popularity had been destroyed by his 'open Catholicity in social matters, and the Spanish troubles. The bulk of English Trade Unionists are anti-Franco and no amount of talk will do any good.'[42]

All of the parties on the Left were aware of the problem, although they handled it in rather different ways. The Communists (and some members of the ILP) sought to challenge Catholics by equating the Nationalists with fascism, and arguing that many Spanish Catholics actually supported the Republic. While some of the Labour Party's propaganda followed this line, it had more to lose electorally from Catholic dissent and adopted a conciliatory attitude. Sir Walter Citrine of the TUC met Cardinal Hinsley, and the two were able to dissipate some of the tension by emphasising their shared anti-communism. In the latter stages of the Civil War the Labour Party rarely made an issue of Spain in by-elections. The Labour MP Josiah Wedgwood's offer to speak at the 1938 Stafford by-election was declined on the grounds that his views on Spain 'might alienate the Roman Catholic vote'.[43]

These problems occurred despite the fact that in the first year of the war the Labour movement and the Catholic hierarchy both supported non-intervention. However, Labour's intention of expressing its solidarity with the Spanish workers primarily through fundraising, which was not enough to satisfy its left-wing critics, was extremely offensive to many Catholics. They found themselves either being asked to contribute to funds, or watching as their trade union subscriptions were given to funds that, they believed, were going to help 'Red Spain'. Thus, it was the issue of humanitarian aid which was the most common battleground for Catholic trade unionists in the early phase of the war.

A small number of Catholics associated with the Labour movement did support the Republic vocally. For instance, the ILP MP John McGovern caused a storm by visiting the Republic and publishing a pamphlet on *Why Bishops Back Franco* on his return. Monica Whatley, a London county councillor for Limehouse, drafted leaflets replying to Bishop Amigo's anti-Republican sermons that were distributed outside his cathedral. When she went to speak on Spain in Paris, Hinsley wrote in person to warn Cardinal Verdier that she 'in no way represents Catholic opinion in England and . . . is distinctly on the side of the Reds'.[44] In 1938 the chairman of Chichester Labour Party was able to persuade twenty-eight fellow Catholics, including an MP and two London councillors, to sign a letter to Cardinal Hinsley asking him to denounce the Nationalist bombing of cities.[45] However, seven other MPs that he had approached refused to sign, and for many Catholics in positions of authority discretion on this issue was the better part of valour.

Hostility to the Republic was, therefore, if by no means uniform, certainly widespread amongst working-class Catholics. But hostility to the Republic need not imply support for Franco, and this crucial distinction deserves to be emphasised. Catholic workers' opinions on Spain were primarily defensive – a logical extension of the defence of their own community against attack. Catholic journalists attempted to put words into their mouths at their own peril. For instance, a report based on interviews with East End dockers in the *Catholic Herald* claimed that 'Catholic Labour is overwhelmingly pro-Franco.' In fact, the interviewed dockers saw themselves as 'Labour men' who would have supported the Spanish socialists in elections, and only changed their sympathies when they realised that the Republican government was failing to protect the churches from the Anarchists. Far from expressing keen support for Franco, the men's comments reflected their ambivalent feelings towards a Republican government that 'represented their political principles [but] was really out to destroy their faith'.[46] This encapsulated the conflict felt by many Catholic workers, torn between their political and trade union loyalty, and their identification with suffering Catholics in Spain. The result was a painful mixture of emotions that was hostile to the Republic but far from convinced that Franco was the workers' friend.

While the sympathy of working-class Catholics appears to have been tempered by suspicion about Franco's regime, many prominent Catholics felt no inhibition in embracing Nationalism – not only as the defender of the Church against communism, but also as the agent for radical social reconstruction on Catholic lines. This support was in many respects the mirror image of left-wing and liberal support for Republican Spain. On both sides there was a similar intensity of feeling for what was seen as a fateful struggle between good and evil, and a shared conviction that neutrality was impossible. Moreover, Catholics were just as attuned as pro-Republicans to seeing the Nationalist movement as ushering in a better and juster New Spain – even if one based on the extermination of all internal enemies.

There are a number of factors specific to the Catholic perception of New Spain. English Catholics had a profound attachment to Spain as a bastion of the faith, and victory for communism in Spain would have been just as traumatic as a fascist victory was for the Left. At the same time, Catholics recognised Spain as a nation in decline that had, to a degree, been failed by its Church. Thus, national and religious revival were inextricably connected – but would also have to be very radical in order to be effective. In the words of the Catholic quarterly *Arena*, 'That a revolution was needed in Spain nobody can deny.'[47] Thus, Catholic pro-Nationalism was composed of two elements: national regeneration, and a new social and political order applying Catholic social principles.

For Catholics the Nationalist movement represented a dramatic turning back of the clock to Spain's Golden Age after centuries of decline. The *Tablet* characterised the Civil War as 'the recovery of a great nation' and the reaction of a 'healthy organism' ridding itself of a poison.[48] The extent of this regeneration was noted by a number of Catholic visitors to Spain. One, touring in August 1937, reported that idleness was a thing of the past, and that even the aristocracy was now working hard![49] Another, Alfonso de Zulueta, noted in 1938 that the struggle had 'called out the latent energies of the race'.[50] According to the *Month*, not only Franco's Christian soldiers, but even his Moors were 'fired with the enthusiastic vision of a national and reviving Spain'.[51]

While looking to the past and Spain's greatness, however, the New Spain also looked to the future, pioneering a new order that would no longer simply defend wealth and privilege. The writer Raymond Lacoste met General Mola (architect of the rebellion), who said that the Nationalists would 'increase the social standing of the workers and peasants'. He travelled on to Valladolid, sipped Manzanilla while 'Reds' were being executed and reflected that 'from this terrible accumulation of horrors a New Spain will arise'.[52] The *Tablet* gave its own imprimatur to the Nationalist New Spain in May 1937 following Franco's formation of the Falange Española Tradicionalista y de las JONS. It welcomed the fact that the Nationalist movement could no longer be called 'reactionary':

> the strength of such movements as these come from the enthusiastic support of large numbers of young men, without personal wealth or desire for it, men in no way anxious to preserve an existing regime but full of enthusiasm to build a new one.

While there would be a concentration of power in the corporate state, this would be balanced by the strong role for the family in the new order. Thus, 'the fascism of Spain, resting on the age-old and ingrained individualism of the Spaniard, will be something new in Europe' (and not a replica of Italian fascism or Nazi Germany).[53]

Catholic enthusiasm for the Nationalists was particularly pronounced because they were believed to be applying Catholic social principles. This was attractive to English Catholics who were not in a position to change social policy in Britain, and saw the opportunity to see such ideas put into practice in Spain. The Nationalists had shovelled aside hated and corrupt politicians and were 'beginning anew' using a Catholic blueprint.[54] A letter from Marie Louise Maxwell-Scott, written from a mining village near Huelva in 1938, drew attention to the new spirit of 'social service' in Nationalist Spain. The creches built in poor areas of Seville were a 'paradise' – 'I wished we had the like in England.' She praised the work of the Auxilio Social (the female wing of the Falange) in running orphanages and soup kitchens: 'Thus National Spain has begun her great work for her people. And her teaching is unity of service, not class against class. No communism and no fascism. Spanish customs and not foreign importations.' Spain would be 'united again under a Christian regime'.[55]

There is, therefore, considerable evidence that within influential Catholic circles there was widespread positive support for Franco that went far beyond the fact that he was a defender of the faith. His Nationalist movement represented a Spanish national revival which would combine all that was 'good' in Spain's Catholic past (the 'true Spain') with all that was 'good' in the Catholic-inspired anti-democratic European regimes of the present. The most famous echo of this is to be found in Cardinal Hinsley's congratulatory letter to Franco on 28 March 1939, in which he thanked the Generalissimo for sending him a signed photograph. He went on:

> I look upon you as the great defender of the true Spain, the country of Catholic principles where Catholic social justice and charity will be applied for the common good under a firm and peace-loving government.
>   May God bless your work for reconstruction and reconciliation.[56]

While Hinsley was expressing here his hope of how Franco's regime might develop (and reconciliation was hardly in evidence), it is also clear that in Hinsley's mind Franco was now the best (and only) option for Spanish Catholicism.

It is almost impossible to discover analogues to this positive endorsement for Francoism amongst working-class Catholics. Occasional examples are found. For instance, Pat Tolhurst of the London Catholic Worker group made a lengthy visit to Nationalist Spain and wrote enthusiastically on social work there – 'the spirit of new Spain is manifesting itself in constructive works'.[57] But this was balanced out by the scepticism of the editor Bob Walsh. The Catholic Social Guild, which united middle- and working-class Catholics in promoting Catholic social principles, carried occasional reports in its journal praising the building of cheap workmen's houses, creches, and free dinners to poor children in the rebel-held area.

Thus, probably the most significant difference within the Catholic community was between those who positively identified with Franco's Nationalism as a model for political and religious reconstruction (a group that dominated the organs of Catholic opinion), and those who saw the Spanish Republican 'Reds' as the enemy of religion, but had little enthusiasm for Franco's cause (the dominant view amongst working-class Catholics). This was not a division that created friction, however, because there was a common denominator available in hostility to the Spanish Republic and communism. Catholic workers were not keen on the Spanish Republic, but they were not willing to leave their trade unions or political parties over the issue. The matter only came to a head on rare occasions when Catholics were actually expelled from the Labour Party for their stance on the Civil War. Otherwise, Catholic workers appear to have tolerated the more pro-Franco leanings of their religious leaders – so long as they were not expected to join in with their 'Crusade'.

EPILOGUE

In the troubled years following the end of the Civil War, both pro-Republicans and pro-Nationalists in Britain faced fresh challenges that sometimes undermined the certainties that had sustained them during the war itself. Republican sympathisers had to come to terms with the defeat of a cause that had seemed so just as to be invincible: the representatives of the New Spain were now scattered in exile in Europe and the Americas. Moreover, defeat served to widen the ideological and personal divisions in the Republican ranks, so that disunity rather than unity was now the hallmark of their cause. In particular, the bitter animosities between the Communists and their critics that had flared up at the end of the Civil War continued to form a rift in exile politics long after 1939. However, there were also problems for pro-Nationalists in their hour of victory. With the outbreak of European war in September 1939, and especially with the fall of France in June 1940, their conviction that Franco would not side with the Axis powers would be sorely tested.

The immediate aftermath of the Civil War brought with it familiar humanitarian problems of caring for refugees (especially in southern France), assisting the escape of political leaders, and appealing for clemency on behalf of those arrested in Franco's ruthless repression. Aid organisations created during the Civil War remained in existence to cater for this new crisis. The National Joint Committee for Spanish Relief, for instance, chartered a steamer to carry 1,600 Republicans to safe haven in Mexico. Less likely benefactors also took an interest. With a rare zeal for bureaucratic self-preservation Francis Hemming of the Non-Intervention Board sought to give it a new lease of life, and employment for its staff, by administering camps for Spanish militiamen in France.[1] (Of course, these refugees may well have blamed their current plight precisely on non-intervention and its servants!)

However, the miserable aftermath of the Civil War was a concern primarily for those British activists who were already committed to the Republican cause – Spain was now of only marginal interest in Britain.

This changed with the outbreak of the Second World War, when the lessons of the Civil War could no longer be ignored. Pioneering work on blood transfusions and the treatment of war wounds now received the wider audience that they deserved, while the observations of the scientist J. B. S. Haldane and others on the need for deep civilian shelters against air raids were also vindicated. Fred Copeman was even invited to lecture to the royal household in Windsor Castle on the dangers of aerial bombardment. As Britain's situation became more perilous after the evacuation of the British forces from Dunkirk, the experience of the Civil War loomed ever larger. Despite the pressing need to conciliate Franco, Churchill's 'finest hour' broadcast of 18 June 1940 paid tribute to the 'brave men of Barcelona' as an example of how the British too would withstand a bombing campaign from the air.

The example of the Spanish people was at its most inspirational when Britain faced possible defeat in the summer of 1940. On 13 May Anthony Eden, restored to government at the War Ministry, launched the idea of a Home Guard to resist a German invasion. Maverick left-wingers such as Tom Wintringham (thrown out of the Communist Party in 1938) and George Orwell (who had left the anti-war ILP) saw the Home Guard as the basis for a 'people's war' such as that fought by the Republican militias. Wintringham became the organisation's unofficial leader when he persuaded the Picture Post proprietor Edward Hulton to fund a training school at Osterley Park in west London. His staff included other Spanish veterans such as Hugh Slater and 'Yank' Levy, and the school trained some 5,000 men in its first six months in the face of War Office hostility. (John Langdon-Davies, another prominent pro-Republican, also established a training school at Burwash in Sussex.) Tom Wintringham wrote prolifically throughout the war, constantly drawing on his Civil War experiences. Above all, he referred back constantly to the battle of the Jarama where the British Battalion had defended 'the last road into Madrid' against an enemy 'twenty times greater in fire power'.[2]

The Civil War was also never far from Orwell's mind in his brilliant polemic *The Lion and the Unicorn* (1941), in which he argued that only a revolution in English society could make victory over the Nazis possible. His belief that 'The war and the revolution are inseparable'[3] came straight from the analysis of the ill-fated POUM. The dreams of Orwell and Wintringham were never to be realised. Osterley Park was eventually given official status, but Wintringham was edged out and resigned in June 1941. He committed himself instead to the left-wing Common Wealth Party that shattered the wartime political truce and won a number of by-election seats from the Conservatives. Orwell was disenchanted by the failure of his 'English Revolution': the entry of the USSR and the United States into the war in 1941 might have made eventual victory more likely, but seemed to preclude the possibility of radical change in Britain.

The case of Wintringham and Orwell shows how one interpretation of the lessons of the Civil War could be applied to Britain in its war against Nazi Germany. More generally, some historians have argued that the campaigns for Republican Spain laid the foundation for the anti-fascist mobilisation of Britain during the Second World War: that the frustrated Popular Frontism of 1936–9 found its fulfilment in the wartime unity of 1941–5.[4] The degree to which the Second World War was perceived as an ideological war against fascism, a view never wholly accepted by officialdom, undeniably owed much to the political education that the Civil War had offered. The activists of the Civil War years were to the fore in all fields during the Second World War – air raid protection, medicine, propaganda, and, of course, the military. Many of the former International Brigade volunteers fought and died in the British forces and, although some suffered petty discrimination in being given lowly ranks and unrewarding postings, others did not. Bill Alexander received the rank of captain in the British army to match that which he had been awarded at Teruel.

However, too great an emphasis on the continuities between these two struggles overlooks the immense discontinuity imposed by Communist policy between the Nazi–Soviet Pact of August 1939 and the German invasion of the Soviet Union in June 1941. After bitter debate the British Communist leaders endorsed Moscow's line in October 1939 by opposing what they regarded as the 'imperialist war' between Britain and Germany. The ludicrous idealism of the Communist policy – it was hoped that the war would be ended by the German and British people overthrowing their political masters – could not conceal the fact that the short-term dictates of Soviet foreign policy had triumphed. The Communists' stance appalled erstwhile anti-fascist allies such as Victor Gollancz, while appearing to confirm the judgement of Labour leaders as to their unreliability. None felt this betrayal of the anti-fascism of the 1930s more keenly than Harry Pollitt, who privately confessed to his sense of shame that 'we have not been able to treat the Warsaw resistance in the same way that we treated Madrid and Valencia and Barcelona'.[5] For resisting the new 'line' he was removed from his post as the party's general secretary, to be eventually restored following the Nazi attack on the Soviet Union. In the interim the Communists opposed the war. In June 1940 Isabel Brown, star of so many Spanish Medical Aid rallies, won a derisory vote when contesting the Poplar by-election on an anti-war platform. For the many Communists who never felt happy with the party line, the German invasion of the Soviet Union was in many respects a relief; only now could they fully resume the anti-fascist politics that they had espoused so enthusiastically during the 1930s.

After June 1940 the response of the Franco regime to the German victory in western Europe acquired immense significance for Britain's survival. Whether Spanish forces themselves attacked Gibraltar (a long-standing Nationalist goal) or merely allowed German troops passage through Spain, the danger to Britain's imperial communications was obvious. In this darkest period of the war considerable energy was expended in ensuring that Franco did not side openly with the Axis. In this struggle the British Left could have no influence on the Spanish government; it was the moment for the British pro-Nationalists to seek their reward for supporting Franco during the Civil War.

In May 1940 Sir Samuel Hoare, an arch-appeaser and until recently air minister, was appointed as ambassador to Madrid just as the German armies were triumphing in western Europe. The arrival of German troops on the Pyrenees and Mussolini's decision to join the war on the German side in June 1940 added to the pressure on Franco to do likewise. The dramatic shift in the fortunes of war threatened to undermine the British government's strategy, pursued since the end of the Civil War, of using its economic strength to win Franco's friendship. Indeed, as recently as March 1940 Britain had extended a package of aid including £2 million in trade credits. In June 1940 Spain shifted from neutrality to 'non-belligerency' in the war, and seized control over the internationally administered port of Tangier. Despite these blows, Hoare's policy was to trust Franco not to join the Axis, and to draw him towards Britain through food aid. At the same time he encouraged those elements sympathetic to Britain in the government and army, while offering the regime tantalising prospects of territorial gains (at French expense). Hoare was joined in the Embassy by other former pro-Nationalists such as the young Catholic press attaché Tom Burns, who had driven an ambulance to Nationalist Spain in 1938. Mgr Edwin Henson, rector of the English College in Valladolid and an even more fervid pro-Nationalist during the Civil War, worked closely with the Embassy in promoting British interests and propaganda.

In Britain, this was above all a moment for the Catholic Church. Lord Perth, a Catholic at the Ministry of Information, wrote that 'It is clear that if friendship and understanding are to be established between England and Spain it must be largely through the Catholic Church.'[6] Such a role appealed to Cardinal Hinsley, an ardent anti-Nazi who played an important part in the formation of the Sword of the Spirit movement in 1940 to campaign for Christian values against Nazi 'paganism'. He was eager to see that English Catholicism's special relationship with both the Franco regime and the Spanish Church should work to Britain's advantage in the war. In the spring of 1940 the remnants of the Bishops' Committee funds were used to buy gifts to re-equip some of Spain's burnt-out churches, and a deputation was sent to present them to Cardinal Gomá. Later in the year Hinsley sponsored the appointment of the Irish writer Walter Starkie as director of the British Institute in Madrid. Hinsley made very clear the political role that he envisaged for Starkie: 'I am sure that you will do immense good in Spain. Your efforts will constitute a spear-head against Nazism and Fascism.'[7] Hinsley was able to reconcile his support for Franco (whose signed photograph he proudly displayed on his desk) with his hostility to Nazism. However, the war years broke the influence of the right-wing Catholic intellectuals who had been so prominent in the 1930s and had toyed dangerously with some forms of fascism. One bishop complained that the exclusion of laymen like Douglas Jerrold from the Sword of the Spirit 'causes a suspicion in my mind that Catholics who stood up for Franco and tried hard to explain the meaning of the Civil War to English audiences will not be very welcome'.[8] The Friends of National Spain, renamed simply the Friends of Spain and still chaired by Lord Phillimore, were kept at arm's length by the hierarchy in its Spanish projects.

What was not always appreciated at the time was that, in seeking to keep Franco from wholeheartedly siding with the Axis, the British were kicking on an open door. This was not from any lack of pro-Axis enthusiasm on Franco's part – far from it. However, the price that Franco demanded was always too high for the Nazis to pay. In addition to requiring massive economic and military assistance for his devastated country, he also demanded much of the French empire in North Africa (forcing Hitler to choose between Franco and his collaborationist allies in Vichy France). At their sole meeting at Hendaye on the French border in October 1940 Hitler and Franco failed to reach agreement, and no more propitious occasion would occur during the war.[9] However, while Franco was later to present his wartime policy as a masterful strategy to stay out of war, his government undoubtedly supplied valuable help to the Axis. Some 47,000 Spaniards fought in the volunteer Blue Division on the eastern front, facilities were offered to German U-boats on the Atlantic coast, and German intelligence was provided with information on the passage of Allied vessels through the Straits of Gibraltar. Spain also traded heavily with Nazi Germany in both manufactured goods and vital minerals such as wolfram (large quantities of which were also bought up as a pre-emptive measure by the Allies).

Despite his good fortune in staying out of the war, Franco's assistance to the Axis would form a major part of the indictment against his regime after 1945, and could not be easily overlooked. In 1944, when Franco appealed directly to Churchill for a *rapprochement* between the two 'virile' European nations and an alliance against communism, he received a frosty reply. Churchill made it clear that Franco could not expect his conduct to be ignored: 'throughout the war German influence in Spain has constantly been permitted to embarrass the war effort of Great Britain and her Allies'.[10] Even so, the Allies were unwilling to create a new enemy at this late stage in the war, and Churchill was also adamant that Franco would not be removed by force. In a speech in the House of Commons on 25 May 1944 he had concluded: 'Internal political problems in Spain are a matter for the

Spaniards themselves. It is not for us — that is, the government — to meddle in such affairs.'[11]

The end of the war in Europe and the defeat of Franco's sponsors Hitler and Mussolini brought great hope for the exiled Republicans. These hopes were shared by the British Left, which believed that Franco's regime would soon be replaced. In the May 1945 British election campaign hostility to Franco's regime, as unfinished business from the Second World War, was frequently expressed. A Labour candidate such as George Jeger could proudly proclaim his role in Spanish Medical Aid in his election leaflet, and win his seat in Winchester as part of Labour's landslide victory over Churchill's Conservatives.

And yet, despite the dramatic Labour victory and the hopes for a 'socialist' foreign policy, the moment for the Left in Spanish policy did not come in 1945 as it had for the Right in 1940. Franco's regime, defying the great hostility towards it in Britain and the Allied nations, survived the post-war years with an ease that appears hard to comprehend. Internationally, the regime was a pariah and an un-pleasant reminder of the dictatorships of the 1930s. Spain was excluded from membership at the formation of the United Nations in 1945, and in March 1946 Britain, the United States, and France (which had closed its border on the Pyrenees) issued a joint declaration calling for the 'peaceful withdrawal' of Franco and the disman-tling of his regime. The height of official disapproval came in 1946 when a UN resolution called for ambassadors to be withdrawn from Madrid. This symbolic measure, however, was considerably less than the complete break in diplomatic relations and economic sanctions for which many on the Left wished. The Labour government denounced the Franco regime rhetorically, and offered limited support to the exiled Republicans, but in practice had little appetite for attempting to overthrow it. British diplomats at the UN worked to soften proposed anti-Franco measures, and Britain almost immediately restored its ambassador to Madrid when the UN resolution was rescinded in November 1950. When Franco's first choice for ambassador to London, a veteran of the anti-Soviet Blue Division, was rejected, his successful second choice was almost as provocative: Miguel Primo de Rivera, brother of the executed Falangist leader.

The unconfrontational British policy of these years has been explained as a continuation of the 'non-intervention' of the Civil War;[12] in both cases British aversion to intervention in Spain worked to Franco's advantage. More directly, Spanish policy was but one example of the strong continuity between the foreign policy of the wartime Churchill coalition and that of the new Labour government: defending Britain's position as a great power and seeing the main international threat as coming from the Soviet Union. Certainly, the anti-communism of Labour's new foreign minister Ernest Bevin made him unwilling to contemplate any radical measures against the Franco regime, fearing that the destabilisation of Spain would result in a communist regime there. If a peaceful transition to a moderate democratic regime (preferably a monarchy) could not be effected, then the continuation of Francoism was more acceptable than a new civil war. The government was also profoundly influenced by the great expansion of trade with Spain after 1945, as Spain became an important market for British goods and the leading source of imported fruit and vegetables. Any economic sanctions would have significant repercussions for Britain's own shattered economy.

The degree of continuity in British policy between 1936 and 1950 should not, however, be exaggerated. The context in which Spanish policy was formulated was fundamentally different after 1945. With the defeat of the dictators, Franco's regime remained an unpleasant one, but no longer one that threatened world peace. Compared to the massive tasks that faced Bevin and his colleagues in reconstructing the post-war world, Spain was, sadly, a trivial concern. The Labour government's inactivity is easy to chastise with hindsight, but it is more difficult to identify an active policy that would have brought constructive results. There was no prospect of direct allied military intervention once the war in Europe had finished, while economic sanctions would only have hurt the already impoverished Spanish people. The exiled opposition was divided and (although a limited guerrilla war raged for some years after 1945) internal opposition was heavily suppressed. Franco was by now an old hand at presenting foreign hostility against him and his regime as an affront to the Spanish nation. By 1950 even Gerald Brenan, having made a return visit to Spain, would argue that there was very little prospect either of forcing Franco out or of installing parliamentary democracy. Only economic assistance could provide the Western democracies with some influence: 'There can surely be no object in condemning the Spanish working classes to starvation and misery or driving naturally honest people into corruption and starvation.'[13]

In other respects the political campaigns of the post-1945 period differed from the Civil War era. While many familiar figures remained involved, such as Wilfred Roberts, others had moved on to new preoccupations. In 1944–5 the Duchess of Atholl took up the cause of the Baltic peoples and the Poles under Soviet domination, and became chairman of the British League of European Freedom, critical of the extension of Soviet power under the Tehran and Yalta agreements. Leah Manning returned to Spain in 1947 to observe a political trial, but was then refused a visa for a further visit and 'lost the urge to go'. She disengaged herself from Spanish activities still dreaming that a statue of her with the Basque children would one day be erected in Bilbao.[14]

Increasingly the campaign was carried forward by the International Brigades Association (Spanish Medical Aid having been wound up in 1941, and the National Joint Committee's work having finished at the end of the Second World War). Formed in March 1939 as a focus of support for the Spanish Republic, the Association confirmed the Brigades' veterans as the elite of the anti-Franco cause in Britain. After 1943 it was chaired by Nan Green, who had herself served as a nurse in Spain and whose husband, George, had died just before the British Battalion was pulled out of the battle of the Ebro. While initially concerned with rescuing foreign volunteers from wartime Europe and assisting imprisoned Republicans, the Association became after 1945 an effective campaigning organisation for Spanish democracy. Although having a largely Communist membership, the heroism of its members gave it a legitimacy which could not be denied, allowing it to transcend the often bitter Labour/Communist divide of the Cold War years.

Even so, the Association spoke for only a small proportion of the volunteers. By the end of 1948 it was in touch with 550 members, of whom 200 were involved with events in Spain.[15] Some had abandoned active politics or found another focus for their energies, while others had changed their allegiance. Fred Copeman had broken with communism to become a Catholic, and eventually adopted the cause of moral rearmament. Hamish Fraser, who had served in Spanish military intelligence and was a Communist activist on the Clyde during the Second World War, eventually turned to a highly traditionalist and anti-communist Catholicism. In 1956 he led opposition to a visit by Bulganin and Khrushchev (the 'enemies of humanity')[16] with an intensity that alarmed even his religious superiors. Like many Catholics, he campaigned vigorously for Spain's reintegration into the international community.

For the International Brigade Association the fight against Franco was a fight to the death rooted in the personal commitment that the volunteers had long since made to Republican Spain. For the Left as a whole, however, the Spanish cause was emotive, but no longer central. Indeed, the Left's failure to shift government policy on Spain between 1945 and 1951 was but one aspect of its wider failure to impose a distinctive socialist foreign policy during these years of Cold War polarisation. As it had done so effectively during the Civil War, the institutional discipline of the Labour movement (now strengthened by the need to support a Labour government) overpowered the brittle idealism of the Left. For many on the Left, moreover, the idealism that had been channelled into the Republican cause now found new outlets with greater prospects of success. There were now other new worlds being created in Yugoslavia and China – and even in Britain itself.

If the return of the Conservatives to power in 1951 alleviated what little pressure the Attlee government had exerted on Franco, it was the continuing intensification of the Cold War that allowed his complete rehabilitation. By the early 1950s the United States rather than Britain was taking the initiative in relations with Spain, and this culminated in the 1953 military and economic agreements that brought millions of dollars as well as bases for American military aircraft into Spain. This deal, combined with the perfection of the regime's internal repression, the continuing disunity of the exiles, and the signing of a long-desired Concordat with the Vatican, marked 1953 as the apex of Franco's achievement. When President Eisenhower paid a state visit to Spain in 1959 Franco could finally believe that he had won the Civil War.[17]

After 1953 Franco's hold on power may have been finally assured, but new challenges were already developing. As the economy was liberalised in the late 1950s internal resistance revived in the form of clandestine trade unions under local leadership. From a less expected angle, the regime was also criticised by a new generation of Catholic priests inspired by the principles of the Second Vatican Council (1962–5), and their calls for democratic reform threatened to remove one of the main pillars of Franco's regime. Basque opposition also revived, and the urban guerrillas of ETA brought violence to the heart of the regime when Franco's closest adviser Admiral Carrero Blanco was spectacularly assassinated in 1973.

Changed circumstances in Spain brought a changing response in Britain. Although there was now no prospect of overthrowing the regime, the growth of internal conflict in Spain created the need for legal and political support in a series of high-profile trials of trade unionists and other opposition activists. (Many trials were a mockery of justice, and some executions were carried out by the particularly brutal method of garrotting.) The change was symbolised by the creation of the Labour Party's Spanish Democrats' Defence Fund in 1959, which sent observers to the trials. This committee enjoyed the support of Civil War volunteers who had by now matured into prominent trade union leaders, including Will Paynter (leader of the mine workers), Jack Jones (of the transport workers), and Bob Edwards (leader of the ill-fated ILP contingent in Spain and a Labour MP).

Generational change had other consequences. Franco's bitter enemies were growing older alongside the dictator that they so despised. Interest in Spain and its Civil War began to revive in Britain in the 1960s, not least because of the publication of Hugh Thomas' epochal history of the conflict in 1961. But the contemporary anti-Franco struggle was but one rather specialised left-wing cause amongst many, and for students and the young lacked the immediacy of the Campaign for Nuclear Disarmament or the struggle against the Vietnam War. The campaign was also growing old in other ways. Since the 1950s Spain had begun to develop the package holiday industry. A country that has been continually rediscovered by the British in the twentieth century was, in the 1960s, increasingly familiar to working-class Britons as a place for cheap holidays in the sun. While the British veterans of the Civil War kept alive their memory of the Spanish Republic, it was one that co-existed increasingly uneasily with this popular, hedonistic and apolitical perception of modern Spain.

Franco died on 20 November 1975 and, despite the hopes of the

Falangists, his appointed heir King Juan Carlos (grandson of the monarch deposed in 1931) had no wish to perpetuate the dictatorship. In alliance with his prime minister Adolfo Suárez the king steered Spain through a rapid transition to democracy, with even a legalised Communist Party contesting the first free elections in 1977. Under the constitution of 1978 Spain became a constitutional monarchy. The genuine danger of a Francoist backlash degenerated into near-deadly farce with Colonel Tejero's storming of Parliament in October 1981. In the face of hostility from the king and mass popular resistance the plot soon collapsed, and within a year Spain had its first Socialist prime minister (Felipe González) since 1939. Spain's remarkable transformation was completed with its entry to the European Economic Community in 1984 and (far more controversially within Spain) NATO in 1986.

Franco's death and the rapid transformation of Spain brought to a close not only a chapter in British foreign relations, but a chapter in British politics and, indeed, in Britain's view of the world. Franco's achievement had been to isolate Spain from Europe, so that its remoteness and distinctiveness was artificially perpetuated. Churchill's May 1944 speech alluded to this mystique when he referred to Spain as 'once the most famous empire in the world and down to this day a strong community in a wide land, with a marked personality and distinguished culture among the nations of Europe'.[18] Halifax, the former foreign secretary, writing his memoirs in 1957, could still blame British aversion to Franco's regime on the legacy of the Armada, the Inquisition, and other folk memories that left the 'impression that Spain is something to be kept as far away as possible'.[19] Even in the 1950s such a view was anachronistic. Since 1975 democratisation and involvement in the European Community and NATO have spectacularly broken down Spain's remoteness: the New Spain has ended up looking remarkably like the rest of western Europe.

Since 1939 the Spanish Civil War has made a deep and lingering impact on British politics and culture, although affecting the Left far more than the Right. While Franco continued to have his right-wing admirers, these were a dwindling band – mainly of Catholics. Many Conservatives wanted to see the Franco regime shed its pariah status (for instance, R. A. B. Butler's comment in Spain in 1961 that it was 'an essential factor against the communist danger, especially today'),[20] but they did not feel that it had anything to teach them. The Second World War, and the autarkic chaos of post-war Spain, destroyed the relevance of Franco's regime as any kind of political model to the mainstream Right. It is the memory of Munich, rather than the Civil War, that has been salvaged by the Conservatives from the 1930s, justifying robust military action against dictators from the Falkland Islands to the Gulf.

For the Left, however, the Civil War has been central to a series of vital (if often contradictory) political myths. While Franco's Spain was eventually discredited by its failures in peacetime, the Republic has lived on in the minds of the Left as a cherished memory of popular valour and a just cause. In 1993 the former Labour leader Michael Foot would say that he was 'as furious about Sarajevo as we were about Spain'.[21] The Spanish Civil War may have been the last great war of national liberation in Europe, but within British politics it was a prototype for the many post-war anti-imperialist liberation struggles. The idea of an oppressed people united against foreign aggression and in pursuit of a better society has sustained the Left's interest in conflicts from Vietnam to Palestine, from Nicaragua to Bosnia. The *Brigadistas* who went to Nicaragua in the 1980s (to pick coffee rather than to fight) were paying conscious homage to the ideals and to the idealists of the 1930s.

Since the 1960s, however, this memory has been a contested one. The revival of Trotskyism and anarchism and the withering of Stalinism has given new life to the Orwellian interpretation of the Spanish Civil War in both academic and political circles: in recent decades apologias for the suppression of the POUM, even from former International Brigaders, have no longer carried much weight. Old wounds were reopened by Ken Loach's openly Orwellian film *Land and Freedom* (1995), with one veteran reported as saying that he would not want his grandchildren to see it.[22] As Spain has found peace, reconciliation, and forgetfulness, it is above all the Left in Britain and elsewhere that has found both inspiration and division in the memory of the Spanish Civil War.

NOTES

All books published in London unless otherwise stated.

INTRODUCTION

1 N. Branson, *History of the Communist Party of Great Britain, 1927–1941* (1985), p. 163.
2 B. Crick, *George Orwell: A Life* (Harmondsworth, 1980), p. 312.
3 *Seaman*, 22 June 1938.
4 Bodleian Library, Oxford, Gilbert Murray papers, dep. 228, 8 April 1937, Murray to Eden.
5 World Student Association, *Spain Assailed: Student Delegates to Spain Report* (1936), p. 22 (article by Hugh Gosschalk, chairman of the University of London Liberal Association).
6 H. Thomas, *The Spanish Civil War* (1961), p. 348, n. 2. The comment is apocryphal but consistent with Pollitt's fixation with Byron during the Civil War (see pp. 121–2 in this volume).
7 *Daily Worker*, 30 November 1936.

1 OLD SPAIN, NEW SPAIN

1 In J. B. Priestly, *et al.*, *Spain and Us* (1936), p. 3.
2 Radio broadcast by Prime Minister Neville Chamberlain, 27 September 1938. He was referring to the conflict between Czechoslovakia and the Sudeten Germans, manipulated by Germany, which culminated in the Munich conference.
3 *House of Lords Debates*, vol. 105, 19 November 1936, col. 437.
4 From 'Spain' (1937), in V. Cunningham (ed.), *The Penguin Book of Spanish Civil War Verse* (1980), p. 99.
5 Unattributed comment in summary of discussion, PRO, CAB 23/86, Cabinet minutes, 16 December 1936, p. 6.
6 *Tablet*, 19 September 1936.
7 H. Brinton, *Christianity and Spain* (1938), p. 26.
8 Quoted in A. C. Guerrero, *Viajeros británicos en la España del siglo XVIII* (Madrid, 1990), p. 109.
9 R. Carr, *Spain, 1808–1975* (Oxford, 1982 edn), pp. 105–10.
10 G. Borrow, *The Bible in Spain* (1843; 1906 edn), p. 1.
11 R. Skidelsky, *Oswald Mosley* (1975), p. 215.

12 D. Little, *Malevolent Neutrality: The United States, Great Britain, and the Origins of the Spanish Civil War* (Ithaca, N. Y., 1985), p. 37.

13 J. Walton, 'British Perceptions of Spain and Their Impact on Attitudes to the Spanish Civil War', *Twentieth-Century British History*, 5:3, 1994, pp. 283–300, p. 291. In September 1936 Lloyd George told Hitler that 'Primo de Rivera had at least built roads on which motor-cars could travel with some degree of safety': cited in M. Gilbert, *The Roots of Appeasement* (1966), p. 203.

14 Little, *Malevolent Neutrality*, p. 54.

15 G. Young, *The New Spain* (1933), p. xviii. Sir George Young, a former diplomat, later organised relief work on the Republican side during the Civil War.

16 Note by W. H. Montagu-Pollock, 23 June 1936, DOBFP, 2nd series, vol. 17, p. 1.

17 On Franco's Civil War strategy, see P. Preston, *Franco* (1993), especially chapter 11.

18 D. S. Birn, *The League of Nations Union, 1918–1945* (Oxford, 1981), p. 2.

19 Frontispiece to W. Lippman, *The Phantom Public* (New York, 1927).

20 Hoare had, in association with his French counterpart Pierre Laval, sought to prevent the complete Italian conquest of Abyssinia by giving much of its territory to the aggressor.

21 PRO, FO 371 21343, W14544/7/41, 25 July 1937, Atholl to Eden.

22 A. Livingstone, *The Peace Ballot: The Official History* (1935).

23 R. Eatwell, 'Munich, Public Opinion, and the Popular Front', *Journal of Contemporary History*, 6:4, 1971, pp. 122–39, pp. 136–8.

24 C. Madge and T. Harrisson, *Britain by Mass Observation* (1939), p. 12.

25 Ibid., p. 8.

26 D. P. F. Lancien, 'British Left-Wing Attitudes to the Spanish Civil War', BLitt. thesis, University of Oxford, 1965, appendix 1.

27 Madge and Harrisson, *Britain by Mass Observation*, p. 30.

28 A. Aldgate, *Cinema and History: British Newsreels and the Spanish Civil War* (1979), p. 107.

29 P. de Azcárate, *Mi embajada en Londres durante la guerra civil española* (Barcelona, 1976), pp. 26–7.

30 F. Lannon, *Privilege, Persecution, and Prophecy: The Catholic Church in Spain, 1875–1975* (Oxford, 1987), p. 201; on atrocity stories in the press, see K. Martin, 'Spain and British Public Opinion', *Political Quarterly*, 7:4, 1936, pp. 573–87, pp. 579–82.

31 Quoted in R. A. C. Parker, *Chamberlain and Appeasement: British Policy and the Coming of the Second World War* (Basingstoke, 1993), p. 89.

32 Churchill College, Cambridge, Philip Noel-Baker Papers, Spain Correspondence, vol. I, 19 September 1936, Noel-Baker to Attlee.

33 F. Ryan (ed.), *The Book of the XV Brigade* (Newcastle upon Tyne, 1938; 1975 edn), p. 15.

34 T. Buchanan, 'A Far Away Country of Which We Know Nothing? Perceptions of Spain and Its Civil War in Britain, 1931–1939', *Twentieth-Century British History*, 4:1, 1993, pp. 1–24, pp. 11–14.

35 *Left Review*, October 1936 (emphasis added). On Bates, see pp. 154 and 163 in this volume.

36 G. L. Steer, *The Tree of Gernika: A Field Study of Modern War* (1938), pp. 12–13.

37 J. Langdon-Davies, *Air Raid* (St Albans, 1938), p. 13.

38 K. W. Watkins, *Britain Divided: The Effect of the Spanish Civil War on British Political Opinion* (Edinburgh, 1963), p. vii.

39 King's College, London, Liddell Hart papers, LH/11/1938, 'Reflections', 7 February 1938.

40 Quoted in P. Stansky and W. Abrahams, *Journey to the Frontier: Two Roads to the Spanish Civil War* (1966), p. 316.

41 G. Orwell, *Homage to Catalonia* (1938), p. 8.

42 University of Kent, Hewlett Johnson papers, diary, 9 April 1937.

43 K. Atholl, *Searchlight on Spain* (1938), p. 144.

44 University of Liverpool, Eleanor Rathbone papers, R P XIV 2.12, 26, 23 April 1937, Rathbone to Mrs D. Verstage.

45 *Left Review*, September 1937.

2 GOVERNMENT

1 PRO, FO 371 20520, W8416/62/41, letters of 11 August and 13 August 1936. Lord Halifax, who would become foreign secretary in 1938, was Lord Privy Seal and acting as Anthony Eden's deputy while he was on holiday.

2 PRO, CAB 23/86, Cabinet Minutes, 16 December 1936, comment by the home secretary, Sir John Simon.

3 J. Edwards, *The British Government and the Spanish Civil War, 1936–1939* (London and Basingstoke, 1979), p. 65.

4 Little, *Malevolent Neutrality*, p. 264.

5 Quoted in Edwards, *The British Government*, p. 212.

6 PRO, FO 371 21343, W14544 17/41, minute by Sir G. Mounsey, 3 August 1937.

7 J. Harvey (ed.), *The Diplomatic Diaries of Oliver Harvey, 1937–1940* (1970), p. 188; O. O'Malley, *The Phantom Caravan* (1954), p. 197; M. Peterson, *Both Sides of the Curtain* (1950), p. 184; C. Duff, *No Angel's Wing* (1947), p. 119.

8 DOBFP, 2nd series, vol. 17, p. 590, n. 4.

9 See Warwick University, MRC, Mss 126, T&GWU papers, sack 96: 21 October 1936, A. E. Huart to Bevin; 24 July 1936, Huart to Bevin; and 5 October 1937, W. G. Ormesby Gore to A. Creech Jones.

10 G. Thompson, *Front-Line Diplomat* (1959), p. 125.

11 Bodleian Library, Oxford, Gilbert Murray papers, dep. 225, 20 August 1936, Eden to Murray.

12 E. Moradiellos, 'British Political Strategy in the Face of the Military Rising of 1936 in Spain', *Contemporary European History*, 1:2, 1992, pp. 123–37, p. 137.

13 Quoted in G. Post, *Dilemmas of Appeasement: British Deterrence and Defense, 1934–1937* (Ithaca, N. Y., 1993), p. 260.

14 DOBFP, 2nd series, vol. 17, note of 5 August 1936, pp. 62–3.

15 Ibid., minute of 12 August 1936, pp. 90–1.

16 A view expressed in two recent books: Little, *Malevolent Neutrality*; and E. Moradiellos, *Neutralidad benévola: el gobierno británico y la insurrección militar español de 1936* (Oviedo, 1990).

17 Parl. Debs., vol. 319, 19 January 1937, col. 95.

18 Edwards, The British Government, p. 5.

19 DOBFP, 2nd series, vol. 17, p. 664.

20 Moradiellos, 'British Political Strategy', p. 131.

21 On 23 July a confidential telegram from the Foreign Office to the prime ministers of the Dominions noted that in Barcelona the situation was critical as the government there was 'at the mercy of the armed workers': quoted in E. Moradiellos, 'The Origins of British Non-Intervention in the Spanish Civil War: Anglo-Spanish Relations in Early 1936', European History Quarterly, 21:3, July 1991, pp. 339–64, p. 359.

22 DOBFP, 2nd series, vol. 17, p. 34, n. 5.

23 Ibid., pp. 61–3.

24 Ibid., pp. 136–8.

25 Ibid., pp. 151–4.

26 Edwards, The British Government, pp. 16–17.

27 T. Jones, A Diary with Letters, 1931–1950 (1959), p. 231, diary reference for 27 July 1936.

28 DOBFP, 2nd series, vol. 17, p. 72.

29 Edwards, The British Government, p. 27.

30 DOBFP, 2nd series, vol. 17, p. 49, n. 3.

31 Cited in Edwards, The British Government, p. 137.

32 PRO, FO 371 21333, W9357/7/41, 17 May 1937.

33 PRO, FO 371 20583/84, W14679/9549/41, 27–8 October 1936.

34 Parl. Debs., vol. 322, 6 April 1937, col. 25.

35 PRO, FO 371 21394, W22711/1786/41, 21 December 1937, W. Malkin.

36 DOBFP, 2nd series, vol. 17, p. 193, n. 1.

37 N. J. Padelford, International Law and Diplomacy in the Spanish Civil Strife (New York, 1939), pp. 7–10.

38 R. Hodgson, Spain Resurgent (1953), p. 85.

39 University of Liverpool, Eleanor Rathbone papers, XIV 2.14, letters to M. Stewart, organising secretary of the Parliamentary Committee for Spain, 18 and 28 November 1938.

40 A. Eden, Facing the Dictators (1962), p. 413.

41 Parl. Debs., vol. 317, 19 November 1936, col. 1923.

42 Edwards, The British Government, p. 147, n. 68.

43 Memorandum by Sir Auckland Geddes, quoted in C. E. Harvey, The Rio Tinto Company: An Economic History of a Leading International Mining Concern, 1873–1954 (Penzance, 1981), p. 261.

44 DOBFP, 2nd series, vol. 18, p. 665.

45 See chapter 4 in this volume.

46 PRO, FO 371 22667, W3384/203/41, 12 March 1938, letter from Norman Brook (of the Home Office).

47 Parl. Debs., vol. 328, col. 1523, 8 November 1937, Lt Commander Fletcher.

48 Bodleian Library, Oxford, Francis Hemming papers, Ms CCC 536, diary entry for 29 October 1938.

49 On Alba's political connections, see E. Moradiellos, *La perfidia de Albión: el gobierno británico y la guerra civil española* (Madrid, 1996), p. 191.

50 *The Times*, 16 October 1937.

51 DOBFP, 2nd series, vol. 19, p. 1092.

52 Edwards, *The British Government*, p. 131.

53 I. McLeod, *Neville Chamberlain* (1961), p. 222.

54 PRO, CAB 23/95, Cabinet minutes, 9 November and 30 November 1938.

55 Comment by Charles Howard Smith, quoted in Edwards, *The British Government*, p. 157.

3 POLITICS

1 E. Hobsbawm, *Age of Extremes: The Short Twentieth Century, 1914–1991* (Harmondsworth, 1994), p. 160; J. Saville, 'May Day 1937', in Saville and A. Briggs (eds.), *Essays in Labour History, 1918–1939* (1977).

2 See University of Hull, National Council for Civil Liberties papers, DCL, 8/6, files on 'Police – Demonstrations'.

3 On the committee, see S. Bruley, 'Women Against War and Fascism: Communism, Feminism, and the People's Front', in J. Fyrth (ed.), *Britain, Fascism, and the Popular Front* (1985), p. 145.

4 *Labour Discussion Notes*, July 1939.

5 *Stornoway Gazette*, 10 January 1938.

6 NMLH, CP papers, CC minutes, 16 January 1937, p. 16.

7 Quoted in F. Brockway, *Bermondsey Story: The Life of Alfred Salter* (1949), p. 200.

8 Bodleian Library, Gilbert Murray papers, dep. 226, 12 October 1936, Murray to Lord Cecil.

9 NMLH, CP papers, CC minutes, 16 January 1937.

10 PRO, FO 371 21343, W14544/7/41, 25 July 1937, Atholl to Eden. In February 1933 a resolution had been passed at the Oxford Union that 'this House would not fight for King and Country'.

11 Ted Bramley quoted in *Daily Worker*, 14 September 1936.

12 NMLH, CP papers, CC minutes, 10 October 1936.

13 NMLH, CP papers, Political Bureau minutes, 11 September 1936.

14 *Daily Worker*, 21 July 1936.

15 *Daily Worker*, 9 October 1936.

16 *Daily Worker*, 6 August 1936. In the first flush of enthusiasm at the start of the Civil War, the *Daily Worker* had called for the creation of a 'Spanish Soviet Republic' (22 July 1936).

17 NMLH, CP papers, CC minutes, 16 January 1937.

18 *Daily Worker*, 31 May and 10 June 1937.

19 Lancien, 'British Left-Wing Attitudes to the Spanish Civil War', p. 54.

20 NMLH, CP papers, CC minutes, November 1936.

21 P. Drake, 'Labour and Spain: British Labour's Response to the Spanish Civil War with Particular Reference to the Labour Movement in Birmingham', MLitt. thesis, University of Birmingham, 1977.

22 H. Francis, *Miners Against Fascism: Wales and the Spanish Civil War* (1984), p. 118.

23 M. Squires, *The Aid to Spain Movement in Battersea, 1936–1939* (1994).

24 NMLH, CP papers, CC minutes, 16 August 1937, comments by Idris Cox, William Rust, George Brown, and Rajani Palme Dutt.

25 On the history of the ILP, see R. Dowse, *Left in the Centre: The Independent Labour Party, 1893–1940* (1966).

26 *New Leader*, 14 and 28 August 1936.

27 *New Leader*, 31 July 1936 (emphasis in original).

28 *New Leader*, 28 May 1937.

29 Harvester, Archives of the ILP, Series II, Card 25, NAC minutes, Treasurer's Report for 1937, 11–12 December 1937.

30 *New Leader*, 4 December 1936.

31 Harvester, Archives of the ILP, Series II, Card 25, NAC minutes, 11–12 December 1937.

32 Captain Ramsay brought McGovern's pamphlet to the attention of the Foreign Office as further proof of Soviet clandestine activity in Spain: PRO, FO 371 22625, W5988/29/41, FO minute, W. Roberts, 10 May 1938.

33 Harvester, Archives of the ILP, Series II, Card 25, 13 November 1937, report by F. Brockway on 'A Survey of the Party Position', p. 4.

34 Dowse, *Left in the Centre*, pp. 190–8.

35 See T. Buchanan, *The Spanish Civil War and the British Labour Movement* (Cambridge, 1991).

36 See chapter 7 in this volume.

37 PRO, FO 371, W13175/9549/41, FO minute, 9 October 1936. Dolores Ibarruri ('La Pasionaria') was one of the leaders of the Spanish Communist Party and the best-known orator of the war-time Republic. Isabel de Palancia spoke so effectively that many of those who attended the Edinburgh conference later believed that they had listened to La Pasionaria herself.

38 Buchanan, *The Spanish Civil War and the British Labour Movement*, pp. 120–36.

39 PRO, CAB 23/90A, Cabinet minutes, 22 December 1937,

40 *Parl. Debs.*, vol. 330, 9 December 1937, cols. 565 and 821–4. Attlee was alluding to Labour's handsome victory earlier in the year in the elections for the London County Council.

41 *Parl. Debs.*, vol. 337, 21 June 1937, col. 1013.

42 Quoted in Lancien, 'British Left-Wing Attitudes to the Spanish Civil War', p. 76.

43 House of Lords Records Office, Lloyd George papers, G/1/14/6, 14 December 1936, Noel-Baker to Lloyd George.

44 Warwick University, MRC, W. Roberts papers, Mss 308/3/NC/1–55, 21 April 1938, H. Elvin to Roberts.

45 Quoted in M. Baines, 'The Survival of the British Liberal Party, 1932–1959', DPhil. thesis, University of Oxford, 1989, p. 40.

46 L. S. Amery, *My Political Life*, vol. III, *The Unforgiving Years, 1929–1940* (1955), p. 193

47 N. Nicolson (ed.), *Harold Nicolson: Diaries and Letters, 1930–1939* (1966), p. 307; R. Rhodes James, 'Chips': The Diaries of Sir Henry Channon (1967; 1993 edn), p. 153. See

also Martin Gilbert, *Winston S. Churchill*, vol. V, *Companion Part 3, 1936–1939* (1982), p. 297.

48 Quoted in Little, *Malevolent Neutrality*, p. 226.

49 Quoted in Moradiellos, 'British Political Strategy', p. 129, n. 17.

50 R. Rodriguez-Moñino Soriano, *La misión diplomática de Don Jacobo Stuart Fitz James y Falcó XVII Duque de Alba, en la embajada de España en Londres* (Valencia, 1971), p. 34.

51 Drake, 'Labour and Spain', p. 106.

52 House of Lords Record Office, Lloyd George papers, G/1/11/5, 11 January 1939, Atholl to Lloyd George.

53 S. Ball, 'The Politics of Appeasement: The Fall of the Duchess of Atholl and the Kinross and West Perth By-election, December 1938', *Scottish Historical Review*, 187, April 1990, pp. 49–85.

54 Moradiellos, *Neutralidad benévola*, p. 173.

55 Azcárate, *Mi embajada en Londres durante la guerra civil española*, p. 27.

56 Brigadier Pakenham-Walsh's diary for 17 October 1937, cited in Gilbert, *Companion Part 3, 1936–1939*, p. 800.

57 R. Rhodes James, *Churchill: A Study in Failure, 1900–1939* (1973), p. 409.

58 *Daily Worker*, 29 April 1937.

59 *Tablet*, 9 January 1937.

60 *Highway*, December 1937. For more on Bryant's support for Franco, see A. Roberts, *Eminent Churchillians* (1994), pp. 291–3.

61 King's College London, Liddell Hart papers, 1/27/11, 23 December 1937, Atholl to Liddell Hart.

62 *Middleton Gazette*, 29 January 1938.

63 Warwick University, MRC, Mss 292, TUC papers, file 946/521.

64 *Action*, 6 August 1936.

65 Hull University Library, Union of Democratic Control papers, DDC 5/373, BUF speakers' notes no. 19, September 1936.

66 PRO, FO 371 22666, W1934/203/41, 3 February 1938, report from Hull Immigration Office, dated 31 January 1938.

67 Parker, *Chamberlain and Appeasement*, p. 91; N. Thompson, *The Anti-Appeasers: Conservative Opposition to Appeasement in the 1930s* (Oxford, 1971), pp. 116–19.

68 H. Dalton, *The Fateful Years: Memoirs, 1931–1945* (1957), p. 202.

4 AID

1 This was the Voluntary Industrial Aid for Spain Committee. See D. Lampe, *Pyke: The Unknown Genius* (Aylesbury and Slough, 1959), pp. 64–8.

2 G. Finlayson, *Citizen, State, and Social Welfare in Britain, 1830–1990* (Oxford, 1994), pp. 220–2.

3 *Parl. Debs.*, vol. 318, 16 December 1936, cols. 2433–4.

4 M. Alpert, 'Humanitarianism and Politics in the British Response to the Spanish Civil War, 1936–1939', *European History Quarterly*, 14:4, 1984, pp. 423–40, p. 436.

5 PRO, FO 371 21370, W9147/37/41, 5 May 1937, Foreign Office to British Consul in Bilbao.

6 PRO, CAB 23/90A, Cabinet minutes, 15 December 1937.

7 I. MacDougall (ed.), *Voices from the Spanish Civil War: Personal Recollections of Scottish Volunteers in Republican Spain, 1936–1939* (Edinburgh, 1986), p. 78.

8 D. Hyde, *I Believed* (Bungay, Suffolk, 1950), pp. 58–9. Hyde was later to leave the Communist Party and convert to Catholicism.

9 National Library of Scotland, Acc. 9083, Thomas Murray papers, 26 June 1938, J. Murray to T. Murray.

10 Friends Service Council papers, SP/1/4, 30 December 1938, D. Thompson to A. Jacob.

11 See especially J. Fyrth, *The Signal Was Spain: The Aid Spain Movement in Britain, 1936–1939* (1986).

12 Warwick University, MRC, W. Roberts papers, Mss 308/3/NJC/1, typed report, undated.

13 Friends' Service Council papers, FSC minutes, 13 January 1937.

14 Save the Children Fund papers, Council minutes, 17 June 1937.

15 D. Legarretta, *The Guernica Generation: Basque Refugee Children of the Spanish Civil War* (Reno, Nev., 1984), p. 128.

16 FO 371 21370, W1945/37/41, 21 April 1937, minute by W. H. Montagu-Pollock.

17 Save the Children Fund papers, Council minutes, 17 March 1938.

18 *Parl. Debs.*, vol. 321, 2 March 1937, cols. 208–9.

19 Save the Children Fund, Council minutes, 21 October 1937.

20 Ruskin College, Oxford, James Middleton papers, MID 59, 14 January 1937, T. Baxter to Middleton.

21 Warwick University, MRC, TUC archive, Mss 292/946/41, Spanish Medical Aid (1), 9 April 1937, Bolton to Citrine; Mss 292/946/42, report by Morgan, 18 August 1937.

22 Warwick University, MRC, TUC archive, Mss 292/946/41, Spanish Medical Aid (1), 11 August 1936, verbatim report of meeting.

23 Ibid., p. 6.

24 P. Churchill, *All My Sins Remembered* (1964), p. 158.

25 Warwick University, MRC, TUC archive, Mss 292/946/41, memorandum dated 30 November 1936.

26 MML, IB papers, Box C, 7/5, 30 November 1936, 'A. P.' to R. Robson.

27 MML, IB papers, Box C, 12/3, W. Tapsell, report on 'position in the British Medical Unit', 21 April 1937.

28 *Guardian*, 24 April 1993.

29 Warwick University, MRC, TUC archive, Mss 292/946/42, report on International Conference for Aid to Spain, 1938.

30 R. Rees, *A Theory of My Time: An Essay in Didactic Reminiscence* (1963), p. 104; Fyrth, *The Signal*, pp. 85–7.

31 Bodleian Library, Oxford, Addison papers, 14 June 1937, B. Barnard and A. Ware to Addison; Churchill, *All My Sins*, p. 167.

32 Warwick University, MRC, TUC archive, Mss 292/946/42, 14 June 1938, G. Jeger to Citrine.

33 Squires, *The Aid to Spain Movement in Battersea*, pp. 12–17.

34 Bodleian Library, Oxford, Addison papers, 20.2, notes by organising secretary, 27 September 1937.

35 Bodleian Library, Oxford, Addison papers, file 20.2, report.

36 Bodleian Library, Oxford, Addison papers, 20.2, notes by organising secretary, 27 September 1937.

37 Warwick University, MRC, TUC archive, Mss 292/946/43, Spanish Medical Aid Committee minutes, 13 July 1938.

38 Fyrth, *The Signal*, p. 120.

39 Warwick University, MRC, TUC archive, Mss 292/946/42, 21 April 1939, Stevenson to Citrine.

40 Warwick University, MRC, TUC archive, Mss 292/946/41, 12 November 1936, P. Dollan to Citrine.

41 Warwick University, MRC, TUC archive, Mss 292/946/41, 12 November 1936, telephone conversation with W. Elgar.

42 Warwick University, MRC, TUC archive, Mss 292/946/41, 30 March 1937, L. Crome, R. McFarquhar, and M. Linden to National Council of Labour.

43 Fyrth, *The Signal*, p. 190.

44 PRO, FO 371 21370, W9147/37/41, memorandum, 5 May 1937.

45 Friends' Service Council papers, FSC minutes, 26 May 1937.

46 PRO, FO 371 21377, W18793/37/41, 6 October 1937, Hinsley to Hoare.

47 Warwick University, MRC, TUC archive, Mss 292/946/39, Basque Children's Committee, minutes, 31 May 1937.

48 Ibid.

49 Fyrth, *The Signal*, p. 224.

50 PRO, FO 371 21372, W12532/37/41, 5 July 1937, Mounsey to Chilton.

51 Warwick University, MRC, TUC archive, Basque Children's Committee minutes, 1 October 1937.

52 Warwick University, MRC, W. Roberts papers, Mss 308/3/RO, 2 April 1938, F. Pittman to Mr Turner.

53 Legarretta, *The Guernica Generation*, p. 134.

54 C. M. Skran, *Refugees in Inter-War Europe: The Emergence of a Regime* (Oxford, 1995), pp. 58–9.

55 Friends Service Council papers, Spain committee minutes, 16 February 1938.

56 Friends Service Council papers, FSC/R/SP/1/1, 3 October 1936, Jacob to F. Tritton.

57 Friends Service Council papers, FSC/R/SP/3/2, 5 May 1938, B. Wood to E. Hughes.

58 Friends Service Council papers, FSC/R/SP/1/1, 7 October 1936, Jacob to F. Tritton.

59 Friends Service Council papers, FSC/R/SP/1/3, 14 March 1937, A. Jacob and N. Jacob to F. Tritton.

60 Save the Children Fund papers, Council minutes, 15 July 1937.

61 Alpert, 'Humanitarianism and Politics', p. 428.

62 Diocese of Southwark, Amigo papers, 1 September 1936, G. Damard to Amigo.

63 Westminster Diocese, Hinsley papers, Hi 2/217, 17 September 1937, M. Melvin to Hinsley.

64 T. Moloney, *Westminster, Whitehall, and the Vatican: The Role of Cardinal Hinsley, 1935–1943* (1985), p. 68.

65 Diocese of Southwark, Amigo papers, report dated 22 October 1937.

66 *Tablet*, 26 February 1938.

67 Diocese of Southwark, Amigo papers, 1 December 1936.

5 VOLUNTEERS

1 Bodleian Library, Oxford, Nevinson papers, Ms.Eng.Misc.e.626, journal entry for 10 December 1936.

2 F. M. Leventhal, *The Last Dissenter: H. N. Brailsford and His World* (Oxford, 1985), p. 252.

3 J. Lehmann, T. A. Jackson, and C. Day Lewis (eds.), *Ralph Fox: A Writer in Arms* (1937), p. 6.

4 Thomas, *The Spanish Civil War*, appendix III, pp. 634–9.

5 R. D. Richardson, *Comintern Army: The International Brigades in the Spanish Civil War* (Lexington, Ky., 1982).

6 The unit was named in honour of Tom Mann (1856–1941), the militant trade unionist and Communist.

7 P. Sloan (ed.), *John Cornford: A Memoir* (1938), pp. 210–11.

8 T. Wintringham, *English Captain* (1939), p. 29.

9 MML, IB archive, Box C, 5/3, 10 September 1936, Wintringham to Pollitt.

10 Francis, *Miners Against Fascism*, pp. 161–2.

11 NMLH, CP papers, CC minutes, 10 October 1936; MML, IB papers, Box C, 7/2, Wintringham to Pollitt.

12 Elstob had, in fact, been making notes with a view to publication. See B. Bridgeman, *The Flyers* (Reading, 1989), pp. 185–6.

13 MML, IB papers, Box C, Bates to Pollitt, n.d.

14 E. Romilly, *Boadilla* (1937), p. 56.

15 MML, IB papers, Box C, 10/5, 7 February 1937, P. Kerrigan to Pollitt. Nathan had a murky past, which included an alleged part in the assassination of two Irish Republicans in 1921 (see V. Brome, *The International Brigades: Spain, 1936–1939* (1965), p. 279, and Richard Bennett, 'Portrait of a Killer', *New Statesman*, 24 March 1961).

16 R. Crossman (ed.), *The God That Failed: Six Studies in Communism* (1950), p. 245.

17 MML, IB papers, Box C, 1/1, note on analysis of British Battalion members.

18 King's College London, Liddell Hart papers, LH/1/758, 16 September 1938, Wintringham to B. Liddell Hart.

19 *New Statesman*, 9 January 1937.

20 PRO, FO 371 21331, W7469/7/41, 14 April 1937, Peck to Roberts.

21 C. Haldane, Truth Will Out (1949), p. 114.

22 J. Cook, Apprentices of Freedom (1979), p. 65.

23 C. Haden Guest (ed.), David Guest: A Scientist Fights for Freedom (1939), p. 175.

24 Quoted in Francis, Miners Against Fascism, p. 272.

25 Warwick University, MRC, Mss 21/1449, 26 December 1937, 'Ken' to 'Ted'.

26 Sloan, John Cornford, p. 197.

27 Wintringham, English Captain, p. 205.

28 J. Sommerfield, Volunteer in Spain (1937), p. 102.

29 PRO, FO 371 21320, W1136/7/41, 13 January 1937, report on meeting of London District Communist Party.

30 W. Gregory, The Shallow Grave: A Memoir of the Spanish Civil War (1986), pp. 19–21.

31 R. Felsted, No Other Way: Jack Russia and the Spanish Civil War (Port Talbot, 1981), p. 35.

32 H. Francis, '"Say Nothing and Leave in the Middle of the Night": The Spanish Civil War Revisited', History Workshop Journal, 32, Autumn 1991, pp. 71–2.

33 Ryan, Book of the XV Brigade, p. 218.

34 MML, IB papers, Box C, 10 February 1937, Kerrigan to Pollitt.

35 NMLH, CP papers, Political Bureau minutes, 11 March 1937.

36 King's College London, Liddell Hart papers, LH/1/758, 16 September 1938, Wintringham to Liddell Hart.

37 MML, IB papers, Box C, 17/7, statement by G. Aitken.

38 MML, IB papers, Box C, 9/8, 19 January 1937, Springhall and Kerrigan to Pollitt.

39 MML, IB papers, Box C, 9/3, 6 January 1937.

40 MML, IB papers, Box C, 9/10, 23 January 1937, Springhall to Pollitt.

41 MML, IB papers, Box C, 9/11, 24 January 1937, Kerrigan to Pollitt.

42 Francis, Miners Against Fascism, p. 175.

43 T. Buchanan, 'The Death of Bob Smillie, the Spanish Civil War, and the Eclipse of the Independent Labour Party', forthcoming Historical Journal, 1997.

44 MML, IB papers, Box C, 10/5, 7 February 1937.

45 J. Gurney, Crusade in Spain (1974), p. 107.

46 T. A. R. Hyndman in P. Toynbee (ed.), The Distant Drum: Reflections on the Spanish Civil War (1976), p. 125.

47 Cunningham, Penguin Book of Spanish Civil War Verse, p. 75.

48 B. Alexander, British Volunteers for Liberty: Spain, 1936–1939 (1982), p. 81.

49 J. Angus, With the International Brigade in Spain (Loughborough, 1983), pp. 7–8.

50 NMLH, CP papers, Political Bureau minutes, 25 March 1937.

51 Francis, Miners Against Fascism, pp. 230–1.

52 Felsted, No Other Way, p. 112.

53 MML, IB papers, Box C, 13/1, May 1937, Tapsell to Pollitt.

54 V. Cunningham, Spanish Front: Writers on the Civil War (Oxford, 1986), p. 308.

55 MML, IB papers, Box C, 15/6, J. Hinks to W. Paynter.

56 Communist Party of Great Britain, Report of the Central Committee to the Fourteenth National Congress, 1937, p. 9.

57 Francis, Miners Against Fascism, p. 232.

58 W. Rust, *Britons in Spain: The History of the British Battalion of the XVth Brigade* (1939), p. 98.

59 Francis, *Miners Against Fascism*, p. 283.

60 MML, IBA papers, Box C, 12/4, 25 April 1937, Tapsell to Pollitt.

61 Alexander, *British Volunteers for Liberty*, p. 202.

62 D. Corkill and S. Rawnsley (eds.), *The Road to Spain: Anti-Fascists at War, 1936–1939* (Dunfermline, 1981), p. 120.

63 NMLH, CP papers, report to CC, 2 July 1938.

64 Alexander, *British Volunteers for Liberty*, p. 215.

65 See p. 55, in this volume.

66 NMLH, CP papers, CC minutes, October 1937.

67 Francis, *Miners Against Fascism*, p. 173.

68 Ibid., pp. 173–4.

69 *Parl. Debs.*, vol. 338, 27 July 1938, cols. 3185–92.

70 MML, IB papers, Box C, 24/1, 1 August 1938, Rust to Communist Party Secretariat.

71 NMLH, CP papers, CC minutes, 16 January 1937.

72 National Library of Scotland, David Murray papers, Accs. 7914, Box 1, File 2, 2 August 1937, J. Lacey to Murray.

73 MRC, TUC archive, file 946/535, 16 September 1938, Mr Boswell to Citrine.

74 National Library of Scotland, David Murray papers, Accs. 7914, Box 1, File 2, July 1937, D. Donald to Murray.

75 *Parl. Debs.*, vol. 326, 30 July 1937, col. 3558.

76 Thompson, *Front-Line Diplomat*, pp. 119–20.

77 Rust, *Britons in Spain*, p. 8.

78 Interview with volunteer Hugh Sloan, cited in MacDougall, *Voices from the Spanish Civil War*, p. 199.

79 Lehmann *et al.*, *Ralph Fox*, p. 6.

6 INTELLECTUALS

1 A. Malraux, *Days of Hope* (first published in French as *L'Espoir*, 1938; 1982 edn), p. 133 (emphasis in original).

2 King's College London, Liddell Hart papers, LH/11/1937/23a, 18 April 1937.

3 Quoted in S. Hynes, *The Auden Generation: Literature and Politics in England in the 1930s* (1976), p. 65.

4 *Daily Worker*, 11 September 1935, quoted in J. Coombes, 'British Intellectuals and the Popular Front', in F. Gloversmith (ed.), *Class, Culture, and Social Change: A New View of the 1930s* (1980), p. 75.

5 S. Spender, *World Within World* (1951), p. 211.

6 Branson, *History of the Communist Party of Great Britain, 1927–1941*, p. 209.

7 Quoted in S. Samuels, 'The Left Book Club', *Journal of Contemporary History*, 1:2, 1966, pp. 65–86, p. 68.

8 I am grateful to David Bradshaw for allowing me to consult his unpublished paper on 'British Writers and Anti-Fascism in the 1930s'.

9 Quoted in Cunningham, *Penguin Book of Spanish Civil War Verse*, p. 29.

10 *The Times*, 19 August 1936.

11 From Spender's contribution to *Authors Take Sides*.

12 K. Martin, 'Thoughts on Spain', in E. Allen Osborne (ed.), *In Letters of Red* (1938), p. 191.

13 World Student Association, *Spain Assailed*, pp. 29–30.

14 *Listener*, 12 January 1938.

15 Articles in *Dublin Review*, April 1937 and January 1938.

16 *Fortnightly*, March 1936 and January 1939.

17 Haldane, *Truth Will Out*, pp. 90–1.

18 See in particular N. Chomsky, 'Objectivity and Liberal Scholarship', in *American Power and the New Mandarins* (London, 1969), and B. Bolloten, *The Spanish Civil War: Revolution and Counter-Revolution* (Chapel Hill, N. C., 1991).

19 G. Orwell, *Collected Essays, Journalism, and Letters*, 4 vols. (Harmondsworth, 1970), vol. I, p. 308.

20 Crick, *George Orwell*, p. 341.

21 *New Statesman*, 22 May 1937.

22 R. Bates, *The Olive Field* (1936), p. 477.

23 R. G. Collingwood, *An Autobiography* (Oxford, 1939; 1978 edn), p. 159.

24 F. Jellinek, *The Civil War in Spain* (1938), p. 21.

25 'Impressions of Valencia', *New Statesman*, 30 January 1937.

26 In Cunningham, *Spanish Front*, p. 307.

27 J. Langdon-Davies, *Behind the Spanish Barricades* (1936), p. 204.

28 H. Gannes and T. Repard, *Spain in Revolt* (1936), p. 165.

29 *New Statesman*, 15 May 1937.

30 *New Statesman*, 22 May 1937.

31 H. Runham Brown, *Spain: A Challenge to Pacifism* (n.d.), p. 7.

32 A. Huxley, *Ends and Means* (1937), p. 145.

33 From her contribution to *Authors Take Sides*.

34 R. Crossley, *Olaf Stapledon: Speaking for the Future* (Liverpool, 1994); Liverpool University Library, Olaf Stapledon papers, F.45, notes for lecture on 'International Brigade'.

35 Cunningham, *Penguin Book of Spanish Civil War Verse*, pp. 67–8.

36 MML, IBA papers, Box C, 7/1, report dated 9–10 October 1936.

37 Francis, *Miners Against Fascism*, p. 102.

38 Jellinek, *The Civil War in Spain*.

39 Imperial War Museum, Sound Archives, 0010059/4, Sir Geoffrey Cox.

40 *Left News*, May and October 1938.

41 Quoted in Cunningham, *Spanish Front*, p. 51.

42 A. Chisholm, *Nancy Cunard* (1979), p. 240.

43 V. Cunningham, 'Neutral? 1930s Writers and Taking Sides', in Gloversmith, *Class, Culture, and Social Change*, pp. 45–69.

44 Orwell, *Collected Essays*, vol. I, p. 346.

45 N. Sherry, *The Life of Graham Greene*, vol. I, 1904–1939 (1989), pp. 612–13.

46 W. Lewis, *The Revenge for Love* (1937); *Count Your Dead: They Are Alive or The New War in the Making* (1937).

47 Cunningham, *Spanish Front*, p. 71.

48 T. Burns, *The Uses of Memory: Publishing and Further Pursuits* (1993), p. 74.

49 MML, IBA papers, Box C, 12/3, report by W. Tapsell on 'Case of Comrade O'Donnell'.

50 J. Poster, *The Thirties Poets* (Buckingham, 1993), pp. 17–19.

51 In J. Pike (ed.), *Modern Canterbury Pilgrims* (1956), p. 41.

52 *New Statesman*, 1 May 1937.

53 Spender, *World Within World*, pp. 239–43, and in Crossman, *The God That Failed*, pp. 251–2.

54 Rees, *A Theory of My Time*, pp. 95–110.

55 L. Lee, *A Moment of War* (1991), pp. 49 and 46.

56 Orwell, *Homage to Catalonia*, p. 101.

57 Quoted in C. Norris (ed.), *Inside the Myth. Orwell: Views from the Left* (1984), p. 93.

58 *Observer*, 5 November 1989.

59 Letter to F. Jellinek, 20 December 1938, in *Collected Essays*, vol. I, p. 404.

60 'Caesarean Section in Spain', *Highway*, March 1939; R. Stradling, 'Orwell and the Spanish Civil War: A Historical Critique', in Norris, *Inside the Myth*.

61 Orwell, *Collected Essays*, vol. II, pp. 286–306.

62 F. Borkenau, *The Spanish Cockpit* (1937), p. 256.

63 A. Koestler, *The Invisible Writing: An Autobiography* (1954), p. 383.

64 Orwell, *Collected Essays*, vol. II, p. 294.

7 RELIGION

1 M. Shelden, *Orwell: The Authorised Biography* (1991), p. 308.

2 Francis, *Miners Against Fascism*, p. 123; on the political context, see D. Bebbington, 'Baptists and Politics Since 1914', in K. W. Clements (ed.), *Baptists in the Twentieth Century* (1983), p. 76.

3 *The Times*, 13 October 1936.

4 Quoted in *The Times*, 1 October 1936.

5 *The Times*, 8 September 1937.

6 Lambeth Palace, Lang papers, 166, 11 November 1938, Lang to W. Temple; 3 January 1939, A. Don to Temple, and reply, 5 January 1939.

7 *House of Lords Debs.*, vol. 105, 29 April 1937, col. 92.

8 Lambeth Palace, Bell papers, Ms 210, correspondence, 2 September and 13 October 1937.

9 Lambeth Palace, Lang papers, Ms 149, 24 April 1937, H. Johnson to Lang.

10 The report is contained in the Parliamentary Committee for Spain's pamphlet, *Religion and Spain* (1938), pp. 20–7.

11 D. R. Davies, *In Search of Myself* (1961), pp. 163–4.

12 Ibid., pp. 166 and 176–85.

13 *Morning Post*, 19 April 1937.

14 Lambeth Palace, Lang papers, Ms 149, memorandum by Revd A. C. Don, 7 June 1937.

15 *Church Times*, 25 June 1937.

16 Lambeth Palace, Ms 2864, A. C. Don, diary for 1936, 9 June 1937.

17 K. G. Grubb, *Evangelical Christianity in Spain* (1937), p. 5.

18 *Methodist Recorder*, 18 February 1937.

19 Friends Service Council papers, FSC/R/SP/3/2, 5 May 1938, B. Wood to E. Hughes.

20 *Tablet*, 25 March 1939, obituary for Sir Henry Lunn by Christopher Hollis.

21 Lambeth Palace, Bell papers, Ms 210, 21 July 1938.

22 *Tablet*, 25 September 1937.

23 Westminster Diocesan archives, Hinsley papers, Hi 2/217, 12 February 1938, Hinsley to Marquis del Moral.

24 *Tablet*, 26 March 1938.

25 *The Times*, 13 October 1936.

26 Westminster diocesan archives, Hinsley papers, Hi 2/76, 4 February 1938, Hinsley to Fr Gosling.

27 J. M. Sanchez, *The Spanish Civil War as a Religious Tragedy* (Notre Dame, Ind., 1987), p. 123.

28 *Tablet*, 25 July 1937; *Catholic Herald*, 31 July and 21 August 1937.

29 *The Times*, 7 August 1936.

30 Westminster diocesan archives, Hinsley papers, Hi 2/217, 7 November 1937, Gomá to Hinsley.

31 M. Clifton, *Amigo: Friend of the Poor* (Leominster, 1987), p. 143.

32 See, for instance, J. Flint, 'Must God Go Fascist? English Catholic Opinion and the Spanish Civil War', *Church History*, 56, 1987, pp. 264–74.

33 *Blackfriars*, September and October 1936.

34 Author's interview with Bob Walsh, 31 January 1985.

35 *Blackfriars*, July 1937.

36 J. Keating, 'Looking to Europe: Roman Catholics and Christian Democracy in 1930s Britain', *European History Quarterly*, 26:1, January 1996, pp. 57–79, p. 66.

37 *Colosseum*, March 1937.

38 *Ibid.*

39 *Blackfriars*, April 1939.

40 Cited in Moloney, *Westminster, Whitehall, and the Vatican*, p. 65.

41 Westminster diocesan archives, Hinsley papers, Hi 2/55.

42 Plater College Archives, Oxford, John Ford file, 14 May 1938, Ford to Fr O'Hea.

43 University of Liverpool, Eleanor Rathbone papers, RP xiv 2.11, 13 June 1938, Rathbone, letter to the press.

44 Westminster diocesan archives, Hinsley papers, Hi 2/55, 22 January 1937.

45 Buchanan, *The Spanish Civil War and the British Labour Movement*, pp. 189–90.

46 *Catholic Herald*, 22 January 1937.

47 *Arena*, April 1937.

48 *Tablet*, 24 October 1936.

49 *Tablet*, 21 August 1937.

50 *Tablet*, 18 June 1938.

51 *Month*, November 1936.

52 *Tablet*, 19 and 26 September 1936.

53 *Tablet*, 1 May 1937.

54 *Month*, April 1937.

55 *Tablet*, 26 February 1938.

56 Westminster Diocesan Archives, Hinsley papers, Hi 2/217.

57 *Catholic Worker*, August 1936.

EPILOGUE

1 Bodleian Library, Oxford, Hemming papers, CCC 536, diary for 13–15 March 1939.

2 T. Wintringham, *New Ways of War* (1940), pp. 92–3. On the impact of the Spanish Civil War on the creation of a Home Guard, see S. P. Mackenzie, *The Home Guard: A Military and Political History* (Oxford, 1996), pp. 68–76.

3 Orwell, *Collected Essays*, vol. II, p. 113.

4 B. Alexander, *No to Franco: The Struggle Never Stopped, 1939–1975* (1992), p. 20.

5 K. Morgan, *Harry Pollitt* (Manchester, 1993), p. 109.

6 M. E. Williams, *St Alban's College, Valladolid: Four Centuries of English Catholic Presence in Spain* (1986), p. 217.

7 Westminster diocesan archives, Hinsley papers, Hi 2/217, 15 June 1940, Hinsley to Starkie.

8 Quoted in S. Mews, 'The Sword of the Spirit: A Catholic Cultural Crusade of 1940', in W. J. Shiels (ed.), *Studies in Church History*, 20 (1983), p. 421.

9 See P. Preston, 'Franco and Hitler: The Myth of Hendaye 1940', *Contemporary European History*, 1:1, 1992, pp. 1–16.

10 Quoted in Watkins, *Britain Divided*, p. 252.

11 Quoted ibid., p. 251.

12 Q. Ahmad, *Britain, Franco Spain, and the Cold War, 1945–1950* (New York, 1992), p. 16.

13 G. Brenan, *The Face of Spain* (1950), p. xvii.

14 L. Manning, *A Life for Education: An Autobiography* (1970), p. 140.

15 Alexander, *No to Franco*, p. 57.

16 Scottish Catholic archives, Edinburgh, Bishop of Galloway papers, DG 19/9, 4 January 1956, Fraser to Bishop McGee.

17 Carr, *Spain, 1808–1975*, p. 715.

18 Watkins, *Britain Divided*, p. 249.

19 Earl of Halifax, *Fulness of Days* (1957), pp. 192–3.

20 Watkins, *Britain Divided*, p. 209.

21 *Guardian*, 7 August 1993.

22 *Guardian*, 29 September 1995.

BIBLIOGRAPHY

All books published in London unless otherwise stated.

1 ARCHIVAL SOURCES

The largest single archive concerned with British involvement in the Civil War is the Public Records Office at Kew, London, which holds the papers of the Cabinet and Foreign Office as well as other interested ministries such as the War Office, Admiralty, and Board of Trade. The work of the Non-Intervention Committee can also be studied through the Francis Hemming papers in the Bodleian Library, Oxford.

Archival sources are far fuller for political parties of the Left than for the Conservatives: see, in particular, the Labour Party and Communist Party archives at the National Museum for Labour History (NMLH) in Manchester and the papers of the Labour Spain Committee at Churchill College, Cambridge. The Modern Records Centre (MRC) at the University of Warwick holds the archives of the Trades Union Congress (TUC), the International Transport Workers' Federation, and a number of leading trade unions, such as the Amalgamated Engineering Union and the Transport and General Workers' Union. Papers of many politicians also deal with the Civil War to some degree, including Stanley Baldwin and Samuel Hoare (Lord Temple-wood) (both held in the University Library, Cambridge), Neville Chamberlain and Anthony Eden (both held in Birmingham University Library), R. A. B. Butler (Trinity College, Cambridge), Sir Stafford Cripps (Nuffield College, Oxford), Philip Noel-Baker (Churchill College, Cambridge), Eleanor Rathbone (Liverpool University), Wilfred Roberts (Warwick University), and David Lloyd George (House of Lords Record Office, Westminster).

Although none of the *ad hoc* aid organisations have left formal archives, the work of Spanish Medical Aid, the Basque Children's Committee, and the National Joint Committee for Spanish Relief can be studied at the University of Warwick in the Wilfred Roberts and TUC collections. For letters from nursing volunteers in Spain, see the correspondence of Molly Murphy (Murphy papers, NMLH, Manchester) and Anne Murray (Tom Murray papers, National Library of Scotland). Other sources include the Public

Records Office, the Marx Memorial Library (MML; Clerkenwell, London), and the Addison papers (Bodleian Library, Oxford). For the archives of other important relief organisations, see the Religious Society of Friends (Friends House, London) and the Save the Children Fund (Mary Datchelor House, London).

The main archive pertaining to the British volunteers is that of the International Brigade Association at the Marx Memorial Library, Clerkenwell, London. This collection, in addition to the central records of the British Battalion, contains the private papers of many individual volunteers. See also the Tom Murray papers (National Library of Scotland), the Peter Kerrigan papers (NMLH, Manchester), and, for the ILP contingent, the Bob Edwards papers (NMLH, Manchester). Documents relating to the Cornford–McLaurin Memorial Fund, which raised money for the British volunteers and their families, are in the Joseph Needham papers (Cambridge University Library). The Imperial War Museum, London, has a collection of recorded interviews with volunteers and other Britons involved in the Civil War.

Papers of intellectuals dealing with the Spanish Civil War include those of George Orwell and Richard Rees (both in University College, London), Kingsley Martin (University of Sussex), and Joseph Needham (Cambridge University Library). The archive of For Intellectual Liberty has recently been deposited in Cambridge University Library, where there is also related material in the papers of J. D. Bernal. The papers of Artists International Association are held at the Tate Gallery Archive, London.

Roman Catholic responses can be studied through the archives of the archdiocese of Westminster (Hinsley papers) and the diocese of Southwark (Amigo papers). For Anglican responses, see the Lang papers at Lambeth palace and the Hewlett Johnson papers at the University of Kent, Canterbury.

2 THE SPANISH CIVIL WAR

a The Second Republic and the Spanish Civil War

Raymond Carr's Spain, 1808–1975 (Oxford, 1982 edn) provides the historical context. Hugh Thomas, The Spanish Civil War (first published 1961), is a masterly narrative, and also deals fully with the international aspects of the conflict. Other standard works are Gabriel Jackson, The Spanish Republic and the Civil War (Princeton, 1965), Raymond Carr, The Spanish Tragedy: The Civil War in Perspective (1977), Ronald Fraser, Blood of Spain: The Experience of Civil War, 1936– 1939 (1979), Paul Preston, The Spanish Civil War (1986), and Preston, Franco (1993). George Esenwein and Adrian Shubert's Spain at War: The Spanish Civil War in Context, 1931–1939 (1995) is an excellent recent work of synthesis. Burnett Bolloten's The Spanish Civil War: Revolution and Counter-Revolution (Chapel Hill, N. C., 1991) is overwhelmingly concerned with Republican politics; Helen Graham's Socialism and War: The Spanish Socialist Party in Power and Crisis, 1936–1939 (Cambridge, 1991) provides a valuable corrective to Bolleten's interpretation. On the origins of the Civil War, see Paul Preston, The Coming of the Spanish Civil War: Reform, Reaction, and Revolution in the Second Republic (1978), and Richard A. H. Robinson, The Origins of Franco's Spain: The Right, the Republic, and Revolution, 1931–1936 (Newton Abbot, 1970). There are a number of important collections of essays, including Paul Preston (ed.), Revolution and War in Spain, 1931–1939 (1984), and Martin Blinkhorn (ed.), Spain in Conflict, 1931–1939: Democracy and Its Enemies (1986).

b International intervention

Dante A. Puzzo, Spain and the Great Powers, 1936–1941 (New York, 1961), provides a good overview. For a more recent summary, see Michael Alpert's A New International History of the Spanish Civil War (1994) and Glyn Stone's 'The European Powers and the Spanish Civil War, 1936–1939', in Robert Boyce and Esmonde Robertson (eds.), Paths to War: New Essays on the Origins of the Second World War (Basingstoke, 1989). International aspects of the Civil War are dealt with in a number of the essays in P. Preston and A. Mackenzie (eds.), The Republic Besieged: Civil War in Spain, 1936–1939 (Edinburgh, 1996). On the role of the Soviet Union, see David Cattell's Communism and the Spanish Civil War (Berkeley, 1955) and Soviet Diplomacy and the Spanish Civil War (Berkeley, 1957), and E. H. Carr, The Comintern and the Spanish Civil War (1984). The memoirs of the Soviet ambassador in London during this period provide an interesting commentary on both Soviet policy and the working of the Non-Intervention Committee: Ivan Maisky, Spanish Notebooks (1966). The French stance on non-intervention is critically appraised in Glyn Stone's 'Britain, France, and the Spanish Problem, 1936–1939', in Dick Richardson and Glyn Stone (eds.), Decisions and Diplomacy: Essays in Twentieth-Century International History (1995). On the role of Italy, see John Coverdale, Italian Intervention in the Spanish Civil War (1975). German attitudes are analysed in Denis Smyth's 'Reflex Reaction: Germany and the Onset of the Spanish Civil War', in Paul Preston (ed.), Revolution and War in Spain (1984), Robert Whealey, Hitler and Spain (Lexington, Ky., 1989), and Christian Leitz, 'Hermann Göring and Nazi Germany's Economic Exploitation of Nationalist Spain, 1936–1939', German History, 14:1, 1996, pp. 21–37. On Portugal, see Glyn Stone, The Oldest Ally: Britain and the Portuguese Connection, 1936–1941 (1994). On other important international aspects, see Richard Veatch, 'The League of Nations and the Spanish Civil War, 1936–1939', European History Quarterly, 20:2, April 1990, pp. 181–207; and Maria Rosa de Madariaga, 'The Intervention of Moroccan Troops in the Spanish Civil War: A Reconsideration', European History Quarterly, 22:1, January 1992, pp. 67–97.

c Eye-witness accounts in English

On Spain before the Civil War, see Laurie Lee, As I Walked Out One Midsummer Morning (1969), Charles Graves, Trip-tyque (1936), Kate O'Brien, Farewell Spain (1937), Gerald Brenan, South from Granada (1957), and Leah Manning, What I Saw in Spain (1935).

The outstanding first-hand accounts of the Civil War were written by independent-minded left-wingers: George Orwell's *Homage to Catalonia* (1938) and Franz Borkenau's *The Spanish Cockpit* (1937). Both chart the rise and fall of the revolution in the Republican zone. G. L. Steer's account of the Basque campaign in 1937, *The Tree of Gernika: A Field Study of Modern War* (1938), is also exceptional. Arthur Koestler's *Spanish Testament* (1937) and Peter Chalmers Mitchell's *My House in Malaga* (1938) both deal with the fall of Málaga and Koestler's subsequent incarceration. John Langdon-Davies' *Behind the Spanish Barricades* (1936) is a vivid account of the opening months of the Civil War in Catalonia and Madrid.

There are no accounts from the Nationalist side to match the acuity of those of Orwell and Borkenau. For journalistic and politically coloured reports, see Harold Cardozo, *The March of a Nation: My Year of Spain's Civil War* (1937); Cecil Geraghty, *The Road to Madrid* (1937); Florence Farmborough, *Life and People in Nationalist Spain* (1938); and Eleanora Tennant, *Spanish Journey: Personal Experiences of the Civil War* (1936). Francis Horace Mellor's *Morocco Awakens* (1938) is an account of conditions in Morocco.

3 BRITAIN IN THE 1930S

The standard histories are C. L. Mowat, *Britain Between the Wars, 1918–1940* (1955), A. J. P. Taylor, *English History, 1914–1945* (1965), and John Stevenson, *British Society, 1914–1945* (1984). For a concise modern synthesis, see Andrew Thorpe, *Britain in the 1930s* (1992). Other surveys of the period include Christopher Cook and John Stevenson, *The Slump: Society and Politics During the Depression* (1977), and Noreen Branson and Margot Heinemann, *Britain in the 1930s* (St Albans, 1973). There is no comprehensive history yet of the National Government, although there are a number of detailed studies on its formation, including Robert Skidelsky, *Politicians and the Slump: The Labour Government of 1929–1931* (1967), Philip Williamson, *National Government and National Crisis: British Politics, the Economy, and Empire, 1926–1932* (Cambridge, 1992), and Andrew Thorpe, *The British General Election of 1931* (Oxford, 1991). Tom Stannage's *Baldwin Thwarts the Opposition: The British General Election of 1935* (1980) dissects mid-1930s electoral politics. Martin Ceadel, *Pacifism in Britain, 1914–1945: The Defining of a Faith* (Oxford, 1980), is the best introduction to the pacifist politics of the 1930s. For biographies of the leading politicians, see Keith Middlemass and John Barnes, *Baldwin: A Biography* (1969), Keith Feiling, *The Life of Neville Chamberlain* (1946), David Carlton, *Anthony Eden: A Biography* (1981), Andrew Roberts, *'The Holy Fox': A Biography of Lord Halifax* (1991), Kenneth Harris, *Attlee* (1982), Alan Bullock, *The Life and Times of Ernest Bevin*, vol. I (1960), Ben Pimlott, *Hugh Dalton* (1985), and Robert Skidelsky, *Oswald Mosley* (1975).

On culture and the information media, see D. L. LeMahieu, *A Culture for Democracy: Mass Communication and the Cultivated Mind in Britain Between the Wars* (Oxford, 1988), Herbert Rutledge Southworth, *Guernica! Guernica! A Study of*

Journalism, Diplomacy, Propaganda, and Illusion (Berkeley and Los Angeles, 1977), Franklin Reid Gannon, The British Press and Germany, 1933–1939 (Oxford, 1971), Anthony Aldgate, Cinema and History: British Newsreels and the Spanish Civil War (1979), and Richard Cockett, Twilight of Truth (1989).

4 THE BRITISH GOVERNMENT

For the background to British foreign policy, see F. S. Northedge, The Troubled Giant: Britain Among the Great Powers, 1916–1939 (1966); R. A. C. Parker, Chamberlain and Appeasement: British Policy and the Coming of the Second World War (Basingstoke, 1993); A. R. Peters, Eden at the Foreign Office, 1931–1938 (Aldershot, 1986); and Lawrence Pratt, East of Malta, West of Suez: Britain's Mediterranean Crises, 1936–1939 (Cambridge, 1975).

The most significant published source is Documents on British Foreign Policy: the second series (W. N. Medlicott, ed.) covers most of the period of the Spanish Civil War. The standard works on the subject are Jill Edwards, The British Government and the Spanish Civil War, 1936–1939 (London and Basingstoke, 1979), and, most recently, Enrique Moradiellos' La perfidia de Albión: el gobierno británico y la guerra civil española (Madrid, 1996). Unlike earlier studies such as William Kleine-Ahlbrandt, The Policy of Simmering: A Study of British Policy During the Spanish Civil War, 1936–1939 (The Hague, 1962), and Patricia van der Esch, Prelude to War: The International Repercussions of the Spanish Civil War (The Hague, 1951), both books were written after the release of Foreign Office documents. Pasión y farsa: franceses y británicos ante la guerra civil española (Madrid, 1994) by Juan Avilés Farré is also mainly concerned with British government policy and Farré, like Moradiellos, uses Spanish diplomatic sources.

The question of British involvement in the making of the non-intervention policy was debated by David Carlton, 'Eden, Blum, and the Origins of Non-Intervention', Journal of Contemporary History, 6:3, 1971, pp. 40–55, and Glyn Stone, 'Britain, Non-Intervention, and the Spanish Civil War', European Studies Review, 9, 1979, pp. 129–49. The tendency in recent publications has been to criticise the British government for its ideological antipathy towards the Spanish Republic: see Douglas Little, Malevolent Neutrality: The United States, Great Britain, and the Origins of the Spanish Civil War (Ithaca, N. Y., 1985) and Enrique Moradiellos, Neutralidad benévola: el gobierno británico y la insurrección militar español de 1936 (Oviedo, 1990). Much of Moradiellos' work is available in English, in articles such as 'Appeasement and Non-Intervention: British Policy During the Spanish Civil War', in Peter Catterall and C. J. Morris (eds.), Britain and the Threat to Stability in Europe, 1918–1945 (1993); 'The Origins of British Non-Intervention in the Spanish Civil War: Anglo-Spanish Relations in Early 1936', European History Quarterly, 21:3, July 1991, pp. 339–64; 'The Gentle General: The Official British Perception of General Franco During the Spanish Civil War', in P. Preston and A. Mackenzie (eds.), The Republic Besieged: Civil War in Spain, 1936–1939 (Edinburgh, 1991); and 'British Political Strategy in the Face of the Military Rising of 1936 in Spain', Contemporary European History, 1:2,

1992, pp. 123–37. On the final phase of Britain's Civil War policy, see Paul Stafford, 'The Chamberlain–Halifax Visit to Rome: A Reappraisal', *English Historical Review*, 98:386, January 1983, pp. 61–100.

There are a number of studies of the role of the Royal Navy: see Michael Alpert, *La guerra española en el mar* (Madrid, 1987); Peter Gretton, 'The Nyon Conference: The Naval Aspect', *English Historical Review*, 90:354, January 1975, pp. 103–12; and *El factor olvidado: la marina británica y la guerra civil española* (Madrid, 1984). For the political context of Nyon, see William C. Mills, 'The Nyon Conference: Neville Chamberlain, Anthony Eden, and the Appeasement of Italy in 1937', *International History Review*, 15:1, February 1993, pp. 1–22. James Cable's *The Royal Navy and the Siege of Bilbao* (Cambridge, 1979) deals with the political and humanitarian, as well as the naval, ramifications of the Bilbao crisis. See also P. M. Heaton, *Welsh Blockade Runners of the Spanish Civil War* (Newport, Gwent, 1985).

On British–Spanish economic relations, see C. E. Harvey, *The Rio Tinto Company: An Economic History of a Leading International Mining Concern, 1873–1954* (Penzance, 1981); S. G. Checkland, *The Mines of Tharsis* (1967); and David Avery, *Not on Queen Victoria's Birthday: The History of the Rio Tinto Company* (1974).

Memoirs and diaries include Anthony Eden, *Facing the Dictators* (1962); the Earl of Halifax, *Fulness of Days* (1957); John Harvey (ed.), *The Diplomatic Diaries of Oliver Harvey, 1937–1940* (1970); Robert Hodgson, *Spain Resurgent* (1953); Lord Templewood (Sir Samuel Hoare), *Nine Tempestuous Years* (1954); Geoffrey Thompson, *Front-Line Diplomat* (1959); and Owen St Clair O'Malley, *The Phantom Caravan* (1954).

5 BRITISH POLITICS

The main published sources are the *Parliamentary Debates* of both Houses of Parliament, and the *Annual Reports* of the TUC and the Labour Party Conference. For a good overview, written without access to archival material, see K. W. Watkins' *Britain Divided: The Effect of the Spanish Civil War on British Political Opinion* (Edinburgh, 1963).

There has been little work on Conservative or right-wing attitudes to the Civil War. On the Tory dissidents, see Neville Thompson, *The Anti-Appeasers: Conservative Opposition to Appeasement in the 1930s* (Oxford, 1971), and Sheila Hetherington, *Katharine Atholl, 1874–1960: Against the Tide* (Aberdeen, 1989). Right-wing attitudes are touched on in Richard Griffiths, *Fellow Travellers of the Right: British Enthusiasts for Nazi Germany, 1933–1939* (1980), and G. C. Webber, *The Ideology of the British Right, 1918–1939* (1986).

On the Communist Party in the 1930s, see Noreen Branson, *History of the Communist Party of Great Britain, 1927–1941* (1985); Kevin Morgan, *Harry Pollitt* (Manchester, 1993), and *Against Fascism and War: Ruptures and Continuities in British Communist Politics, 1935–1941* (Manchester, 1989); Nina Fishman, *The British Communist Party and the Trade Unions, 1933–1945* (Aldershot, 1995); and Henry Felix Srebrenik, *London Jews and British Communism, 1935–1945* (Ilford, 1995).

Memoirs include Douglas Hyde's *I Believed* (Bungay, Suffolk, 1950) and Phil Piratin's *Our Flag Stays Red* (1948).

On the non-communist Left, see Robert E. Dowse, *Left in the Centre: The Independent Labour Party, 1893–1940* (1966); James Jupp, *The Radical Left in Britain, 1931–1941* (1982); Mark Shipway, *Anti-Parliamentary Communism: The Movement for Workers' Councils in Britain, 1917–1945* (Basingstoke, 1988); and Robert Kern, 'Emma Goldman and the Spanish Civil War', *Journal of Contemporary History*, 2:2–3, July 1976, pp. 237–59. On the ILP's Spanish ally, see V. Alba and S. Schwartz, *Spanish Marxism Versus Soviet Communism: A History of the POUM* (New Brunswick, N. J., 1988).

Although interest has tended to focus on the Labour Party, Tom Buchanan, *The Spanish Civil War and the British Labour Movement* (Cambridge, 1991) is the only full-length study. See also C. Fleay and M. L. Sanders, 'The Labour Spain Committee: Labour Party Policy and the Spanish Civil War', *Historical Journal*, 28:1, 1985, pp. 187–98; Victor Kiernan, 'Labour and the War in Spain', *Journal of the Scottish Labour History Society*, 11, May 1977, pp. 4–16; and John F. Naylor, *Labour's International Policy: The Labour Party in the 1930s* (1969). Ben Pimlott's *Labour and the Left in the 1930s* (Cambridge, 1977) provides the context for the Labour Party rank-and-file movements during the Civil War. There are also a number of significant unpublished theses: D. P. F. Lancien, 'British Left-Wing Attitudes to the Spanish Civil War', BLitt. thesis, University of Oxford, 1965; Peter Drake, 'Labour and Spain: British Labour's Response to the Spanish Civil War with Particular Reference to the Labour Movement in Birmingham', MLitt. thesis, University of Birmingham, 1977; Heather Mary Errock, 'The Attitude of the Labour Party to the Spanish Civil War', MA thesis, University of Keele, 1980; Marja Lynne Mueller, 'The British Labour Party's Response to the Spanish Civil War', Ph.D thesis, University of Alabama, Birmingham, 1979.

On the Liberal Party, see Malcolm Baines, 'The Survival of the British Liberal Party, 1932–1959', DPhil. thesis, University of Oxford, 1989; and Chris Cook, *A Short History of the Liberal Party, 1900–1976* (1976).

On Irish politics north and south of the border, see J. Bowyer Bell, 'Ireland and the Spanish Civil War, 1936–1939', *Studia Hibernica*, 9, 1969, pp. 137–62; Robert Stradling, 'Battleground of Reputations: Ireland and the Spanish Civil War', in P. Preston and A. Mackenzie (eds.), *The Republic Besieged: Civil War in Spain, 1936–1939* (Edinburgh, 1991); and Graham S. Walker, *The Politics of Frustration: Harry Midgley and the Failure of Labour in Northern Ireland* (Manchester, 1985). Welsh political reactions are assessed in Hywel Francis, *Miners Against Fascism: Wales and the Spanish Civil War* (1984); on Scotland, see Ian S. Wood, 'Scotland and the Spanish Civil War', *Cencrastus*, 18, Autumn 1984, pp. 14–16.

Political memoirs dealing more or less candidly with the Civil War (other than those of government ministers listed in section 3 above) include Fenner Brockway, *Inside the Left* (1942); Clement Attlee, *As It Happened* (1954); Hugh Dalton, *The Fateful Years: Memoirs, 1931–1945* (1957); Lord Citrine, *Men and Work:*

The Autobiography of Lord Citrine (1964); John McGovern, *Neither Fear Nor Favour* (1960); Charles Duff, *No Angel's Wing* (1947); John McNair, *Spanish Diary* (n.d.); Katharine Atholl, *Working Partnership* (1958); and Leah Manning, *A Life for Education: An Autobiography* (1970).

6 AID

The most comprehensive account is Jim Fyrth's *The Signal Was Spain: The Aid Spain Movement in Britain, 1936–1939* (1986). There is a summary of Fyrth's findings in John Saville, 'The Aid for Spain Movement in Britain, 1936–1939', *Dictionary of Labour Biography*, vol. IX (Basingstoke, 1993), pp. 25–32. Fyrth's interpretation is questioned in Tom Buchanan, 'Britain's Popular Front? "Aid Spain" and the British Labour Movement', *History Workshop Journal*, 31, Spring 1991, pp. 60–72; for Jim Fyrth's reply, see 'The Aid Spain Movement in Britain, 1936–1939', *History Workshop Journal*, 35, 1993, pp. 153–65. Michael Alpert's 'Humanitarianism and Politics in the British Response to the Spanish Civil War, 1936–1939', *European History Quarterly*, 14:4, October 1984, pp. 423–40, makes good use of Foreign Office archives. Mike Squires' *The Aid to Spain Movement in Battersea, 1936–1939* (1994) is a detailed local study.

The context for the case of the Basque refugee children is provided by Panikos Panayi, *Immigration, Ethnicity, and Racism in Britain, 1815–1945* (Manchester, 1994), and Claudena M. Skran, *Refugees in Inter-War Europe: The Emergence of a Regime* (Oxford, 1995). The best detailed study is Dorothy Legarretta, *The Guernica Generation: Basque Refugee Children of the Spanish Civil War* (Reno, Nev., 1984), which examines the world-wide Basque diaspora of the Civil War. See also Adrian Bell, *Only for Three Months: The Basque Children in Exile* (Norwich, 1996). One aspect of the story is covered in Tom Buchanan, 'The Role of the British Labour Movement in the Origins and Work of the Basque Children's Committee, 1937–1939', *European History Quarterly*, 18:2, April 1988, pp. 155–74. Oliver Marshall's *Ship of Hope* (1991) contains interviews with three children who remained in Britain.

On the problems encountered by some trade unions in raising funds, see Tom Buchanan, 'The Politics of Internationalism: The Amalgamated Engineering Union and the Spanish Civil War', *Bulletin of the Society for the Study of Labour History*, 53:3, 1988, pp. 47–55, and 'Divided Loyalties: The Impact of the Spanish Civil War on Britain's Civil Service Trade Unions, 1936–1939', *Historical Research*, 65:156, February 1992, pp. 90–107. David Lampe, *Pyke: The Unknown Genius* (Aylesbury and Slough, 1959), is a biography of the eccentric founder of Voluntary Industrial Aid for Spain Committee.

On the involvement of women – especially in aid work – see Sue Bruley, 'Women Against War and Fascism: Communism, Feminism, and the People's Front', in Jim Fyrth (ed.), *Britain, Fascism, and the Popular Front* (1985), and Pamela M. Graves, *Labour Women: Women in British Working-Class Politics, 1918–1939* (Cambridge, 1994). Jim Fyrth and Sally Alexander, *Women's Voices from the*

Spanish Civil War (1991), contains many recollections by volunteer nurses. Penelope Fyvel, *English Penny* (Ilfracombe, Devon, 1992), is a memoir by one such British nurse. See also Jim Fyrth's article on Isabel Brown in the *Dictionary of Labour Biography*, vol. IX (Basingstoke, 1993).

7 VOLUNTEERS

There have been three official histories of the British Battalion and its Brigade: Frank Ryan (ed.), *The Book of the XV Brigade* (Newcastle upon Tyne, 1938; 1975 edn); William Rust, *Britons in Spain: The History of the British Battalion of the XVth Brigade* (1939); and Bill Alexander, *British Volunteers for Liberty: Spain, 1936–1939* (1982). Alexander's book is the standard modern history of the British volunteers, dealing also with Britons who volunteered in other capacities. An essential complement is Hywel Francis' 'Welsh Miners and the Spanish Civil War', *Journal of Contemporary History*, 5:3, 1970, pp. 69–76, and *Miners Against Fascism: Wales and the Spanish Civil War* (1984). His argument is updated, if not fundamentally revised, in his article ' "Say Nothing and Leave in the Middle of the Night": The Spanish Civil War Revisited', *History Workshop Journal*, 32, Autumn 1991, pp. 69–76. Peter Stansky and William Abrahams, *Journey to the Frontier: Two Roads to the Spanish Civil War* (1966), while only dealing with Julian Bell and John Cornford, contains much of interest on the early volunteers. On British volunteer airmen, see Brian Bridgeman, *The Flyers* (Reading, 1989). Some of the military lessons of the Civil War are discussed in David Fernbach, 'Tom Wintringham and Socialist Defence Strategy', *History Workshop Journal*, 14, Autumn 1982, pp. 63–91. The commemoration of the British volunteers is the subject of Colin Williams, Bill Alexander, and John Gorman's *Memorials of the Spanish Civil War* (1996).

The British contribution is also dealt with in the more general studies of the Brigades. The most important – Andreu Castells, *Las brigadas internacionales de la guerra de España* (Barcelona, 1974) – is unfortunately not in translation. Vincent Brome's *The International Brigades: Spain, 1936–1939* (1965) is colourful but rather dated. R. Dan Richardson's *Comintern Army: The International Brigades in the Spanish Civil War* (Lexington, Ky., 1982) is written from a passionately anti-communist standpoint, although it contains some useful insights.

There are a number of important oral history collections. Ian MacDougall (ed.), *Voices from the Spanish Civil War: Personal Recollections of Scottish Volunteers in Republican Spain, 1936–1939* (Edinburgh, 1986), gives the text of interviews with Scottish volunteers; D. Corkill and S. Rawnsley (eds.), *The Road to Spain: Anti-Fascists at War, 1936–1939* (Dunfermline, 1981), also offers verbatim texts. Judith Cook's *Apprentices of Freedom* (1979) is a history of the British Battalion based on interviews with surviving members.

There is a large amount of memoir and memorial literature. Esmond Romilly's *Boadilla*, John Sommerfield's *Volunteer in Spain*, and Keith Scott Watson's *Single to Spain* (all 1937) were all written soon after the events described and capture the passion of the early volunteers. Tom Wintringham's *English Captain* (1939) offers a more self-analytical account. Fred Copeman's *Reason in Revolt* (1948) and Charlotte Haldane's *Truth Will Out* (1949) were both written after their authors had acrimoniously left the Communist Party, but are fair in their treatment of the International Brigades. Two more recent memoirs are of value, Jason Gurney's *Crusade in Spain* (1974) for its irreverence and Laurie Lee's *A Moment of War* (1991) for its sense of tragedy and futility.

Other recollections (including those of T. A. R. Hyndman and James Jump) are collected in Philip Toynbee (ed.), *The Distant Drum: Reflections on the Spanish Civil War* (1976). *My Generation*, by the former commissar Will Paynter (Plymouth, 1972), gives little away.

On the Irish volunteers who fought with the Nationalists, see Maurice Manning, *The Blueshirts* (Dublin, 1970); Robert Stradling, 'Franco's Irish Volunteers', *History Today*, 45:3, 1995, pp. 40–7; and Seamus McKee, *I Was a Franco Soldier* (1938).

8 INTELLECTUALS

Much of the relevant contemporary literature is collected in two books edited by Valentine Cunningham, *The Penguin Book of Spanish Civil War Verse* (1980), and *Spanish Front: Writers on the Civil War* (Oxford, 1986). The former has a marvellously iconoclastic introduction, which was challenged by John Saville in 'Valentine Cunningham and the Poetry of the Spanish Civil War', *Socialist Register*, 1981. A shorter collection of British writing is in Alun Kenwood (ed.), *The Spanish Civil War: A Cultural and Historical Reader* (Oxford, 1993).

On the intellectual background, see David Caute, *The Fellow Travellers: A Postscript to the Enlightenment* (1977); Neal Wood, *Communism and the British Intellectuals* (1959); John Coombes, *Writing from the Left: Socialism, Liberalism, and the Popular Front* (1989); David Blaazer, *The Popular Front and the Progressive Tradition* (Cambridge, 1992); and Lynda Morris and Robert Radford, *The Story of the Artists' International Association, 1933–1953* (Oxford, 1983). The literary context is provided by Samuel Hynes, *The Auden Generation: Literature and Politics in England in the 1930s* (1976), and Valentine Cunningham, *British Writers of the Thirties* (Oxford, 1988). Frank Gloversmith (ed.), *Class, Culture, and Social Change: A New View of the 1930s* (1980), contains a number of significant essays. See also Stuart Samuels, 'The Left Book Club', *Journal of Contemporary History*, 1:2, 1966, pp. 65–86, and John Lewis, *The Left Book Club: An Historical Record* (1970).

There are a number of studies on the Civil War itself. Katherine Hoskins' *Today the Struggle: Literature and Politics in England During the Spanish Civil War* (Austin, Tex., 1969) offers detailed criticism of specific texts. Stanley Weintraub, *The Last Great Cause: The Intellectuals and the Spanish Civil War* (1968), offers a more historical approach. See also Hugh D. Ford, *A Poet's War: British Poets and the Spanish Civil War* (Philadelphia, 1965), and Nicholas Jenkins, 'Auden and Spain', in Katherine Bucknell and N. Jenkins (eds.), *W. H. Auden. 'The Map of All My Youth': Early Works, Friends and Influences* (Oxford, 1990).

George Orwell's Spanish experiences are analysed in Bernard Crick's *George Orwell: A Life* (Harmondsworth, 1980), in Michael Shelden's *Orwell: The Authorised Biography* (1991), and in Peter Stansky and William Abrahams' *Orwell: The Transformation* (1979). Orwell's reliability is questioned, if hardly discredited, in essays by Bill Alexander and Robert Stradling in Christopher Norris (ed.), *Inside the Myth. Orwell: Views from the Left* (1984).

There are many memoirs that touch on intellectual involvement. See, for instance, Stephen Spender, *World Within World* (1951); Arthur Koestler, *The Invisible Writing: An Autobiography* (1954); John Lehmann, *The Whispering Gallery* (1955); C. Day Lewis, *The Buried Day* (1960); Jack Lindsay, *Fanfrolico and After* (1962); Kingsley Martin, *Editor: A Second Volume of Autobiography, 1931–1945* (1968); T. C. Worsley, *Behind the Battle* (1939); R. G. Collingwood, *An Autobiography* (Oxford, 1939; rpt, 1978). Richard Crossman (ed.), *The God That Failed: Six Studies in Communism* (1950), contains contributions from both Koestler and Spender.

9 RELIGION

Apart from Catholicism, this is the least-researched aspect of the British response to the Civil War. On the background, see Alan Wilkinson, *Dissent or Conform? War, Peace, and the English Churches, 1900–1945* (1986), and Adrian Hastings, *A History of English Christianity, 1920–1990* (5th edn, 1991). While not dealing directly with the Civil War, Stephen Koss, *Nonconformity in Modern British Politics* (1975), helps to explain the Nonconformists' lack of political involvement in it.

Anglican biographies and memoirs that touch on Spain include Hewlett Johnson, *Searching for Light: An Autobiography* (1968); D. R. Davies, *In Search of Myself* (1961); S. C. Carpenter, *Duncan-Jones of Chichester* (1956); C. H. Smyth, *Cyril Foster Garbett* (1959); and John Kent, *William Temple* (Cambridge, 1992).

On Spanish Catholicism, see Frances Lannon, *Privilege, Persecution, and Prophecy: The Catholic Church in Spain, 1875–1975* (Oxford, 1987). José M. Sanchez, *The Spanish Civil War as a Religious Tragedy* (Notre Dame, Ind., 1987), sets the British Catholic response within a Spanish and international context; see also Tom Buchanan and Martin Conway (eds.), *Political Catholicism in Europe, 1918–1965* (Oxford, 1996). Thomas Moloney, *Westminster, Whitehall, and the Vatican: The Role of Cardinal Hinsley, 1935–1943* (1985), is an excellent monograph. Articles on British Catholicism include Thomas R. Greene, 'The English Catholic Press and the Second Spanish Republic, 1931–1936', *Church History*, 45:1, 1976, pp. 70–84; James Flint, ' "Must God Go Fascist?" English Catholic Opinion and the Spanish Civil War', *Church History*, 56, 1987, pp. 264–74; Tom Gallagher, 'Scottish Catholics and the British Left, 1918–1939', *Innes Review*, 34:1, Spring 1983, pp. 17–42; and Joan Keating, 'Looking to Europe: Roman Catholics and Christian Democracy in 1930s Britain', *European History Quarterly*, 26:1, January 1996, pp. 57–79. Michael E. Williams, *St Alban's College, Valladolid: Four Centuries of English Catholic Presence in Spain* (1986), covers an important aspect.

Stuart Mews, 'The Sword of the Spirit: A Catholic Cultural Crusade of 1940', in W. J. Shiels (ed.), *Studies in Church History*, vol. 20 (1983), pp. 409–30, considers the longer-term impact of the Civil War on English Catholicism.

10 BRITAIN AND FRANCO'S SPAIN

The best introduction to the foreign relations of the Franco regime is Paul Preston's *Franco* (1993). K. W. Watkins' *Britain Divided: The Effect of the Spanish Civil War on British Political Opinion* (Edinburgh, 1963) provides an overview of the post-Civil War era, along with some of the most important documentary sources. Denis Smyth, *Diplomacy and Strategy of Survival: British Policy and Franco's Spain, 1940–1941* (Cambridge, 1986), offers a detailed survey of two critical years. See also Hoare's own account of his years in Madrid in Lord Temple-wood, *Ambassador on a Special Mission* (1946), and the memoirs of his predecessor Maurice Peterson, *Both Sides of the Curtain* (1950). Qasim Ahmad, *Britain, Franco Spain, and the Cold War, 1945–1950* (New York, 1992), is a most detailed, and unremittingly hostile, study of the Attlee government's policy towards Spain. Bill Alexander's *No to Franco: The Struggle Never Stopped, 1939–1975* (1992) deals primarily with the International Brigade Association. See also Christopher Crompton, 'British Political Opinion and the Franco Regime, 1939–1951', MPhil. thesis, University of Birmingham, 1991; and Christian Leitz, 'The Economic Relations Between Nazi Germany and Franco Spain, 1936–1945', DPhil. thesis, University of Oxford, 1994.

INDEX

Hinsley, Archbishop Arthur, 110, 111,
119, 120, 176, 178, 180, 183, 184,
187, 193
Hoare, Sir Samuel, 22, 39, 43, 53, 55,
56, 58, 86, 192, 193, 203n
Hoare–Laval Pact (1935), 22, 203n
Hodgson, Sir Robert, 53, 59
Home Guard, 190
Home Office (British), 42, 50, 57, 58,
110, 141
Hood, HMS, 56–7
Hope, Arthur, 119
Horsfall Carter, W., 152
Housman, Laurence, 159
Houston, Lady, 119
Howard, Lord, of Penrith, 119
Huesca, 133
Hulton, Edward, 190
Huxley, Aldous, 150, 156, 159
Hyde, Douglas, 96, 209n
Hyndman, T. A. R., 136

Immingham, 58, 91
Independent Labour Party, 50, 72, 74–8,
95, 122, 133–4, 146, 152, 159,
164–5, 183, 184, 190, 199
military unit of, 133–4, 164–5, 199
Inge, Dean, 176
Inquisition, Spanish, 10, 200
International Brigades, 6, 19, 20, 55, 61,
68, 69, 71, 93, 95, 103, 106, 108,
121–45, 155, 156, 157, 162, 163,
164, 165
British Battalion of, 71–2, 73, 83,
103, 121–45, 190, 197
commissars in, 129, 131–2, 133, 135,
138, 139, 140, 163
desertion from, 135, 136, 139
XI Brigade of, 122, 125
XIV Brigade of, 103, 125
XV Brigade of, 103, 125, 129, 130,
131
International Brigades Association,
197–8

International Commission for Assistance
of Child Refugees, 94, 118
International Federation of Trade Unions,
79, 100
International Peace Campaign, 68
International Solidarity Fund, 100
International Writers' Association, 35,
148
Iredell, Revd E. O., 173, 174
Irish Christian Front, 176
Irwin, Major, 112
Isherwood, Christopher, 147, 162
Italy, 2, 18, 19, 20, 21, 27, 32, 37, 39,
40, 42, 43, 44, 47, 48, 49, 50, 53,
54, 58, 59, 60, 61, 62, 67, 80, 84,
91, 123, 140, 146, 151, 186, 203n

Jacob, Alfred, 116–18, 175
Jacob, Norma, 116–18
Jacobsen, Fernanda, 108–9
Jarama, battle of, 131, 132, 134–5, 136,
141, 157
Jeger, George, 104, 105, 195
Jeger, Santo, 105
Jellinek, Frank, 158
Jerrold, Douglas, 16, 89, 90, 161, 193
Jews,
in Britain, 66, 126
in Germany, 171, 175–6
Joad, C. E. M., 155
Johnson, Hewlett, 34, 171–4, 175
Jones, Jack, 199
Jones, Lewis, 158
Juan Carlos, King, 200

Kemp, Peter, 122
Kerrigan, Peter, 129, 131–2, 134
King, Norman, 41
Kinross and West Perth, 1938 by-
election in, 87
Koestler, Arthur, 163, 167–8
Komsomol, 157

Labour and Socialist International, 81, 100